Beyond Well-Being

Spirituality and
Human Flourishing

Beyond Well-Being

Spirituality and
Human Flourishing

edited by

Maureen Miner

*University of Western Sydney
and Wesley Institute*

Martin Dowson

Wesley Institute

Stuart Devenish

Booth College

INFORMATION AGE PUBLISHING, INC.
Charlotte, NC • www.infoagepub.com

Library of Congress Cataloging-in-Publication Data

Beyond well-being : spirituality and human flourishing / edited by Maureen
Miner, Martin Dowson, Stuart Devenish.
   p. cm.
 ISBN 978-1-61735-804-3 (pbk.) – ISBN 978-1-61735-805-0 (hardcover) –
ISBN 978-1-61735-806-7 (ebook) 1. Success–Religious
aspects–Christianity. 2. Well-being–Religious aspects–Christianity. 3.
Quality of life–Religious aspects–Christianity. 4. Spirituality. 5.
Christianity–Psychology. 6. Positive psychology. I. Miner, Maureen. II.
Dowson, Martin. III. Devenish, Stuart.
 BV4598.3.B49 2012
 248–dc23
                                                        2012006587

Printed in the United States of America

CONTENTS

SECTION III

PRACTICING HUMAN FLOURISHING

FOREWORD

This volume arose out of a concern to assist people in their struggle to lead a *flourishing life*. Fractured, stressed, relationally broken and spiritually empty people instinctively reach for the panacea of happiness. But happiness is a fair weather friend, which often evaporates on contact. More stable and worthwhile than happiness is leading a *flourishing life*, which is able to integrate our impulses, desires, longings, and experiences into a stable theatre on whose stage we are able to *perform* our lives. Flourishing describes both the journeying and arrival that turns broken hearts and homeless minds into purposeful pilgrims whose journeys are engaged in living life on a *grand scale*, and are subsequently filled with hope, expectation and the sense of something "more."

The origins of the present volume lie among a small group of researchers who collaborated around the question, "In what way might spirituality contribute to human flourishing?" Those researchers were members of the Psychology and Spirituality Society (PASS), which operated out of the Psychology Department of the University of Western Sydney (UWS). Under the leadership of Dr Maureen Miner, PASS applied for and received funding from the Metanexus Institute (Philadelphia, PA, USA), and the UWS. Metanexus promotes a transdisciplinary approach to the interface of religion and science; firstly in intellectual dialogue around the most profound questions of nature, culture and human "being"; and secondly by making a positive contribution to increasing emotional, experiential, communal and spiritual capital in the lives of ordinary people.

Over a period of three years (2007–2009), a group of PASS researchers from the social sciences, humanities, human service professionals, theol-

Beyond Well-Being: Spirituality and Human Flourishing, pages vii–x
Copyright © 2012 by Information Age Publishing
vii

ogy, religious studies and spiritual practitioners met each month to discuss aspects of spirituality and human life. The group organized conferences, lectures, workshops and discussion meetings that were open to the public. The interactions were inter-disciplinary in nature, and contributions from the major world religions and spiritual traditions were invited. All types of spirituality were discussed, and how spirituality as it is defined by various traditions related with, and contributed to, the social environment and the quality of individual experiences. Throughout those years of shared research the central concern was how to assist people in their struggle to lead a *flourishing life.*

In its final year of full funding (2009) the UWS PASS Executive organized a conferral in which participants from the Australasia region were invited to write papers on the topic of spirituality and human flourishing. In order to focus more carefully on the nexus between spirituality and human flourishing, the type of spirituality under investigation was stipulated as *Christian* spirituality. A range of disciplines that had generated material relating to human flourishing was considered, and participants from the following fields were approached: psychology, psychiatry, theology, philosophy, education, community development, and sociology. All participants had an interest in Christian spirituality. Participants were asked to write a paper on human flourishing from a single disciplinary or inter-disciplinary perspective, depending on their expertise. The conferral was held on the 25th and 26th of September, 2009 at the Chevalier Resource Centre, Missionaries of the Sacred Heart Congregation monastery in Kensington, Sydney. Each of the papers was presented, discussed, critiqued and revised. Subsequently they have been edited and compiled into this book.

The aim of this book, then, is to consider how Christian spirituality contributes to human flourishing from a number of different disciplinary perspectives. Many questions are suggested by the basic aim. *First,* concerning spirituality: What is spirituality? In what way does spirituality contribute to human flourishing? What is Christian spirituality? How does Christian spirituality relate to the way people live? Is spirituality necessary for human flourishing and in what way does it provide a unique and important contribution? Why is Christian spirituality important for human flourishing? Each of these questions is addressed in different ways in the chapters that follow.

Second, the book invites consideration of what it means to flourish as a human being. Is it just living, working and enjoying pleasure? Or is there something more—is it possible to live vitally, fruitfully and satisfyingly? If there is *something more* to flourishing than our everyday expectations, how can that *something more* be described and analyzed? How can flourishing be distinguished from, or related to, concepts such as maturity, actualization, and personal integration?

A *third* aim is to consider how professionals can promote positive change among those in their care. Many professionals are change-agents in their personal lives and professional roles as teachers, counselors, therapists, community developers, clergy, social workers, life coaches and so on. They practice in public and private contexts with people of all ages, cultural backgrounds, and demographic indicators. What resources are embedded in Christian spirituality that can be "carried over" from the religious and spiritual realms into professional practice? How might, for example, Christian practitioners make use of resources for flourishing within their own "home" tradition, in the context of their professional practice in the public square?

A *fourth* and final aim considers flourishing from its expressly religious and spiritual aspects. Religious accounts of flourishing are unpopular in our times, especially those which may be related to a specifically *Christian* spirituality. Yet Christian spirituality has traditionally offered an alternative to hedonistic and humanistic values and perspectives on the meaning and purpose of human life. Is there a way to bring Christian spirituality into dialogue with people who are dissatisfied with their lives, who experience inner dissonance, and yet who may be disinclined to commit to practices that increase their overall flourishing? In what ways do spiritual resources for human flourishing differ from those sources promoted by humanistic and secular agencies and ideologies?

No single viewpoint can encompass the totality of human flourishing. The perspectives covered in this volume represent fields from the humanities and social sciences, but there was no attempt to give an exhaustive coverage. Further, there is merit in considering theory, research and practice in any investigation of human life. Therefore an associated aim was to include chapters by writers who adopt a variety of approaches to human flourishing—for example, the theoretical approach of researchers, and the practical approaches preferred by professional practitioners. Overall, the book aims to give complementary yet diverse accounts of human flourishing. Each account argues that Christian spirituality is an important and unique *contributor* to flourishing. Hence, the overall emphasis is on spirituality as necessary but not sufficient for humans to flourish.

The book will be valuable for those who are dissatisfied with popular hedonistic approaches to flourishing. Such people are ready for change but often do not have a clear alternative in view. It is hoped that this book will provide a clear alternative to popular culture's representation of the flourishing person, which is largely vested in conspicuous consumption. This book will also be valuable for those who have considered alternatives to the media's lenses of novelty and sensationalism; such offerings frequently lack a more objective perspective, which this book attempts to furnish. Finally, the book will be valuable for those who are committed to Christian spirituality but may not appreciate the rich resources that Christian faith offers for human flourishing. Among the latter group are included Christian leaders such as priests and pastors, voluntary church workers, and lay people who may or may not be involved in formal religion but who long to flourish in their own lives and to enable others to do the same.

SECTION I

UNDERSTANDING HUMAN FLOURISHING

Preface

Section I of this monograph, Understanding Human Flourishing, utilizes perspectives from the social sciences and theology to consider the nature of human flourishing and how spirituality contributes to human flourishing. Section I provides a conceptual framework for Sections II and III, which provide resources for, and explorations of, human flourishing in different professional contexts. The chapters in Section I are also critical for practitioners because they address the key question: "*Why* is spirituality so important for human flourishing?"

PHILOSOPHY, PSYCHOLOGY, AND FLOURISHING

In Chapter 1, Maureen Miner and Martin Dowson discuss how human flourishing has been understood over the centuries from ancient Greek philosophy to 21st century psychology and contemporary culture. Although a philosophical and psychological emphasis on cultivating virtue as a way of flourishing remains, the culture of consumption, self-gratification, and hedonism undermines this. In contrast, Miner and Dowson present a composite model of flourishing in which flourishing is defined in terms of self-actualization (the ongoing realization of unique human potential, after Maslow, 1970) and altruism as complementary aspects of flourishing.

Beyond Well-Being: Spirituality and Human Flourishing, pages 1–4
Copyright © 2012 by Information Age Publishing
1

Miner and Dowson also note that accounts of flourishing typically either neglect, or provide a superficial account of, how spirituality contributes to human flourishing. However, Miner and Dowson argue that spirituality (and Christian spirituality in particular) has an essential role to play in promoting flourishing, particularly in the context of universal suffering. Spirituality is defined as multi-dimensional (with dimensions of *meaning*, *transformation* and *connectedness*) and multi-modal (with modes of *state*, *trait* and *experience*). A causal sequence from suffering to spirituality to flourishing is proposed, with flourishing reciprocally causing higher attained states of spirituality.

Christian spiritual writings and theology are important resources for human flourishing because they provide concepts and language for understanding, expressing and explaining spiritual experiences. Christian theology also specifies the purpose of human life and flourishing in terms of connection to and unity with God. As a result, actualization (in particular) is not presented as the ultimate "good," but as a means to the end of personal integration in relationships with God and others.

SPIRITUALITY, SUFFERING, AND CONNECTEDNESS

Themes of meaning, transformation, connectedness, the virtues promoted by spiritual disciplines, and flourishing—which is defined as actualization and altruism—are evident in several subsequent chapters of this book. In Chapter 2, Grant Gillett examines how connectedness is vital to spirituality, and considers flourishing in the context of disease and disasters. Large scale epidemics and disasters drive home both our human vulnerability and interdependence. Gillett proposes that human identity is relational—our sense of who we are derives from whom we know and how we know them. Our responses to unpredictable events are shaped by the same social structures that inform our identities and the meanings we give to things. Drawing upon philosophers such as Lacan, Gillett reflects upon the influence of others in forming and sustaining our identity. He suggests that our twin senses of individual identity and connection with others in fact transcend ourselves. Further, identity cannot be reduced to measurable observations or made subject to empirical investigation. This is because spiritual connections between people have a different ontological order from that with which science engages.

Suffering, whether personal or vicarious, also directs our attention to transcendent concerns. Religions with their faith stories of good and evil resonate with our experiences of suffering and direct us to God. When woven into the fabric of our experience, these stories enable us to find significance and flourishing, including a deeper sense of connection with the Ultimate, in all kinds of disasters. In contrast, secular philosophy offers a practical "cure" for disorders and distress caused by suffering through ethical praxes, with some contemporary thinkers such as Ramachandran (1998) arguing that the ethical aspects of human life are evolutionary by-products, and hence fully explicable by science. However, Gillett argues that evolutionary accounts are not sufficient to account for altruism and its contribution to flourishing. Spirituality is also necessary for flourishing because it orients us to what is good and enables us to conceptualize and connect to the good.

HEALTH, HEALING, AND WHOLENESS

Chapters 3 and 4 explore conditions for human flourishing as they are depicted in Christian theology. Stuart Devenish in Chapter 3 considers how Christian teachings promote health, healing, and human flourishing. He defines flourishing in terms of vigor and a subjective sense of well-being, noting distinctions in philosophical approaches between hedonistic (pleasure-focused) and "eudaimonistic" forms of flourishing. Devenish offers a definition of eudaimonia as a state of self-realization. These distinctions are used to highlight different understandings of health (and healing) by proponents of traditional medicine, complementary medicine, and psychotherapy. Devenish argues that Christianity emphasizes a broader cosmic dimension of healing as well as immediate individual wholeness and flourishing. He analyzes the core method, mode and outcome of a variety of healing traditions, including: secular alternative-medical approaches; spiritual, unorthodox, alternative or complementary medicine; psychotherapeutic practices; and religious attitudes. In traditional medicine these are naturalistic, biological and curative; for complementary medicine they are holistic, systemic and harmonizing; for psychotherapy they are developmental, psycho-somatic and integrative; and for Christianity they are ontological, restorative and redemptive. In counterpoint to the restorative emphases in the Christian tradition, Devenish identifies "voluntary vulnerability," in which otherwise healthy and whole individuals eschew self interest in order to benefit those who are suffering. However, the main thrust of the chapter is that Christianity offers a restorative focus that can be incorporated within secular healing traditions or viewed as offering distinct alternative therapies. Devenish argues that embedded within Christian teachings is an account of people as Godlike, yet flawed and alienated from their ideal environment. However, God is restoring the cosmos. As such, humans can flourish as they identify themselves within God's redemptive plan and use spiritual resources to cope with the vicissitudes of life.

KNOWN BY GOD

In Chapter 4, Brian Rosner and Loyola McLean consider the theme of being known by God. Usually the theme of human knowledge of God is more prominent, but the shift in perspective emphasizes the prior ontological reality of the relational God. The ontological reality and stability of the self is also considered in light of post-modern claims about the ephemeral, transitional self. The authors argue that the healthy self is developing towards cohesive wholeness, becoming self-conscious as it matures in, and emerges from, a web of supportive attachment relationships. Such a healthy, stable self is necessary for the individual's flourishing. Yet contemporary culture is not conducive to the development of a stable sense of self. Rosner and McLean further argue that a stable sense of identity must be anchored in transcendent reality—something or someone beyond the material person. They use Christian theology to assert that God offers believers a secure identity, located within a secure relationship with God and including secure relationships between God and the Christian "family" or community. This secure identity does not have to be sought with hard work by the individual—it is bestowed by God. Rosner and McLean discuss Biblical passages that attest to humans being known by God and thus, given identity in relationship with God. Hence, instead of striving to find one's identity, the individual who recognizes she is known by God is able to receive her identity as a gift. She is also able to flourish in a more secure attachment relationship with God because of a heightened sense of significance, comfort in situations of distress, and moral direction.

Both Chapters 3 and 4 consider human flourishing as dependent upon responses to a relational God who provides new (redeemed) identity and purpose. These responses are receptive rather than active: receiving identity and redemption. As a result of receiving God's relational gifts, people can use spiritual resources more effectively for personal and social-moral flourishing.

CHAPTER 1

SPIRITUALITY AS A KEY RESOURCE FOR HUMAN FLOURISHING

Maureen Miner
University of Western Sydney and Wesley Institute

Martin Dowson
Wesley Institute

ABSTRACT

Few voices in our contemporary culture advocate spirituality as a resource for human flourishing in a systematic and convincing manner. Popular culture focuses on hedonism as the way to flourishing. As academic disciplines, philosophy and psychology acknowledge aspects of spirituality and flourishing but fail to construct full accounts of spirituality and human flourishing. In contrast, this chapter seeks to develop a thorough account of the relationship between spirituality and human flourishing. Specifically, we propose that spirituality is a multi-dimensional and multi-modal construct affecting, and reciprocally affected by, flourishing. The chapter further proposes that Christian sacred texts, spiritual writings, and theology provide language, concepts, and explanatory systems that underpin the recognition, understanding, and

Beyond Well-Being: Spirituality and Human Flourishing, pages 5–31
Copyright © 2012 by Information Age Publishing

integration of spiritual experience and further promote flourishing and spirituality. The chapter also notes that Christian sacred texts, spiritual writings, and theology identify suffering as a key cause of spirituality and flourishing and God the ultimate goal of spirituality and flourishing. In so doing, Christian constructions of spirituality and flourishing avoid self-centeredness while simultaneously explaining how flourishing can lead to deeper states of spirituality within a relational universe.

Although we are finite beings, humans nonetheless yearn for more than physical existence. We realize that physical existence is fickle: that pleasure often quickly turns to pain, that chance brings good and ill, and that our choices can have uncertain and often unsatisfying consequences. As the mystical poet St. John of the Cross (c.1618/1983) wrote:

> To find in worldly goods delight
> Is at the most a weariness
> And satiated appetite
> And tired palate, more or less.
> For all life's sweets that have their sting
> I'll never lose my way, if not
> For some unknown I don't know what
> That some most lucky chance may bring...
>
> The man who wants to make his way
> Puts all his care not to what's gained
> But what is yet to be attained.
> So I who wish to mount, not stay
> Below, find it a normal thing
> To scale the heights, climb to the peak
> To choose—I don't know what—and seek
> What some most happy chance may bring. (p. 35)

St. John recognizes that we long for a "way" through life that makes sense of suffering, allows us to make risky but potentially satisfying choices, and helps us find purpose in our actions. We look within and without, but crucially we long to grow and thrive—to flourish. St. John of the Cross found this "way" by focusing on the continuing search, rather than focusing on what he had already gained. Christian spirituality was a central resource for his flourishing. This chapter argues that spirituality in general, and Christian spirituality in particular, continues to provide a key resource for human flourishing today.

POPULAR CULTURE AND FLOURISHING

In contemporary Western societies, popular culture typically depicts flourishing in terms of personal wealth, health and pleasure. Media emphasis on expensive goods and services, gossip concerning the rich, and bias towards the portrayal of young, fit and beautiful people reinforces this interpretation of flourishing. The often implicit, but sometimes blatant, message is: wealth, health and pleasure are desirable for the "good life" and hedonism constitutes *the* valid philosophy for, or orientation towards, life. Yet research suggests that the pursuit of flourishing through the acquisition of wealth, health and pleasure is only weakly associated with actual happiness, mental health and reported wellbeing—at least in developed countries (Campbell, Converse, & Rodgers, 1976; Heller, Watson, & Hies, 2004; Howell & Howell, 2008; Kammann, 1983). For example, people who suddenly acquire wealth (as in a lottery win) may report temporarily increased life satisfaction, but their underlying sense of wellbeing quickly returns to previous levels (Frederick & Loewenstein, 1999). In developing countries, health, wealth and associated pleasure, are more strongly related to reported wellbeing, but the strength of the relationship is still only weak to moderate (Howell & Howell, 2008). These research findings suggest that correlates of hedonism are not strong or consistent predictors of wellbeing, and thus that a hedonistic approach to flourishing is misleading.

Popular accounts of flourishing are not only selective and inaccurate, but often changeable and sensationalized. Popular media often focuses on novelty rather than on what is enduring and typically presents information sensationally. Popular media can, therefore, unreasonably diminish more substantial (e.g., religious and philosophical) claims about, and routes to, human flourishing. They thus exacerbate confusion about what constitutes a truly "good" (flourishing) life—grooming people to consume for no other reason than for the pleasure of consumption (Smith, 2009), and to make changes simply for the sake of novelty.

It is hardly surprising, then, that many people report having lost their way when it comes to flourishing. They desire more than basic existence but are distracted by hedonistic superficialities and competing pathways to flourishing. They perceive they have been let down by political, social, and economic institutions and reject utopian claims based on scientific and social progress, but cannot find a way to return to an idealized village where basic human values of faith, hope, and love underpin a flourishing life. The results are dissonance, dissatisfaction, and disinclination to commit to any worthwhile life-cause.

Despite the dominance of the hedonistic worldview, people nonetheless become aware of other accounts of flourishing through religion, education, art, and literature. Religion and education, particularly by holding in high esteem the lives of those who provided great service to others, typically exhort people to altruism and self-sacrifice as ways of being fully human, and hence, of flourishing. Unfortunately, in the context of a hedonistic culture, such alternative routes to flourishing (which are often posed in oppositions such as poverty versus wealth, service despite ill-health, self-sacrifice over self-gratification) can create guilt, inner conflict, or other forms of cognitive dissonance. Moreover, if altruistic ways of flourishing are belittled or questioned, people may be disinclined to commit to ways of living that might curtail their immediate sense of pleasure even if these alternatives are more likely to lead to flourishing.

OVERVIEW AND AIMS OF THIS PRESENT CHAPTER

This chapter outlines an argument that spirituality in general, and Christian spirituality as a particular example, promotes human flourishing. First, accounts of human flourishing from philosophy and psychology are discussed. These accounts recognize that humans are connected to others through their familial, community, and wider social relationships. They acknowledge human strivings for personal and social goals, including self-actualization (defined broadly as the ongoing realization of unique human potential, after Maslow, 1970). In light of these accounts, flourishing is defined as ongoing self-actualization that promotes the personal *and* inter-personal good. A composite model of human flourishing based on existing philosophical and psychological approaches is also presented. In current philosophical and psychological approaches to wellbeing, spirituality is often vaguely defined as a search for "something" beyond oneself. In contrast, we clearly specify three major dimensions of spirituality, which we argue are *the search for meaning, personal transformation, and connectedness.* We propose not only that spirituality is multidimensional, but that it is also multimodal. In other words, spirituality presents as an experience a trait (people differ in the degree to which they are motivated towards, or committed to, spiritual questing) and a state (people also differ in the degree to which they have attained a sense of meaning, personal transformation and connectedness). Finally, we explore relationships between spirituality (as an experience, a trait, and a state) and flourishing. In particular, we consider how Christian theology enables the integration of spiritual experience in ways conducive to attaining meaning, transformation and connectedness, and hence enhanced states spirituality and flourishing.

THE NATURE OF FLOURISHING

Philosophy and Flourishing

For over two millennia, philosophers have thought about the nature of individual and social good and ways to promote flourishing. Ancient philosophers promoted virtue ethics as the route of human flourishing. In the 5th century BC, for example, Confucius founded his description of the ideal character on the virtues of benevolence, justice, wisdom, truthfulness and respect for piety (Dahlsgaard, Peterson, & Seligman, 2005). Similarly, Plato and Aristotle urged the cultivation of *arête*, or virtue, in the form of courage, justice, temperance, and wisdom as the route to *eudaimonia* (Honderich, 1995; Williams, 1995). The goal of such virtue was not individual happiness alone, but the good of society as individuals actualized their virtuous potential in the service of society and in the pursuit of their own needs. Subsequent moral philosophers have discussed the relative importance of virtuous motives, dutiful action, and due consideration of consequences as indicators of ethical living. Clearly, the approach to flourishing according to moral philosophy is not primarily though pleasure (*hedonism*), but rather through actualizing one's true nature as a person capable of virtue (*eudainomism*). Hence flourishing is defined primarily in terms of the actualization of virtue rather than the sensation of (usually physical) pleasure.

Building upon the legacy of Plato and Aristotle, moral philosophers such as Kant and Bentham have influenced social scientists' studies of ethical decision making as a route to flourishing (Miner, 2006). Lawrence Kohlberg (1968; Kohlberg, Levine, & Hewer, 1983) maintains that "good" ethical decisions reflect the highest stages of moral thinking—expressed in terms of duty and justice. Kohlberg clearly bases his cognitive-developmental theory on the philosophy of Emanuel Kant (Casement, 1983), who proposed that ethical choices must be founded upon the universal imperative to treat others as equal, autonomous human beings. However, critics claim that Kantian approaches cannot resolve conflicts over competing duties (such as is evident in debates over the death penalty where justice *versus* the preservation of life is debated) and cannot consider social contexts (such as in the case of telling a lie in order to save a life) (Casement, 1983). On the other hand, alternative approaches to moral philosophy also lack unanimous support. The weighing of consequences—to do what maximizes personal well-being, for example—as proposed by Jeremy Bentham (Sommers, 1986) has intuitive appeal as a method for choosing a good alternative. However, the consequentialist pathway may implicitly allow the majority to flourish at the expense of a minority (Raphael, 1981). In contrast, newer versions of classical virtue theory propose that right actions require the exercise of good character (in terms of honesty, integrity, courage, compassion, etc.) and are not determined by the outcome of the actions themselves (Foot, 2001; Hursthouse, 1999; Slote, 2000; Swanton, 2001). Among contemporary virtue theories some include additional, theological virtues (e.g., Hursthouse, 1999), echoing Aquinas' addition of the theological virtues to the Aristotelian understanding of the character, which is informed by pursuit of the "fine." Yet although it is a helpful addition to moral philosophy, virtue theory alone does not fully describe a character predisposed to flourishing and cannot specify how to promote flourishing (Williams, 1995).

Since philosophers disagree about the nature of the good life and how it might be attained, philosophy at present provides no clear way forward with respect to flourishing (Miner & Petocz, 2003). People know *about* the good life, duties, and virtues but still do not flourish. Philosophical approaches may need to be supplemented by other understandings of the human person to determine what might help or hinder human flourishing.

Psychology and Flourishing

In the following section, three psychological approaches to flourishing are considered: clinical, positive, and humanistic psychology. After each approach is described, its limitations as a complete account of human flourishing are discussed. In search of a more complete account of flourishing, a composite model of flourishing, including the strengths of philosophical and psychological accounts, is then presented.

Clinical Psychology

Clinical psychology does not encompass the concept of flourishing directly, but according to its closest approximation, a flourishing person displays few or no persistent *psychological symptoms*. Some negative psychological symptoms are expected as relatively transient reactions to environmental stressors (e.g., acute arousal following trauma, bereavement, reactive anxiety). These expected and transient symptoms, however, do not undermine overall flourishing. Conversely, chronic symptoms indicate a psychological disorder and suggest a commensurate lack of flourishing. From a clinical perspective, people intolerant of acute stress-related symptoms, or who continue to suffer from chronic patterns of symptoms, are likely to have problems in their everyday lives. If people find it difficult to work, look after themselves, and maintain good relationships (American Psychiatric Association, 2000), then ongoing self-actualization (realization of their potential) leading to flourishing is highly unlikely. However, despite its descriptive utility, clinical psychology provides a limited framework for considering flourishing because it does not specify the conditions for eliciting and maintaining *positive* emotions and other states that represent positive indicators of flourishing. Other approaches are, hence, needed to move beyond the "flourishing as few-or-no symptoms" approach. Two alternatives are discussed below: positive psychology, with its emphasis on optimum functioning and flourishing, and humanistic psychology, with its focus on needs and self-actualization.

Positive Psychology

Positive psychology began as a corrective to clinical emphases on disease and dysfunction, with a stated mission to understand and promote human strengths and virtues (Seligman & Csikszentmihalyi, 2000). Since positive psychology has been defined as "the study of conditions and processes that contribute to flourishing and optimum functioning of people, groups and institutions" (Gable & Haidt, 2005, p. 104), it is directly relevant to concerns about flourishing. Proponents of positive psychology view flourishing as a core "good" denoted by the term "happiness," which is defined as a pleasant, engaged and meaningful life (Seligman, Ernst, Gillham, Reivich, & Linkins, 2009).

However, several limitations of this definition of flourishing are apparent. First, it is not clear that "happiness" equates to, comprises, or is causally connected to flourishing. Actualization and the good of others are essential to flourishing, whereas happiness can reasonably derive from any positive emotion without actualization or any particular good accruing towards others. Conversely, history and literature provide countless examples where individuals were intensely *un*happy, yet this unhappiness was essential to their growth and development (flourishing) as human beings. Happiness, we could therefore say, is sometimes correlated with flourishing, but not necessarily so.

Second, positive psychology's rationale for the dimensions of happiness (pleasantness, engagement, meaningfulness) is unclear: why these three dimensions and not others? Moreover, the theory does not identify how highly it values causal links (if any) among the three dimensions of happiness. This is despite noting reciprocal interactions among the dimensions (Seligman, Steen, Park, & Peterson, 2005). Furthermore, other indicators of fulfillment and flourishing are invoked, including: "positive emotions (happiness, joy, contentment); rewarding intimate relationships (love, friendship); approval by self and others; mental health and quality of life; vocational satisfaction and success; satisfying leisure and recreational activities; supportive and consistent families; and safe and responsive communities" (Seligman & Petersen, 2003, p. 308). Yet no coherent rationale for the inclusion of these diverse indicators is provided, and the importance of, and associations among, these indicators are not specified.

Positive psychology views human virtues as direct causes of human flourishing. Six ubiquitous virtues are held to be foundations for fulfillment and flourishing: courage, justice, humanity (benevolence), temperance, wisdom, and transcendence (gratitude, hope, spirituality) (Dahlsgaard et al., 2005). These six virtues are supported by designated character strengths. For example, the virtue of humanity is supported by love and kindness, and transcendence is supported by gratitude, hope and spirituality. It is not, however, made clear:

- why these virtues, as opposed to any other virtues were chosen;
- if all (or any) of these six virtues need to be present for flourishing to occur, and if so to what degree;
- what character strengths associated with the six virtues are more or less germane to flourishing; and
- why any or all of these character strengths should be associated with these virtues in general, and with respect to the particular "pairs" suggested.

To be fair, some empirical evidence supports relationships between some character strengths and measures of human flourishing, such as satisfaction with life. For example, strengths associated with the virtues of humanity (love, kindness) and transcendence (hope, gratitude) are strongly related to life satisfaction (Park, Peterson, & Seligman, 2004). Yet strengths related to the virtue of temperance (such as modesty and humility) are only slightly related to satisfaction with life. These weaker relationships suggest the possibility of alternative interpretations of the positive psychology model, and/ or the presence of confounding variables and/or processes in the model. Harvey and Pauwels (2004), for example, suggest that humility and modesty may be derived from experiences of loss; and interactions with other character strengths may better predict thriving than direct relationships between aspects of temperance and life satisfaction. A related concern is whether the proposed character strengths are better able to predict flourishing than known personality characteristics, such as the Big Five personality traits of neuroticism, extraversion, openness, agreeableness, and conscientiousness (Harvey & Pauwels, 2004). Further, if the core virtues are manifest in ways that promote individual and social good, how exactly do they influence pro-social behavior?

Positive psychology also proposes techniques for remedying psychological dysfunction and promoting flourishing. These strategies include instilling hope, building "buffering strengths," and telling life stories (Seligman et al., 2005). Studies do suggest that educational programs to foster character strengths may improve symptoms of depression and increase social skills. However, it is not yet clear whether all aspects of flourishing can be affected by educational programs (Seligman et al., 2009), or whether results so far obtained will prove context-sensitive.

In short, positive psychology attempts to build theory and practical interventions upon a foundation of neo-Aristotelian virtue ethics (Hackney, 2007). It presents structural models of virtues and character strengths that apparently underpin flourishing, but it lacks a clear rationale for the model's components and the relationships among them. Moreover, although flourishing itself is defined in terms of happiness, it is not clear how or why.

Humanistic Psychology

Humanistic psychology emphasizes human choice and integration as means of satisfying basic needs and the fundamental motive of self-actualization. Self-actualization corresponds to a healthy, fulfilled life. Classical theorists linked to humanistic psychology include Abraham Maslow and Gordon Allport. Maslow (1970) developed a hierarchy of needs that, when filled, promote further growth. At the fourth level are esteem needs including competence, independence and freedom; at the fifth and highest level is the need for self-actualization that, when satisfied, is often accompanied by mystical experiences, creativity, spontaneity, curiosity and intimacy. Flourishing, for Maslow, thus involves self-actualization, and spirituality (e.g., experiences of God's presence, unity with the cosmos, etc.) can accompany flourishing. Although self-actualization usually depends upon the fulfillment of lower needs, higher motives can override lower ones (as when spiritual striving overrides the need for food).

Allport (1950) argued that self-control, a self-chosen unifying philosophy of life, and self-knowledge were indicators of the mature, flourishing person with an integrated personality. Since religion is one form of unifying life philosophy, mature religiosity (which can include tentativeness and doubt even in the presence of unification) is a characteristic of the integrated person. As a result of a unifying personal philosophy, the mature person is consistently able to subdue bodily desires, defensive impulses, and self-interest in order to choose actions that promote higher ends such as self-transformation, full self-integration, and the welfare of others. As Wulff (1997) remarked, "Tentative at first and assailed by doubt, mature faith gradually finds strength in the successive acts and helpful consequences of a growing commitment" (p. 589). Hence, Allport includes a dynamic, questing approach to religion as an indicator of flourishing. For both Maslow and Allport, flourishing people may subordinate lower impulses and needs to the higher ends of self-fulfillment and altruism.

Another approach to flourishing by more contemporary humanistic psychologists combines human needs and self-actualization (Ryan & Deci, 2000, 2001). Their self-determination theory (SDT) proposes that when basic human needs of autonomy, competence, and relatedness are satisfied, individuals can experience wellbeing, vitality, growth, and inner harmony (i.e., flourishing). Subsequent research suggests that freely choosing goals rather than being pressured to follow socially or other-mandated goals, choosing non-material goals such as personal growth (Sheldon, Ryan, Deci, & Kasser, 2004), and choosing goals associated with relationships and competence also promotes wellbeing (Ryan & Deci, 2001). Such empirical findings support the approach of SDT but still do not fully explain human flourishing. Identified outcomes are generally limited to feelings of wellbeing, and the predictors account for low to moderate, rather than high, variation in wellbeing. The need-fulfillment perspective of self-determination theory adds to the overall needs-analysis orientation of humanistic psychology. In particular, the need for relatedness gives a fresh emphasis to social connectedness as a pathway to flourishing. Insights drawn from humanistic psychology and SDT are incorporated into our composite model of human flourishing below.

Composite Model of Human Flourishing

Based on our review of the philosophy and psychology of human flourishing, we first make the following foundational statements concerning human flourishing.

1. Human flourishing is a concern of philosophers and psychologists.
2. Human flourishing involves both positive inner states and positive external traits. In other words, flourishing involves inner wellbeing (actualization) and contributions to the wellbeing of others (altruism).
3. Human flourishing involves harmony, balance, and integrity within and between inner states and external traits. In other words, flourishing involves inner wellbeing without self-centeredness, and positive external action on behalf of others without compulsion, with both of these outcomes dynamically supported by the other.
4. Human flourishing involves distinguishable but inseparable cognitive, affective and behavioral elements such that the person flourishes as a whole intellectual, emotional, and moral being.
5. Flourishing acts to "center" and "ground" the person, providing the person with a sense of themselves in the world. This grounding motivates open, purposeful engagement with the world. Purposeful engagement and exploration create conditions conducive to further flourishing—thus allowing for ongoing flourishing across the lifespan.
6. Flourishing has many potential indicators. However, when seeking to develop a thorough understanding of flourishing, it is more important to concentrate on the foundational nature and structure of flourishing than to become distracted by attempts to enumerate or categorize all of its indicators.

Our model of flourishing comprises two aspects and several indicators. The two aspects are an internal aspect, actualization, and an external aspect, altruism. Actualization refers to the ongoing and achieved realization of the individual's human potential across developmental domains (physical, emotional, intellectual and spiritual). Altruism refers to the deployment of the individual's realized potential to the benefit of others. Altruism, then, invokes the moral and relational domains of human development. The inclusion of altruism in our model of flourishing recognizes understandings from psychology, philosophy, and religion that human beings flourish when they can realize their potential—especially through giving and service. Conversely, both unrealized and unexpressed (or inappropriately expressed) potential compromises flourishing. Based on this reasoning, we define flourishing as the holistic realization and altruistic expression of human potential.

Actualization is indicated by three broad cognitive-emotional dimensions consistent with the philosophical and psychological approaches reviewed above:

1. *non-contingent positive affect* (or "underlying contentment") that transcends particular personal or social circumstances but is enhanced by the absence of negative psychological symptoms;
2. a stable and *authentic sense of self and agency*, with associated self-knowledge and capacity for autonomous action, sufficient to enable the individual to adapt positively to changing internal and external circumstances; and
3. *dynamic equilibrium*, including the integration of personal experience, ongoing exploration of self and the world, and further development of the self.

Defined by these indicators, the *inner* aspect of human flourishing (actualization) is consistent with definitions of personal "good" derived from philosophical and psychological understandings.

Flourishing also involves an *outer* aspect: altruism. Altruism is indicated by behaviors that consciously promote the welfare of others. We propose a set of external behaviors linked to the outer aspect of human flourishing: 1) harmonious self-expression derived from underlying contentment that balances self-control and playful or generous impulsivity; 2) integrity as people act in accordance with their true ("stable" and "authentic") self and an associated philosophy of life; and 3) productivity, as people balance individual and social needs, and engage in activities that benefit self and others. Defined by these indicators, the *outer* aspect of human flourishing (altruism) is consistent with definitions of social "good" derived from philosophical and psychological understandings.

A diagrammatic representation of the model of flourishing is presented in Figure 1.1.

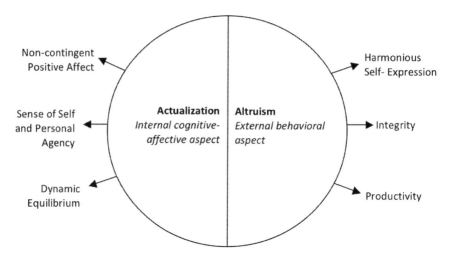

Figure 1.1   Model of flourishing.

Sources of Human Flourishing

Different theories propose different routes to flourishing. Clinical approaches suggest that a lack of flourishing (understood as psychological symptoms and syndromes) develops as a result of genetic factors, life circumstances, and learned responses (e.g., Rieger, 2008). Classical Greek philosophy holds that learning is crucial to flourishing; through experience and reason individuals can develop the skills that promote the good life (Aristotle, 2000). Positive psychology also emphasizes the learning of more appropriate cognitive states and processes, behavioral responses, and life goals as a means of developing the cognitive "flow" and learned optimism that are important causes or correlates of flourishing (Kelley, 2004). On the other hand early humanistic psychologists such as Maslow (1970) posit human nature as inherently good: self-actualization results from following inherent drives towards enhancement and growth. Similarly, self determination theory (SDT) proposes the goal directed nature of humans but also specifies three basic human needs that, when satisfied, result in flourishing.

Barriers to Flourishing

Typically suffering is construed as a barrier to flourishing. However, the inability to explain how suffering might contribute positively to flourishing means that psychological and philosophical accounts are unable to explain experiences where suffering does indeed lead to flourishing. St. John of the Cross indicates that suffering can lead to spiritual transformation, which in turn leads to flourishing. Moreover, life narratives and poetry suggest that spirituality is a cause of flourishing, even in the context of suffering: "Since Love began to work in me his touch transforms me, this I know" (St John of the Cross, c.1618/1983, p. 34). In the sections below, we examine in detail how spirituality can be related to flourishing even in the presence of suffering.

SPIRITUALITY

Spirituality lacks consensual definition (Spilka, 1993) because it is both a multidimensional and multimodal construct, and different definitions of this complex concept focus on different dimensions and modalities of spirituality. As a result, there is little agreement in literature regarding definitions of spirituality. By contrast, we seek to identify the dimensions and modalities of spirituality and so clarify current definitions of spirituality. The constituent elements of spirituality remaining constant across modalities are: meaning, transformation, and connectedness. Park (2005), for example, notes that an important function of spirituality and religion is in providing for, or enabling the development of, an integrated system of global meaning that can be particularly important in times of personal or communal suffering, as well as in the context of experiences of beauty and other forms of ineffability. Similarly, Cottingham (2005) views the pursuit of inner transformation as integral to spirituality. The goal of inner transformation includes radically changed integrative patterns of thinking and emotional response resulting from "systematic self-scrutiny and reflective analysis" (Cottingham, 2005, p. 74). Finally, spiritually is often viewed in terms of connectedness: within and between people, and with the sacred. Of the definitions of spirituality discussed by Zinnbauer and Pargament (2005), over half refer to relationship with God, the divine, or the sacred. For example, they cite a study of 30 years of nursing literature for definitions and associations of the term "spirituality," with the resulting core definition: "a personal life principle which animates a transcendent quality of relationship with God" (Zinnbauer & Pargament, 2005, p. 25). They also cite their own 2002 study where spirituality was characterized by "closeness with God or feelings of interconnectedness with the world and living things" (p. 26).

If the *dimensions* of spirituality may be defined as meaning, transformation and connectedness, it is also important to distinguish various *modes* of spirituality. The modes of spirituality refer to the ways in which the dimensions of spirituality manifest themselves and include: spirituality as an experience (*sensing* meaning, transformation, and connectedness) a trait (*seeking* meaning, transformation, connectedness), and as a state (*attaining* meaning, transformation, connectedness). Some of the confusions in the literature on spirituality would be avoided if clear distinctions were made between definitions of spirituality as an experience, a trait, and an attained state. Accounts of spirituality as an *experience* emphasize feelings of transcendence, connectedness, and awe (e.g., Otto, 1917/1950). Definitions of spirituality as a search or quest emphasize individual differences in the intensity of motivation towards seeking meaning, transformation, and connectedness, and hence conceptualize spirituality as a *trait*. Definitions of spirituality as the relative attainment of personal meaning, transformation, and connectedness conceptualize spirituality as a *state*.

It is also helpful to distinguish between different levels at which different objects of the spiritual search are located—for example, transcendence may be sought at levels of the person, society, environment, and divinity. The spirituality associated with many of the world religions includes experiences, traits and attained states where the transcendent focus is God (or gods). Spiritual dimensions and modalities remain important regardless of the particular "spiritual object" in question. A comprehensive definition of spirituality that combines these considerations is proposed: *In the context of spiritual experience, spirituality is the search, beyond psychology and physicality, for meaning, transformation, and connectedness (trait), success in which leads to new patterns of understanding, becoming, and relating (state).*

Most religious and many philosophical/ideological systems advocate means of attaining spiritual goals. Religions propose spiritual means within a God-focused meaning system. These means, variously termed "personal devotions," "spiritual disciplines," "spiritual behaviors" and so on, include prayer/meditation, reflective study, self-denial, self-scrutiny, acts of charity, and surrender to the Ultimate. Philosophical systems variously advocate self-denial (asceticism), reflective study of virtue (Platonism), beneficence within a particular social group (communitarian systems), and other methods within a human-focused meaning system. Spiritual behaviors are outward signs that an individual is pursuing an inward spiritual quest; hence, they function as *behavioral indicators of the trait* of spirituality. The difference between philosophy-based and religious-based spiritual behaviors lies in the focus of the action: whether the focus is on the material-social world or on the metaphysical "next-world" (including God as Ultimate Being). Figure 1.2 depicts a structural model of spirituality comprising:

(a) core dimensions of spirituality (meaning, transformation, and connectedness);
(b) core modalities of spirituality (trait, state, and experience), with spiritual experience modeled as a cause, correlate, and/or consequence

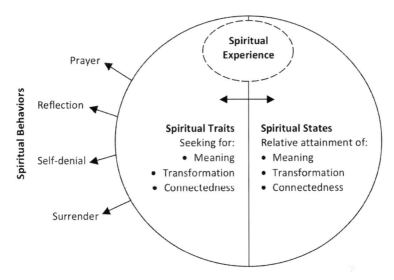

Figure 1.2 Structural model of spirituality.

of spiritual searching that is cognitively and affectively internalized within the person, thus integrating states of spirituality; and

(c) behaviors primarily indicative of spirituality as a trait involving a spiritual "search."

RELATIONSHIPS BETWEEN SPIRITUALITY AND FLOURISHING

Empirical Studies of Spiritual Behaviors and Flourishing

Empirical studies support a causal relationship between spiritual behaviors (indicators of the trait of spiritual seeking) and indicators of actualization and altruism (dimensions of human flourishing). Studies of prayer (including meditation, reflection and self-scrutiny), self-denial, and surrender generally report significant relationships with aspects of flourishing. Moreover, stress or suffering may activate spiritual behaviors that produce subsequent flourishing. Some representative studies relating to these findings are discussed below.

Prayer is a contributor to positive affect, personal integration, and harmonious self-expression. In a review of studies of prayer from 1984 to 2000, Bernard Spilka (2005) concludes that prayer counters depressive feelings; improves marital adjustment; helps individuals cope with the stress of illness, surgery, aging and disability; and contributes to life satisfaction and general wellbeing. The mechanisms underlying these positive effects are not well understood, but prayer facilitates cognitive-affective processing of negative events in ways that converge with the religious person's global meaning system (Spilka, 2005). Such processing may promote the integration of negative events within the person, and hence stabilize both mood and self-expression.

Self-denial (involving a shift from self-preoccupation to a focus on others) increases positive affect and contributes to altruism. Depressed and suffering people can flourish by engaging in behaviors relating to self-denial (see Greenfield & Marks, 2004; Morrow-Howell, Hinterlong, Rozario, & Tang, 2003; Thoits & Hewitt, 2001). Anxious and depressed people are typically preoccupied with their own anxious and depressive feelings. Self-denial, by contrast, de-emphasizes self concerns and so may weaken depressive and anxious symptoms. Other hypothesized mechanisms include the pleasurable qualities of social interaction associated with self-denial, the rewards of positive feedback from others increasing total levels of reinforcement, and changes in brain chemistry as a result of social activity.

Surrender also contributes to positive affect and other indicators of flourishing. In uncontrollable situations, surrender and acceptance denote acknowledgment of the reality of a given situation, construing the situation as part of a broader plan (consistent with one's global meaning system), and acting in conformity to perceptions of transcendent purposes. Surrender and acceptance provide the benefits of mindfulness (non-judgmental ongoing awareness) and facilitate spiritual coping strategies, such as acts of deferring to God (Pargament, 1997). Both mindfulness and acceptance improve positive affect (Baer, 2006; Bishop, 2002; Kabat-Zinn et al., 1992) and allow the person to act in accordance with his or her full potential in a given situation—as in the case of seriously ill people who surrender to what they see as God's purpose in their illness, and use their time to live richly instead of fighting uncontrollable symptoms.

Empirical Studies of Suffering, Spiritual States and Flourishing

Spiritual states associated with the *ongoing* attainment of meaning, transformation and connectedness are also conducive to flourishing in the context of stress and suffering. Events involving stress and suffering often call into question current global *meanings*, especially when global beliefs are violated and important goals are frustrated. Spiritual behaviors and associated cognitive strategizing may, however, result in the development of a revised global meaning system and hence an enhanced ability to derive spiritual meaning from adverse events. Flourishing occurs when suffering prompts a *positive* re-evaluation and revision of aspects of the global meaning system such that the person is better able to adapt and respond to negative events. Suffering may cause a revision of a) beliefs about God and a beneficent providence, b) personal spiritual goals, and c) subjective feelings (Park, 2005). Such positive spiritual interpretations (e.g., "God is bringing good out of the suffering") and positive emotional re-interpretations (e.g., "I find God's peace within the anxiety") appear to be related to better psychological adjustment following bereavement (Pargament, 1997) and greater personal integration following severe stress (Park, 2004). The enlargement of positive global meaning systems can also promote flourishing indirectly through personal transformation.

Such *personal transformation* as a result of suffering can be profound, as illustrated in cases where "sick souls" became "healthy minded" people (James, 1902/1958), or more limited, as in cases where aspects of former functioning are modified but not radically transformed. Transformative changes result from changes in an individual's global meaning system. Following a spiritual conversion, for example, changes in affect, values, personal agency, striving, and inner harmony are reported (Paloutzian, 2005) in directions consistent with self-actualization and altruism.

Suffering can also prompt the direct seeking of *connectedness* with others, including connectedness with the divine. When this connectedness is attained, links to flourishing can be seen. An important type of connectedness between people is "attachment." Attachment behaviors involve care-giving and care-seeking. Experiences of receiving (or not receiving) care inform our sense of self-worth and estimation of others' willingness to care. Empirical studies of attachment bonds between adult spouses show that securely attached people (in more positive relationships where attachment needs are generally met) flourish more than insecurely attached spouses (who experience more negative relationships where attachment needs are inconsistently, or seldom, met). For example, secure adult attachment is associated with general wellbeing and mental health (Bradley & Cafferty, 2001; Cicirelli, 1998), enduring, high quality marriages (Bakermans-Kranenburg & van Ijzendoorn, 1997; Mikulincer, Florian, & Cowan, 2002), and reduced death anxiety (Mikulincer, Florian, & Cowan, 1990). On the other hand, insecure adult attachment is linked to negative psychological symptoms of acute psychological disorders such as anxiety and depression (Eng, Heimberg, Hart, Schneier, & Liebowitz, 2001; Mallinckrodt & Wei, 2005; Tasca, Balfour, Ritchie, & Bissada, 2007; Wei, Mallinckrodt, Russell, & Abraham, 2004; Wei, Vogel, Ku, & Zakalik, 2005) and a greater frequency of chronic personality disorders (Brennan & Shaver, 1998; Crawford et al., 2006; Fonagy et al., 1996; Westen, Nakash, Thomas, & Bradley, 2006). Attachment to God also appears to augment human relationships, affecting symptoms of anxiety and emotional wellbeing (Miner, 2009). This additional effect of attachment to God beyond human attachments shows that connectedness with God holds unique and important psychological consequences for human flourishing.

Causal Model of Spirituality and Human Flourishing

The theoretical, philosophical and empirical findings detailed above can be used to derive a model of spirituality (as experience, trait and state) as a cause of human flourishing. This causal model is depicted in Figure 1.3.

Unique Features and Limitations of the Model
The model in Figure 1.3 represents:

1. suffering as an impetus towards, rather than an impediment to, spirituality and flourishing;
2. a new way of understanding spirituality that combines and, at the same time, clarifies previous definitions and conceptualizations of spirituality;
3. an integrative approach to flourishing that combines internal and external states of flourishing; and
4. reciprocal causal relationships between spirituality and flourishing in the context of suffering such that the "system" of spirituality and its interdependence with flourishing is clearly explicated.

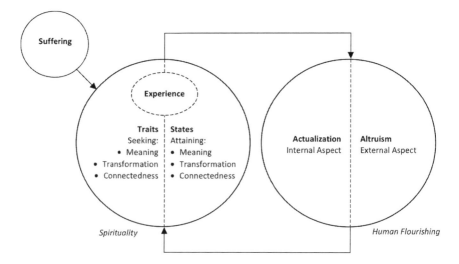

Figure 1.3 Causal model of spirituality and human flourishing.

Spirituality, Theology and Flourishing

The model in Figure 1.3 does not indicate a goal for flourishing either internal or external to the system. Hence, one limitation of the model is that it does not show if or how human flourishing may be related to some greater good, or some greater *object* of the spiritual search (human transcendence, nature, God etc.) outside the self. This limitation is appropriate to the psychological/analytical nature of the model. Below we will consider how theology in general, with Christian theology as a particular case in point, can define external purposes of human flourishing and why defining these purposes is important for human flourishing. We also consider how Christian theology explains spiritual experience itself, thus allowing for the healthy integration of spiritual experience by the Christian believer.

Of spiritual experiences we can say the following:

1. the identification of an experience as spiritual is critical if the individual is to understand and articulate the experience;
2. the expression of spiritual experience is critical if the individual is to communicate the experience to others (especially to those who may have had similar experiences), and hence attain emotional support, personal validation and a sense-of-connectedness regarding it. The uncommunicative individual isolates himself or herself in the context of the experience, thus hindering flourishing.
3. some explanation of spiritual experience is critical if the individual is cognitively to integrate the transcendent experience within their global meaning system. The alternative is cognitive fragmentation and confusion.
4. with appropriate support, validation, and connectedness generated in part through external expressions of transcendent experience and extended meaning developed through internalized explanations of transcendent experience, the individual can accept both the experience and its cognitive (affective) implications, potentially leading to personal transformation.

Philosophy and psychology do provide an objective means of describing and analyzing aspects of spiritual experiences, but not of fully expressing or explaining their ineffable qualities. On the other hand, music, literature and the arts are often used to give partial expression to spiritual traits, states and experiences. Yet, there is always a sense of incompleteness in musical, literary and artistic expressions of the spiritual because they lack the capacity for a systematic explanation and contextualization of the experience.

In this final section of the chapter, we use Christian sacred texts, spiritual writing, and theology to suggest how this corpus of writing provides language, concepts and constructs that express and explain personal spiritual

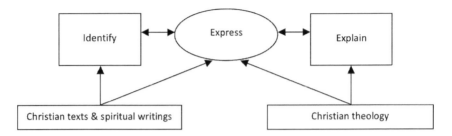

Figure 1.4   Functions of Christian texts, spiritual writings and theology in processing spiritual experiences.

experiences, linking these experiences to a wider and more satisfactory explanatory framework.

As Figure 1.4 shows, Christian texts and spiritual writings help to identify and express experiences that are perceived as having noetic or, more specifically, numinous qualities. Christian theology also expresses spiritual experience, but importantly provides explanations of spiritual experiences—in other words, it provides systematized accounts of the nature, causes, and goals of human life and experience (including spiritual experience) and so provides an explanatory framework for human life and experience.

Christian Sacred Texts and Spiritual Writings

Christian spiritual writings and sacred texts (e.g., the poetry of St. John of the Cross, the Psalms) emanate from experiences of spiritual seeking and attained states of meaning, transformation and connectedness associated with the divine. When a person has an experience of transcendence (perhaps provoked through beauty, an intimate relationship, participation in spiritual behaviors, etc.) and seeks to identify, understand and articulate it, Christian texts and writings provide a means of differentiating the experience from ongoing experiences, assigning a value to the experience as worthy of attention, understanding the experience as numinous and articulating its contours in conscious thought or speech (Schutz & Luckmann, 1974). In so doing, the sacred texts and spiritual writings validate and affirm the person's experience, providing key emotional and cognitive prerequisites for further exploration of the experience.

Christian Theology

If transcendent experience must be explained in order to achieve integration with the person's global meaning system, Christian theology gives one explanation of the origins, purposes, and pathways towards global meaning, spiritual transformation and deepening connectedness with God. In so doing, theological explanations cognitively (and potentially affectively) link transcendent experience to systematized human accounts of God (Hall, 2004). These explanations help embed transcendent experiences in a rich cognitive framework that can promote further spiritual development, and hence flourishing.

According to traditional Christian theology (e.g., McGrath, 1997), God creates the universe and maintains a deep connectedness to His creation. Moreover, (a) God is a community of three persons (called the Trinity) having three distinct functions but existing in perfect unity; and (b) God embeds His perfectly unified communal nature and character in creation itself. In short, theologically, the universe is connected *to* God and *by* God. As the pinnacle of God's universal creation, people are also connected to God and connected by God and thus are whole persons. For both of these reasons, biblical "scholars are increasingly interpreting terms such as 'spirit,' 'soul,' 'heart,' and even 'body' as referring to the whole person under a particular aspect of his or her being in relation" (Shults, 2003, p. 176). For example, commenting on Paul's use of the term "spirit" in the New Testament, Shults (2003) notes that the term "describes the vital principle that animates the person (empowering what we call feeling, thinking, and willing), but in a way that emphasizes human dependence on God for life" (p. 177). The connectedness of the universe and integration of persons are two key theological principles with direct implications for understanding spiritual experience.

Another key theological principle is the spiritual purpose of human life. An emphasis on the causal links between Christian spirituality and flourishing could imply that the purpose of Christian spirituality is simply to attain happiness, self-actualization and social flourishing. However, the goal of the Christian life is deep relationship with God and attaining the likeness of God. This goal is summarized in the Westminster Shorter Catechism—to glorify God and enjoy Him forever (Schaff, 1977). Theologically, relationship with God is dynamic, ending in the transformation into the likeness of God: "The telos of human personality is realized only as persons are stretched beyond the flat confines of human nature in relation to God, as persons are increasingly made in the image and likeness of God" (Rolnick, 2007, p. 256). Thus, Christian theology provides a purpose for spirituality and flourishing (and, indeed for the universe as a whole) that extends beyond the entities themselves. The focus is not upon human actualization and altruism *per se*, but rather on ongoing spiritual transformation, which promotes deep connectedness with humans and with God.

Finally, the centrality of suffering for spirituality and flourishing is a core theological principal. God's purpose for humans—becoming more like God as they live in secure relationship with God—positions suffering as spiritually meaningful and self-actualizing. In Christian theology Christ's suffering is emblematic of the suffering and flourishing relationship. Through his resurrection, Christ flourishes, and makes possible the flourishing of redeemed humanity. This also provides a model for Christians of suffering for faith, and flourishing as a result.

Spiritual experience arises because of God's connectedness to the universe. An important context for Christian spiritual experience is personal suffering, which also leads to flourishing. However, individual human flourishing is not the final goal of life: the telos of flourishing is deep meaning, transformation and connectedness to God within and with the created universe.

Theology, Explanation and Integration

Christian theology explains spiritual experience as a way of:

1. identifying humans as spiritual beings connected to God and dwelling in a universe connected to God. In this way, Christian theology normalizes spiritual experience, making such experience psychologically more amenable to integration.
2. conceptualizing humans as holistic beings, thus anticipating that spiritual experience would affect the whole person. In this way Christian theology normalizes the person-wide impact of spiritual experience—again potentially making such experience easier to accept and integrate both emotionally and cognitively.
3. perceiving humans as embedded in a connected universe, thus anticipating that spiritual experience can involve a deep sense of universal connectedness. In this way, Christian theology normalizes feelings and experiences of interpersonal and cosmic unity in the context of spiritual experience—with commensurate effects on psychological acceptance and integration.
4. positing an external goal for spirituality and flourishing, thus suggesting why spiritual experience need not be experienced as self-centered, self-seeking or self-referential. This explanation may be important where an apparent conflict of values between personal spirituality and service to God and others impedes the integration of spiritual experience.
5. explaining how and why suffering, spirituality and flourishing are not necessarily incongruent.

In short, Christian theology posits that the universe (including human beings) is connected *to*, *by* and *for* God. In this theological context, the Christian believer can find explanation for the occurrence, intra- and interpersonal impact, purpose and conditions for spirituality and flourishing. In addition, Christian theological and spiritual writings provide a language that identifies and expresses the reality of spiritual experiences, over and above identifications and expressions derived from psychology, philosophy, literature, music and the arts. The overall impact of Christian identifications, expressions, and explanations is to situate personal spiritual experience within a wider meaning system that makes spiritual experience more amenable to psychological integration and hence, human flourishing.

CONCLUSION

It has been argued that human longings for flourishing are not met by the hedonism that is widely promoted by the media and other cultural voices. Philosophy has long taught that practicing virtue leads to flourishing, but few claim to be virtuous and flourishing. Psychology proposes therapies and programs to overcome deficits and build strengths, but mental health symptoms are apparently not abating, and self-actualized persons as described by humanistic and positive psychology are not common. There is a need for alternative conceptions of the relationship between spirituality and flourishing.

Christian spirituality in particular is a key resource for human flourishing. As a search for transformation, meaning and connectedness, spirituality promotes the core dimensions of flourishing: actualization and altruism. Spiritual search may result in the attainment of states involving enhanced meaning, inner transformation and deeper connectedness. Sacred texts, spiritual writings and theology provide language, concepts and constructs, embedded in a systematic explanatory system, that promote the integration of spiritual experience. This in turn fosters further search and lifelong flourishing.

REFERENCES

Allport, G. (1950). *The individual and his religion*. New York: Macmillan.

American Psychiatric Association. (2000). *Diagnostic & statistical manual of mental disorders,* (4th ed.).Washington DC: American Psychiatric Assoc.

Aristotle. (2000). *Nichomachean ethics*. R. Crisp (Trans.). Cambridge, UK: Cambridge. (Original work published 350 B.C.E.)

Baer, R. (Ed.). (2006). *Mindfulness-based treatment approaches*. London: Elsevier.

Bakermans-Kranenburg, M. J., & Van Ijzendoorn, M. H. (1997). Adult attachment and the break-up of romantic relationships. *Journal of Divorce and Remarriage, 27*(3/4), 121–139.

Bishop, S. R. (2002). What do we really know about mindfulness-based stress reduction? *Psychosomatic Medicine, 64,* 71–84.

Bradley, J., & Cafferty, T. P. (2001). Attachment among older adults: Current issues and directions for future research. *Attachment and Human Development, 3*(2), 200–221.

Brennan, K. A., & Shaver, P. R. (1998). Attachment styles and personality disorders: Their connection to each other and parental divorce, parental death, and perception of parental care-giving. *Journal of Personality, 66*, 835–878.

Campbell, A., Converse, P. E., & Rodgers, W. L. (1976). *The quality of American life: Perceptions, evaluations, and satisfaction.* New York: Russell Sage Foundation.

Casement, W. (1983, April). Values clarification, Kohlberg and choosing, *Counseling and Values,* 130140.

Cicirelli, V. C. (1998). A frame of reference for guiding research regarding adult attachment and mental health in aging families. In J. Lomranz (Ed.), *Handbook of aging and mental health: An integrative approach* (pp. 341–353). New York: Plenum Press.

Cottingham, J. (2005). *The spiritual dimension: Religion, philosophy and human value.* Cambridge UK: Cambridge University Press.

Crawford, T. N., Shaver, P. R., Cohen, P. A., Pilkonis, O., Gillath, O., & Kasen, S. (2006). Self-reported attachment, interpersonal aggression, and personality disorder in a prospective community sample of adolescence and adults. *Journal of Personality Disorders, 20*(4), 331–351.

Dahlsgaard, K., Peterson, C., & Seligman, M. (2005). Shared virtue: The convergence of valued human strengths across culture and history. *Review of General Psychology, 9*(3), 203–213.

Eng, W., Heimberg, R. G., Hart, T. A., Schneier, F. R., & Liebowitz, M. R. (2001). Attachment in individuals with social anxiety disorder: The relationship among adult attachment styles, social anxiety, and depression. *Emotion, 1*(4), 365–380.

Fonagy, P., Leigh, T., Steele, M., Steele, H., Kennedy, R., Mattoon, G., et al. (1996). The relation of attachment status, psychiatric classification, and response to psychotherapy. *Journal of Consulting and Clinical Psychology, 64*(1), 22–31.

Foot, P. (2001). *Natural goodness.* Oxford: Oxford University Press.

Frederick, S., & Loewenstein, G. (1999). Hedonic adaptation. In D. Kahneman, E. Diener, & N. Schwarz (Eds.), *Well-being: The foundations of hedonic psychology* (pp. 302–329). New York: Russell Sage Foundation.

Gable, S. L., & Haidt, J. (2005). What (and why) is positive psychology? *Review of General Psychology, 9*, 103–110.

Greenfield, E. A., & Marks, N. F. (2004). Formal volunteering as a protective factor for older adults = psychological well-being. *Journal of Gerontology: Social Sciences, 59B*, S258–S264.

Hackney, C. H. (2007). Possibilities for a Christian positive psychology. *Journal of Psychology and Theology, 35*, 211–221.

Hall, T. W. (2004). Christian spirituality and mental health: A relational spirituality framework for empirical research. *Journal of Psychology and Christianity, 23*(1), 66–81.

Harvey, J. H., & Pauwels, B. G. (2004). Modesty, humility, character strength and positive psychology. *Journal of Social and Clinical Psychology, 23*(5), 620–623.

Heller, D., Watson, D., & Hies, R. (2004). The role of person versus situation in life satisfaction: A critical examination. *Psychological Bulletin, 130*(4), 574–600.

Honderich, T. (Ed.). (1995). *The Oxford companion to philosophy.* Oxford: Oxford University Press.

Howell, R. T., & Howell, C. J. (2008). The relation of economic status to subjective well-being in developing countries: a meta-analysis. *Psychological Bulletin, 134*(4), 536–560.

Hursthouse, R. (1999). *On virtue ethics.* Oxford: Oxford University Press.

James, W. (1958). *Varieties of religious experience.* New York: Mentor Books. (Original work published 1902)

Kabat-Zinn, J., Massion, M., Kristeller, J., Peterson, L., Fletcher, K., Pbert, L. et al. (1992). Effectiveness of a meditation-based stress reduction program in the treatment of anxiety disorders. *American Journal of Psychiatry, 149,* 936–943.

Kammann, R. (1983). Objective circumstances, life satisfactions, and sense of well-being: Consistencies across time and place. *New Zealand Journal of Psychology, 12,* 14–22.

Kelley, T. M. (2004). Positive psychology and adolescent mental health: False promise or true breakthrough? *Adolescence, 39*(154), 257–278.

Kohlberg, L. (1968). The child as a moral philosopher. *Psychology Today, 2,* 24–30.

Kohlberg, L., Levine, C., & Hewer, A. (1983). *Moral stages: A current formulation and a response to critics.* New York: Praeger.

Mallinckrodt, R., & Wei, M. (2005). Attachment, social competencies, social support, and psychological distress. *Journal of Counseling Psychology, 52*(3), 358–367.

Maslow, A. H. (1970). *Motivation and personality* (2nd ed.). New York: Harper and Row.

McGrath, A. (1997). *Christian theology: An introduction.* Oxford: Blackwell.

Mikulincer, M. V., Florian, P. A., & Cowan, C. P. (1990). Attachment styles and fear of personal death: A case study of affect regulation. *Journal of Personality and Social Psychology, 58*(2), 273–280.

Mikulincer, M. V., Florian, P. A., & Cowan, C. P. (2002). Attachment security in couple relationships: A systemic model and its implications for family dynamics. *Family Process, 41*(3), 405–434.

Miner, M. (2006). A proposed comprehensive model for ethical decision making. In Morrissey, S. A., & Reddy, P. (Eds.). *Ethics and professional practice for psychologists* (pp. 25–37). Melbourne: Thomson.

Miner, M. (2009). The impact of child-parent attachment, attachment to God and religious orientation on psychological adjustment. *Journal of Psychology and Theology, 37,* 114–124.

Miner, M. H., & Petocz, A. (2003). Moral theory in ethical decision making: Problems, clarifications and recommendations from a psychological perspective. *Journal of Business Ethics, 42*(1), 11–25.

Morrow-Howell, N., Hinterlong, J., Rozario, P., & Tang, F. (2003). Effects of volunteering on well-being of older adults. *Journal of Gerontology: Social Sciences, 58B,* S137–S145.

Otto, R. (1950). *The idea of the holy: An inquiry into the non-relational factor in the idea of the divine and its relation to the rational.* London: Oxford University Press. (Original work published 1917)

Paloutzian, R. (2005). Religious conversion and spiritual transformation. In R. Paloutzian & C. Park (Eds.). *Handbook of the psychology of religion and spirituality* (pp. 331–347). New York: Guilford.

Pargament, K. (1997). *The psychology of religion and coping.* New York: Guilford.

Park, C. (2004). The notion of stress-related growth: Problems and prospects. *Psychological Inquiry, 15,* 69–76.

Park, C. (2005). Religion and meaning. In R. Paloutzian & C. Park (Eds.). *Handbook of the psychology of religion and spirituality* (pp. 295–314). New York: Guilford.

Park, N., Peterson, C., & Seligman, M. (2004). Strengths of character and well-being. *Journal of Social and Clinical Psychology, 23,* 603–619.

Proctor, M. T., Miner, M., McLean, L., Devenish, S., & Ghobary, B. (2009). Exploring Christians' explicit attachment to God representations: The development of a template for assessing attachment to God experiences. *Journal of Psychology and Theology, 37*(4), 245–264.

Raphael, D. D. (1981). *Moral Philosophy.* Oxford: Oxford University Press.

Rieger, E. (2008). *Abnormal psychology: Leading research perspectives.* Sydney: McGraw Hill.

Rolnick, P. (2007). *Person, grace, and God.* Grand Rapids, MI: Eerdmans.

Ryan, R. M., & Deci, E. L. (2000). Self-determination theory and the facilitation of intrinsic motivation, social development, and well-being. *American Psychologist, 55*(1), 68–78.

Ryan, R. M., & Deci, E. L. (2001). On happiness and human potentials: A review of research on hedonic and eudaimonic well-being. *Annual Review of Psychology, 52,* 141–166.

Schaff, P. (1977). *The creeds of Christendom. Volume 3. The Evangelical Protestant creeds, with translations.* Grand Rapids, MI: Baker.

Schutz, A., & Luckmann, T. (1974). *The structures of the life-world.* London: Heinemann.

Seligman, M., & Csikszentmihalyi, M. (2000). Positive psychology: An introduction. *American Psychologist, 55,* 5–14.

Seligman, M., & Peterson, C. (2003). Positive clinical psychology. In L. G. Aspinwall & U. M. Staudinger (Eds.), *A psychology of human strengths: Fundamental questions and future directions for a positive psychology* (pp. 305–317). Washington, DC: American Psychological Association.

Seligman, M., Steen, T., Park, N., & Peterson, C. P. (2005). Positive psychology progress: Empirical validation of interventions. *American Psychologist, 60*(5), 410–421.

Seligman, M., Ernst, R., Gillham, J., Reivich, K., & Linkins, M. (2009). Positive education: Positive psychology and classroom interventions. *Oxford Review of Education, 35*(3), 293–311.

Sheldon, K. M., Ryan, R. M., Deci, E. L., & Kasser, T. (2004). The independent effects of goal contents and motives on well-being: It's both what you pursue and why you pursue it. *Personality and Social Psychology Bulletin, 30*(4), 475–486.

Shults F. L. (2003). *Reforming theological anthropology: After the philosophical turn to relationality.* Grand Rapids, MI: Eerdmans.

Slote, M. (2000). *Morals from motives.* Oxford: Oxford University Press.

Sommers, C. H. (Ed.). (1986). *Right and wrong: Basic readings in ethics.* San Diego: Harcourt Brace Jovanovich.

Spilka, B. (1993, August). Spirituality: Problems and directions in operationalizing a fuzzy concept. Paper presented at the 104th annual meeting of the American Psychological Association, Toronto.

Spilka, B. (2005). Religious practice, ritual, and prayer. In R. Paloutzian & C. Park (Eds.), *Handbook of the psychology of religion and spirituality* (pp. 365–377). New York, NY: Guilford.

St. John of the Cross. (1983). *Centered on love.* M. Flower (Trans.). Varroville, NSW: The Carmelite Nuns. (Original work published 1618)

Smith, J. K. A. (2009). *Desiring the kingdom: Worship, worldview, and cultural formation.* Grand Rapids, MI: Baker.

Swanton, C. (2001). A virtue ethical account of right action. *Ethics, 112*(1), 32–43.

Tasca, G., Balfour, L., Ritchie, K., & Bissada, H. (2007). Change in attachment anxiety is associated with improved depression among women with binge eating disorder. *Psychotherapy: Theory, Research, Practice, Training, 44*(4), 423–433.

Thoits, P. A., & Hewitt, L. N. (2001). Volunteer work and well-being. *Journal of Health and Social Behavior, 42*(2), 115–131.

Wei, M., Mallinckrodt, B., Russell, D. W., & Abraham, T. W. (2004). Maladaptive perfectionism as a mediator and moderator between adult attachment and depressive mood. *Journal of Counseling Psychology, 51*, 201–212.

Wei, M., Vogel, D. L., Ku, T. Y., & Zakalik, R. A. (2005). Adult attachment, affect regulation, negative mood, and interpersonal problems: The mediating roles of emotional reactivity and emotional cutoff. *Journal of Counseling Psychology, 52*, 14–24.

Westen, D., Nakash, O., Thomas, C., & Bradley, R. (2006). Clinical assessment of attachment patterns and personality disorder in adolescents and adults. *Journal of Consulting and Clinical Psychology, 74*(6), 1065–1085.

Williams, B. (1995). Ethics. In A. C. Grayling (Ed.), *Philosophy: A guide through the Subject* (pp. 546–582). Oxford: Oxford University Press.

Wulff, D. M. (1997). *Psychology of religion: Classic and contemporary* (2nd ed.). New York: John Wiley & Sons.

Zinnbauer, B. J., & Pargament, K. I. (2005). Religiousness and spirituality. In R. Paloutzian & C. Park (Eds.), *Handbook of the psychology of religion and spirituality* (pp. 21–42). New York, NY: Guilford.

CHAPTER 2

SPIRITUALITY, HUMAN FLOURISHING, AND DISEASE

Grant Gillett
University of Otago Medical School

ABSTRACT

Spirituality is a vital part of human flourishing, but is difficult to express in terms that do not immediately confine themselves to a faith tradition. One view of spirituality that is derived from Christian mysticism, but is also apt for other traditions, emphasizes a connection with the God of our forebears, the texts of faith, and a great cloud of witnesses. It provokes us to seek something greater than ourselves, particularly at times when ills and mortality become a problem to us. The connection underpins human flourishing, even in the midst of disease or privation, and is exemplified in great stories of faith and healing such as Euripides' *Heracles* and the New Testament healing narratives. What is more, this view of spirituality is able to transcend limited neuropsychological concepts of connectedness, which posit that feelings of connectedness and meaning are derivative only from neurobiological structures and processes.

How do we give substance to a conception of spirituality that does justice to the idea of human flourishing and yet accounts for the importance of spirituality in coping with disease and disaster? We could start by noticing

Beyond Well-Being: Spirituality and Human Flourishing, pages 33–47
Copyright © 2012 by Information Age Publishing

the traditional divisions among *body*, soul/psyche/*mind*, and *spirit* and how these divisions are addressed by the sciences. The body is addressed by physical or biological sciences such as bio-chemistry, physiology, and neuroscience through questions like: In what form does the visual system receive information from the environment? How is the function of the heart connected to the function of the brain? What stimuli does the brain use to monitor hunger? and so on. Psychology (the science of the *psyche)* moves away from the purely biological to ask questions like: How many items of disconnected information can a person remember and what happens, alternatively, if the information is connected together in some meaningful way? Is a human being influenced by the expressed opinions of others in making judgments about stimuli? Do children model their behavior on that of their parents? What contingencies cause people to act in an altruistic way? However, if psychology focuses narrowly on questions of cognition and behavior, what space is left for questions about *spirit?*

Questions that do not merely describe the body or the mind might concern the value or significance of human life. Such questions cannot be answered scientifically and include questions like: What value ought to be attached to a human life? What counts as a good life, and is "the good life" the same as a life in which an individual is content? Are all human beings fundamentally of equal worth? What is truth? (Not what is the truth *about* X, Y or Z?). Wittgenstein (1922) remarks: "How things are in the world is a matter of complete indifference for what is higher. God does not reveal himself in the world" (¶ 6432). Wittgenstein himself professed no particular belief, and he was merely making the point that questions about the spirit did not primarily concern what was in the world and how it functioned, but what significance we ought to attach to our lives.

Significance is found in those connections, relationships, words, images, and stories that inform our thinking. Here our spiritual life is the focus. These aspects of our life are the crucible of identity. A contemporary view of human identity—that it is dispersed, contextual, centered on the body but not contained within it—implies that a lived identity requires us to take a stance informing the regard we have for one another. This stance facilitates the emergence of a different facet of a human being, one that structures attitudes towards and affects relationships with other human beings. That is not just a matter of how a human feels about others, but what evaluation of others those feelings provoke and how we should regard the relevant attitudes. For instance, I might regard you as being of equal value to myself and either be awed by that realization or dismayed because it seems to diminish my own worth. My resulting attitude depends on the way that I connect with the original thought—that you are my equal! This evaluative or attitudinal "field" recalls Wittgenstein's (1953) remark: "My attitude towards him is an attitude towards a soul. I am not of the opinion that he has a soul" (p. 178).

I will argue for a profoundly relational view, linking each of us spiritually to our roots, to the ancestors from whom we have sprung, to the family of which we are a part, to the friendships we form, and to the stories that form our lives together. For many believers, that nexus of relationships itself occurs in a relationship with the divine being (or ground of all being). Even in its non-theistic form, this view of spirituality yields a complex ontology of human identity tied to our ethical and spiritual thinking. It also illustrates why any hope that a new scientific theory of causality could illuminate ethics and religious thought by relating them to so-called brain states is philosophically naïve (see Koch, 2004). In taking this view I will argue that investigating spirituality is best done through an exploration of the duality formed by our unstructured engagement with contingency and the structured layers of meaning in which we operate.

THEOLOGICAL THINKING AFTER LACAN AND POST-STRUCTURALISM

Lacan's post-structuralist influence on the humanities has been widely felt, and I will argue that theology after Lacan should look very different from that often found in standard texts on the philosophy of religion. A Lacanian perspective departs from modernist metaphysics with its apparatus of objects, causes (in the physical or mechanistic sense), durations, absolute positions determinable in space, and so on; rather it entangles us in a world of signifiers. Structuralism directs us to the content of the terms and phrases articulating our beliefs and to the connections between them. Thus, structuralist philosophers have traditionally regarded beliefs as representations of the world, positing an almost-direct relationship between the content of a true belief (the proposition or fact being believed) and the way the world is ("a vertical relation" tying the word directly to the world or a bit of it). This view is problematic when one tries to spell out just what the nature of the link between word and world actually is. For instance, when I believe that a wolf is a type of dog, a certain picture of the world comes to mind, but when I say to a friend, "Watch out, that's a wolf not a dog!" *what* (if any) picture comes to mind? Post-structuralists, therefore, direct us to the human life world and the way that meanings are manufactured in discourses and the events in which they occur in order to discover what is going on. We position ourselves as subjective quilting points (points at which layers of meaning are stitched together—for instance, the biological, the interpersonal, the moral and the mythical), drawing on symbols, stories, and myths to illuminate our engagement with the real, encountered world in order to make some sense of it. In this process, spiritual thinking should help articulate and clarify matters of the spirit (matters to do with human worth, how life should be lived, and our place in the scheme of things) and should respect core connections and resonances of the constituent meanings and myths forming its content.

We might also impose emotive and moral constraints such that the thought concerned should be meaningful in ways that go beyond merely offering closure in a quasi-logical argument. For instance, some find it deeply meaningful to say that the Christian God completed the creation of humankind in the knowledge that it would result in the death of His only begotten Son. This story requires us to interpret it in a way that feels right or satisfies us when we confront the problem of evil. A creation in which there is both suffering and redemption does not gloss over otherwise inexplicable suffering. If we are entangled in a world that is cruel but also a source of joy, then it is unsurprising that we are gripped by the many religious traditions that link good and evil in the person of God—but which refuse to acknowledge God's potential sadism.

Lacan argues that the self is a construct based on the reflection or image-ego of self derived from the reactions, responses, and discourse of others: "the ego is always and as such a meconnaissance" (Lear, 2003, p. 140). We can read this in two ways:

1. If the self is indeed a fiction, then concern about oneself is baseless and should be exploded as it is in Buddhist ontology; there are no actual selves, only the images of selves which are part of a world of illusion.
2. If, on the other hand, Lacan means that the self that I experience as myself here-and-now is a construct of the type envisaged, then that is as good as it gets and the relational and other experiences that seem to transcend one's present life are a kind of non-mortal life (but centered on the body and its presence to others).

This latter view sees the human form as a principle of organization of a living body that holds together a changing aggregation of matter over time. Linked to that view, the human psyche is seen as a longitudinally extended pattern of dispositions and relations from which one abstracts a personality, character, set of beliefs, and so on as patterns evident and salient to us in our dealings with one another. Thus, many discourses—biological, personal, moral, and theological—articulate our understanding of human identity. Creatures of our kind have a story that takes on narrative coherence and therefore unity over time under the influence of discourse with others. I sustain relationships that hold me as an embodied subjectivity and therefore contribute to my individuality and coherence. Others' views constitute the self to be me, and my self-reflection reflects their attitudes and images of me. However, we should not slip too easily into a view of my being itself as based on no more than my "living in the minds of others." The ideas and memories of others are, after all, just aspects of their psyche and do not constitute me as an actual living being.

Perhaps here we find the same elusive kind of truth that is found in attempts to conceptualize love. Why do I love my lover? Do I love him or her because of his or her looks, because of his or her name, because of anything about him or her, any given quality? Would someone else whom I could not tell apart from them do? No, Merleau-Ponty has the right understanding of it when he remarks:

> We weigh the hardihood of the love which promises beyond what it knows, which claims to be eternal when a sickness, perhaps an accident will destroy it . . . but it is true, at the moment of this promise that love extends beyond qualities, beyond the body, beyond time, even though we could not love without qualities, bodies, and time. (1964, p. 27)

Merleau-Ponty captures the inseparability of body and soul and the irreducibility of one to the other. No matter how imaginative one is, the fact of love, so basic to our social and personal world, is not a matter of any subsidiary, contributing other facts that "add up" to love. That irreducibility and indefinability is at the heart of many of our ways of thinking about what goes on in the world even if the origins of those ways of thinking are amenable to evolutionary and psychological explanation. I love my lover as an individual. That love transcends his or her qualities or any complex of features that constitute him or her even if some of them are changed. When we meet, I want to know that the individual with whom I am engaged is still the person I love (and not, for instance, his or her identical twin). No substitute will do even though the needs that my lover fulfils might be fulfilled, even fulfilled better, by some other person.

This particularity and connectedness, un-analyzable as it is, is a recurring theme in our relationships with people. The relationship between lover and beloved is all about identity and spirituality, the irreplaceable value of a particular person. If relatedness and spiritual experience essentially involve irreducibility, it is no wonder that a metaphysics apt for scientific thinking cannot comprehend matters that are eternal, that transcend sickness and death, and that invest bodies, qualities, and peculiarities ("I've grown accustomed to her smile") with an incalculable (and often inexplicable) value. It is hard to separate human flourishing from human relatedness and therefore we should not overlook the fact that our relatedness is itself somewhat resistant to description in purely general terms apt for generalizations and therefore the kinds of entities that can appear in natural sciences. It is hard to say just what it is that flourishing depends on except for a kind of particularity that is, at heart, interpersonal or intersubjective in a way that must be intuitively appreciated.

A Different Thread: Religion and the Brain

I have suggested that in trying to understand the spiritual aspect of human identity and therefore of human flourishing, we should not accept the terms offered by science because those terms deny the centrality of the relationship between humankind and something greater. Kant's two sources of awe—"the starry skies above and the moral law within" (1788/1956)—remind us that our being responds to an apprehension of our place in the order of things and also to a moral law that resides within and embraces all humankind. These sources are traditional loci for beginning the exploration of spirituality so, when we examine the neuroethics of (or a neuroscientifically informed approach to) spirituality and human identity, we should examine the images and symbols that reach beyond biology to disclose important truths about human beings and their flourishing. When we do so, we find that much is wrong in contemporary work relating religion to human brain function.

Koch claims that, for scientists, the metaphysics of ethics and religion require causes to be clear and not just correlations:

> Science seeks a causal chain of events that leads from neural activity to subjective percept...what organisms under what conditions generate subjective feelings, what purpose these serve and how they come about. If such a theory can be formulated...this is bound to have significant consequences for ethics including a new conception of humans. (2004, p. 326)

Writers such as Koch and Ramachandran and Blakeslee (1998) notice the correlations between spirituality (or religious experience) and activity in certain parts of the brain and speculate about the causal links between them, but such questions miss the mark entirely. When we have experiences and think about them, the brain is where those experiences and thoughts are inscribed. But just as a trace in the brain says nothing about the reality of an insult that has deeply affected us, so it tells us nothing about the kind of truth discerned in the connectedness of all things, or my links to my ancestors, or the haunting of the world by sources of meaning that transcend everyday realities. Our appreciation of art indicates for some that we hold aesthetic values and that those are real and not just unscientific ways of talking about the neuroscience of artistic experience. My regard for an ancestor who saw human beings as fundamentally worthy neither mitigates nor explains my commitments to those insights, especially when, at times, they disturb my pursuit of what seem desirable life goals.

The issue of human spirituality touches our thinking both in ethics and religion, whether or not we link an absolute conception of ethics to a context of divine law emanating from a universal Law Giver. The notion of an eternal word that embodies truth about human life and articulates goodness (comprising purpose and worthwhile meaning) in terms of demands conditional only upon the fact that one is a human being, may or may not deserve our respect. But when we ask whether such demands should be heeded, studying the brain and how it enables us to articulate and interrogate such questions does not help us answer such questions.

MacIntyre (1984) makes the disquieting suggestion that our moral discourse draws on "fragments of a conceptual system" that once structured our knowledge of the world and our place in it. Moral thought, he argues, is part of a context that subtends certain attitudes and grounds a sense of belonging according to which "oughts" and "shoulds" have a place. These "oughts" and "shoulds" stand as signposts based on ties of family or kinship to every other human being because of ancient progenitors (such as sky father and earth mother). They underpin our expectations of, and obligations to, one another. They foster a sense in which we are all children of the earth and sky—but what significance this sense should have in our lives and how is it to be applied in our understanding of ourselves is not a matter of deduction or scientific psychology. Rather it requires one to orient oneself within a framework of meaning. Acknowledging another as a *soul* grounds certain ways of regarding and addressing the other that exclude certain kinds of conduct.

These fragments of meaning that move us provide a context that transcends mundane and contingent concerns delineating the horizons of life, and focuses on truths pertaining to our being. Ethical thought sustainable within an ontology of human beings as moral beings can, as Kant says, inspire awe and create reverence in us, thereby providing a basis to explore our self-conceptions and values. There is no immediate connection between this ontology and goal-directed action, yet if the person before me has a place in the order of things that makes them unique, then any relation with them is framed in a certain way that transcends my own views.

This ontological foundation extracts rich but often ignored features of life. They ground a conception of spirituality within our historical situation in a certain human group. Any human group has many kinship relations functioning as our roots and supports, and those connections embrace images and icons of special relevance to the group. In such a context, one's subjectivity is connected to that of others and formed in a deeply relational sense. These aspects of our being-in-the-world-with-others endow us with a conceptual framework about the beginning and ending of life and of the names and self-constructions each of us can apply to ourselves.

The stories, myths, and symbols that humans use in different settings to cope with ethical issues are ways of articulating our spiritual being. They transcend economic conceptions of life, and may even overturn the demands of the ordinary. An understanding of spirituality in this sense appears in the texts of liberation that are increasingly important in an age of reductive biomedicine and its commercialization. Recall Badger's words from the story, *Crow and Weasel*:

> The stories people tell have a way of taking care of them. If stories come to you, care for them. And learn to give them away where they are needed. Sometimes a person needs a story more than food to stay alive. That is why we put these stories in each other's memory. This is how people care for themselves. One day you will be good storytellers. Never forget these obligations. (Lopez, 1990, p. 60)

Narratives of identity and relatedness can take care of us when we contemplate death by telling us that we are held, that we persist, and that there is a significance to our mortal lives. Further and deeper insights can also be found in our spiritual thinking.

CONNECTEDNESS AND THE INNER SELF

Two prominent themes in spiritual life are our connectedness with others and the idea of a self that is inner and may, with discipline and diligence, be developed. If the real basis, the *hypokeimenon* (or underlying reality) of human subjectivity is not individualistic, then these facets of spirituality may be deeply, even internally (i.e., through a conceptual connection in which they are tied up in each other's meaning), related. The themes of connectedness and the inner, or authentic, self appear in different traditions in different ways, but the myths and symbols used are very revealing.

Spirit, as distinct from both body and mind, often shares etymology with the idea of breath or wind moving in and through the individual to create sources of aspiration and inspiration (thus pneuma, noumenal, noemata, norms). We are inspired by taking into the body that non-material component of the source of one's energy and the basis of one's voice. The air we breathe is the present and immediate sign of life itself. In religious terms, fasting is a traditional means of communing with, or living only by, the spirit, and the chakras are exercises focusing on breath as spirit. The air I breathe out, you breathe in, is the medium of life uniting us. This unification, however, becomes a moral challenge in times of plague or epidemic and therefore calls on us to re-evaluate our values at such times.

Spirit reaches beyond time and space and connects us with our beginnings so that the rhythm we see in our own breathing is echoed everywhere. The earth and all living things emerge from the void and share life. In Maori myth, *Tane*, the father of all living things, creates the space between earth mother and sky father so that life can develop and, like the God of Islam and Christianity, *Tane* is personal and omnipresent with those who live; "If you go to the ends of the earth I am there." Hence, in Maori mythology, the queen of the dead has to create and descend into the realm of the dead in order to escape him. We who live relate to each other in a way that death effaces, so that when Achilles meets Odysseus in the land of the dead, he remarks that he would rather be a landless field hand and alive, than be the king of the dead.

In all traditions spirit adds moral significance or purpose and meaning to human life by providing a context of order and belonging within which the moments of life take on a supra-mundane significance and are connected with the transcendent. For Plato, the spirit or soul contemplates the forms used by the intellect to reveal the nature of earthly things, which are themselves only imperfect and corruptible instances of their divine correlates. But a step back into philosophy locates the discussion more readily in traditions of scholarship that inform current bioethics, the latter of which often struggle to find a place for spirituality.

THE PHILOSOPHICAL SPIRIT: KANT, HEIDEGGER AND LEVINAS

Kant (1789/1929), as we have seen, pointed out that our representations of the world are not the world itself but merely ways of rendering our dynamic being-in-the-world tractable for thought. He also has laid before us the idea that an individual is free to act when he or she enacts a way of being that stands under a conception of the order of things (the cosmos) and the moral law. That conception ought to inspire reverence and invokes membership in a kingdom of ends where each member has their own dignity. Therefore our being-there (Heidegger's *dasein*) can be illuminated through the categories of spirit inherited from one tradition or other. It would be silly to think that those traditions and what they tell us about our significance can be grasped or adequately appreciated merely by relating them to brain events. There is a mystery in life searched for through our spirituality and dismissed by what Nietzsche called "the prevailing mechanistic stupidity…offered us by the Darwinists and anti-teleologists," "an uncouth industrious race of machinists and bridge builders" (Nietzsche, 1886/1975, paras. 14 & 21).

The idea of a ground of our being inspires the hope that we are rooted in a reality with an order of its own and that we are entangled in that reality, which is common to a number of spiritual traditions. Christians speak of God the creator and sustainer of all life; Buddhists and Hindus think of human beings as moments of God's self forget-fullness. They claim we are like drops of water rising from the surface of the ocean, forming clouds in the heavens, falling as rain on the earth, coalescing into streams, rivers and lakes or frozen into glaciers and ice fields, and, in each of these states, have definition and finality. For Maori, the origin and center of life from which all life emanates is found in *Tane*, who brings forth from *Papatuanuki*—earth mother—children of men each with an indwelling and distinctive life or *mauri* as a legacy of his or her birth.

Emmanuel Levinas (1996) follows and extends Heidegger's notion of being-in-the-world-with-others, suggesting that engagement with another person allows something radically "other" to erupt into one's world, something indicated by the human face. The face presents an enigma because our representations of the other do not "capture" that other. As a result, we find ourselves "face to face" with the core of ethics—the fact that the world is a shared world and that those sharing it with us have their own ways of representing the world that are not identical to our own. That single realization disrupts the dominance of one's own psychic economy in constructing the world. Levinas reminds us that the face of God is to be encountered in the face of every human being, and upon it is written indelibly the commandment "Thou shalt not murder!" As a result, one is engaged in a series of open-ended encounters that may be transformative in unexpected ways. Because these situations can be transformative, we should embrace them. Levinas provides an orientation that frames a moral psychology and does not form a mere part of it.

But the phenomenology of being-with-others is, necessarily, inarticulate. Derrida explored Heidegger's claim that self-understandings must be articulated, and so deconstructed the subject-as-constructed or as an object of knowledge. Each of us is some-body—an embodied intersection of multiple texts, derived from icons, myths, images, and stories, that lie at the heart of any culture. This culture has inscribed us and drawn us into its disciplines. The texts are, however, combined by each human being in a way that defines a unique story. So where does this leave the inner, authentic self found in many religions and even secular humanist writings?

The inner self discovered by dispelling the fog of unknowing surrounding us is a recurrent theme in spiritual texts. Christian mysticism and the mantras of self renunciation both try to strip away illusions and to reveal the indwelling of the divine in a human being. If we pursue our intertextual nature—that is, as beings inscribed by different traditions linking us and our ancestors to powerful symbols and motifs—the self is revealed as a living or inspir(it)ed node of resonance galvanized and given meaning by the narratives that generate it. In this vein, Giorgio Agamben (2000) directs us to consider the voice that speaks through articulated communication, and by speaking takes on a shape or identity. Spirituality is voice, breath; it animates dust or biological matter, and without its presence that matter is dead, and when that death is a death of spirit or the sense that life is not worth living, such animation can be life-saving.

The energy inspiriting life arises, *inter alia*, from the significances found in mythologies, iconographies, and symbolism. All of these offer us ways to enunciate our vulnerability, mortality, singularity, and contingency. As we enunciate these meanings, we enact significance by locating and describing our current experience in a narrative. Narrative locates us within an order of things, an order that is at least partially laid out and mapped by past generations that have discerned patterns in the world—patterns that would not be evident to any one of us in isolation. The theme of an all-encompassing Word or Truth imparting order and life to human beings and securing their place in the world is widespread—the *logos* of the stoics, the way (*dao*) of Confucius, the path of life and goodness, are all portrayed as written into us to map our life-journeys, and provide guidance when we are lost.

We need a vision of things that transcend the material world in order to understand what happens to us. The sixteen year old girl, more-or-less dead as a result of cerebral anoxia after respiratory arrest at a teenage party, is visited by her father, who cannot come to terms with the monstrous absurdity of her death. The loss is made even more painful as she lingers in a persistent vegetative state, and no one wants to broach the possibility of withdrawal of nutrition and hydration. A wise woman, an elder who came to see her and offer spiritual guidance, articulated her state as one of being held back from her journey to the land of the spirits that wait for her. Her tube is a restraint that holds her among the living where she no longer has a real place. The pain of her loss to her family is as bad, but the loss is seen as more than a mere cessation of function in a body. The girl's death is given depth and meaning along with all the "brief candles" that are human lives. Is the story of spirit the truth? At the very least, the story adjusts our thinking to a sense of what makes us alive, and that it is something to be valued rather than simply preserved. These truths are articulated, but not in the language of biomedicine or anywhere else is the scientific panopticon.

The ineffable, the holy, or that which is not encompassed by cognitive tools captures our attention in a different way. By shrinking this holiness to a point of inner contemplation, we remove its all-embracing significance in relation to the world around us, including its beauty and wonder. By allowing our minds to be touched by the enlivening spirit, we re-expand the boundaries of our being. Thus we can reaffirm each person's uniqueness, and also acknowledge the deep affinity we can find with each other—especially when we look past the many differences that often preoccupy us.

We may wonder how the spirit of a young person can cope with the tragedy that follows an accident in which one of their friends has died. Do we have the stories that equip us for such moments, or are they no longer woven into the fabric of our being? Each tradition offers us stories where life is at its nadir and all seems bleak, but something arises that is unprecedented, transformed and given significance by what has gone before, so that the value (the impetus for flourishing) emerges out of its lived narrative context.

Stories of the spirit transcend historically-situated consciousness and connect us with the wit and wisdom of other ages and their human quests to find meaning in life and the grace to face death with dignity. Stories of the spirit disclose forgiveness where we would otherwise have only the language of legality. Contractual language renders invisible and unthinkable that precious aspect of our being together. For that reason, among others, stories of the spirit are liberating; they allow us to move out of our restrictions and flourish as human souls alive to the world and other people in a responsive and valuable way.

FREEDOM AND CONTESTING MORES

Spirituality lifts our eyes from the possibilities of the everyday world. The divine wind reminds us of the breath that gives us life and the cleansing water that allows healing and refreshment in the arid wastes of suffering. In the most unlikely places we find loving and transformative touches that are things of the spirit. They beatify actions however bloody, messy and unromantic. We are beset by directives and discourses that demean our humanity. We can render life in such terms and try to make it bearable through escapism and pleasure, but there is another way. We live and love in a world where real tragedies happen, real joy is found, and real connections are forged through time and across barriers of culture and history. In those things we discover the resonance in ourselves of inscriptions, utterances, and works that deepen our understanding of ourselves and others.

CARE OF THE SOUL AS SPIRIT WORK AND THE CRAFTING OF FLESH

Foucault's (1994) *cura sui* recalls that the Greeks regarded philosophy as therapy for maladies of the soul. Wittgenstein (1965) echoes this, claiming that ethics is absolute, disinterested and concerned with "the health of the soul" (p. 7). He also refers to ethics as "supernatural," or reaching beyond the scientific descriptions that deliver a certain kind of knowledge. Foucault's (1994) care of the self comprises: *a critical function*, the dynamic of *a struggle*, *a therapeutic function*, and *a disciplinary function*—all aspects of fitting oneself to fulfill the good inherent in one's own being.

The *critical function* reminds us that ethical thought requires reflection upon oneself so as to assess what one has become so that the true value of cultural inscriptions may be discerned.

The dynamic of *a struggle* indicates that one's standing in relation to others and one's place of belonging may conflict with selfish interests. This conflict is not identical to the traditional struggle of the flesh against the spirit, but rather represents struggle between ways of engaging with the world that allow selfish desire to eclipse the needs of others and ways of being that open the soul to the effects of my actions on others so that my desires are de-centered—no longer totally absorbed with my own concerns and point of view. When this conflict is recognized, personal desires are often moderated by mutual recognition, the creation of valued interpersonal relationships, and a sense of one's membership in a kingdom of ends (Kant, 1788/1956).

The *therapeutic function* is often exercised in the company of another who engages with one to help articulate and contextualize one's own feelings through conversations. Such conversations probe one's integrity in moral, personal, and relational terms, and so contribute to truthful wellbeing.

A *set of disciplinary functions* develop one's ability to enact criticism and the deliverances of the therapeutic function. Foucault follows the Greeks in likening these disciplines to the routines and regimen of an athlete preparing him or herself for the games (Foucault, 1994). The disciplines are diverse: some are general, such as listening and writing; others quite specific, such as the meditation on future ills, practices of abstinence and privation, the control of thought, and meditation on death. Heidegger famously regards the last as essential to authentic life in the face of our own mortality, and as a reminder to use our moments well. This ethical work *connects me to the truth* and therefore connects me beyond my self. Wittgenstein (1980) remarks that such truth is not subjective but part of a meaningful discourse that reveals aspects of the world not susceptible to scientific method: "the good is also divine, the good is outside the space of facts" (p. 3), an awareness lacking in those who make a common neuro-ethical mistake.

A NEURO-ETHICAL MISTAKE

Thus it is a mistake to identify spiritual or ethical aspects of our being with any complex of neurological functions arising from structures associated with a localized area of the brain such as the limbic systems. The ethical and spiritual aspects of my identity make me aware of, and give significance to, my actual connectedness to those who go before me, and to the order of things as a whole. These are not fictions, they are actualities—I am produced by them. Moreover, thinking about these aspects closely involves my emotions, my relationships, and my sense of who I am (including integrating memories and inner bodily states).

The temporal and limbic areas of the brain provide the informational substrate for this activity, and so evoke complex thoughts and images relating to the spiritual and ethical aspects of our being-in-the-world-with-others. Nevertheless, the thoughts and images active in these areas have a significance that different individuals relate to in their own way (and therefore they have an objective presence in the world not restricted to the individual subject who thinks about them). These thoughts and images entangle us in such widely connected historico-cultural realities that they move us in ways of which neurobiology can tell us only a little. Neurobiology can tell us the means the nervous system uses to process, record and associate things, and may even prompt us to look at areas of our functioning we would not otherwise have realized were so closely involved, but it does not tell us about the significances animating our dealings with them. Such significance is not a question for neuroscience but for ethics and a kind of enquiry that deals with more things in heaven and earth than are dreamed of in neuro-philosophy.

The tendency of many scientists is to a reductive view, according to which the neural mechanisms underlying our cognitive abilities are exclusively identified with features of what we come to know: Ramachandran and Blakeslee (1998), for instance, write of temporal lobe epilepsy:

> But does this syndrome imply that our brains contain some sort of circuitry that is actually specialized for religious experience? Is there a "God module" in our heads? And if such a circuit exists, where did it come from? Could it be a product of natural selection, a human trait as natural in the biological sense as language or stereoscopic vision? Or is there a deeper mystery at play, as a philosopher, epistemologist or theologian might argue? (p. 175)

This short remark implies that either the neural mechanisms are a product of evolution or that they indicate a deeper mystery; but why not both? It is plausible that everything about us is evolved, and also that our cognitive systems have evolved to track the truth. If so, things that these systems tell us about are, in some sense or another, true of our being-in the-world. Under these conditions, the spiritual aspects of our identity, such as the use of stories to derive value and make sense of our lives, might be as much a part of ourselves as our ability to exploit natural resources in order to adapt to widely diverse ecological contexts. Malcolm Jeeves (1997) makes the point as follows:

> Since each of us is a complex system, simultaneously part of a larger social system and composed of smaller systems which in turn are composed of ever smaller subsystems, any aspect of human behaviour and cognition chosen for investigation may be analyzed at different levels. Each level entails its own questions and appropriate methods for answering them. While the account

given at each level may be complete within itself that does not mean that by itself it constitutes a full account of the phenomenon under investigation. Each level complements the others. (p. 237)

Spirituality relates us to the sources of value in our lives and grounds our ability to conceptualize and connect to these sources. It is no wonder that spirituality retains its recognition of whole human beings as beings with voice, from whom all discourse and all philosophical or psychological inquiry springs. Therefore, we stand, or should stand, in awe of "the starry skies above and the moral law within" (Kant, 1788/1956, p. 166), even following the decade of the brain and the psychology inspired by it.

REFERENCES

Agamben, G. (2000). *Potentialities: Collected essays in philosophy.* D. Heller-Roazen (Trans.). Stanford: Stanford University Press.

Foucault, M. (1994). *Ethics: subjectivity and truth.* London: Penguin.

Jeeves, M. (1997). *Human nature at the millennium.* L. W. Beck (Trans.). Grand Rapids: Baker Books.

Kant, I. (1956). *The critique of practical reason.* Indianapolis: Bobbs Merrill. (Original work published 1788)

Kant, I. (1929). *The critique of pure reason.* N. K. Smith (Trans.). London: Macmillan. (Original work published 1789)

Koch, C. (2004). *The quest for consciousness.* Englewood, CO: Roberts and Co.

Lear, J. (2003). *Therapeutic action.* New York: Other Press.

Levinas, E. (1996). *Enigma and phenomenon.* In A. Peperzak, S. Critchley, & R. Bernasconi, (Eds.), *Basic philosophical writings* (pp. 65–78). Bloomington: Indiana University Press.

Lopez, B. (1990). *Crow and weasel.* Toronto: Random House.

MacIntyre, A. (1984). *After virtue.* Notre Dame: University Press.

Merleau Ponty, M (1964). *The primacy of perception.* Evanston, IL: Northwestern University Press.

Nietzsche, F. (1975). *Beyond good and evil.* R. J. Hollingdale (Trans.). London: Penguin. (Original work published 1886)

Ramachandran, V. S., & Blakeslee, S. (1998). *Phantoms in the brain.* New York: William Morrow.

Wittgenstein, L. (1922). *Tractatus logico philosophicus.* D. Pears & B. McGuiness (Trans.). London: Routledge & Kegan Paul.

Wittgenstein, L. (1953). *Philosophical investigations.* [G.E.M. Anscombe, Trans.] Oxford: Blackwells.

Wittgenstein, L.(1965) Lecture on ethics Philosophical Review,74,3-26.

Wittgenstein, L. (1980). *Culture and value.* P. Winch (Trans.). Oxford: Basil Blackwell.

CHAPTER 3

THE CONTRIBUTION OF SPIRITUALITY TO OUR UNDERSTANDING OF HUMAN FLOURISHING

The Perspective of Christian Theology

Stuart Devenish
Booth College, The Salvation Army

ABSTRACT

This chapter explores spirituality's contribution to human flourishing from the perspective of Christian theology. It puts forward three basic theses: firstly that spirituality is a primary category in contributing to human health and wellbeing; secondly that Christian spirituality is itself a potent resource for generating human wellbeing; and thirdly, that as well as being a religious tradition, Christianity can be understood as a healing tradition, which offers its adherents a variety of practical, theological and existential "therapies." Four healing "traditions" are explored in the chapter, and their approaches to human health and wholeness identified: (a) traditional Western medicine's naturalistic-biological-curative approach, (b) complementary medicine's ho-

Beyond Well-Being: Spirituality and Human Flourishing, pages 49–64
Copyright © 2012 by Information Age Publishing
All rights of reproduction in any form reserved.

listic-systemic-harmonizing approach, (c) the psycho-therapeutic tradition's developmental-psycho-somatic-integrative approach, and (d) Christianity's cosmic-restorative-redemptive approach.

This chapter defines spirituality both in terms of a category intrinsic to the intra-psychic operations within the human person, and from the perspective of a human "response" to God's redemptive animation of the soul and being grasped by life itself. It concludes by offering an understanding of wholeness, health and healing from the perspective of Christian theology and spirituality, suggesting that the redemption at the heart of the Christian gospel should be understood as a therapeutic *re-creation*.

> *Thou art the physician, I am the sick man.*
>
> —Augustine, *Confessions*, X

Thomas Hobbes described human life as "solitary, poor, nasty, brutish and short" (Hobbes, 1651, p. 78). Every living person can readily acknowledge from his or her own experience as a finite human creature that to be human is to suffer and to be vulnerable to a range of limit-conditions that threaten his or her wellbeing. *Physically* such limit-conditions are encountered through illness, aging, morbidity and death. *Emotionally* they are encountered through anxiety, despair, depression and mental illness. *Relationally* they are encountered through conflict, isolation, marginalization and social exclusion. On the other hand, it can be argued that spirituality is a force that counteracts these limit-conditions by offering human subjects a form of potency that knits the fragmented parts of their existence—body, emotions, identity and life-history—into a single integrated *whole*, and that offers a series of resources for re-charging this integrated whole with a renewed *élan vital*.

Spirituality is a slippery term capable of being defined in multiple ways. For the purposes of this chapter, spirituality is defined as a mode of functioning: (a) that is intrinsic to humans, (b) that integrates both corporeal and transcendental aspects of the human person into a single unified whole, (c) that produces in the animated soul the sense of being grasped by life itself, thus elevating the whole person—body, mind and soul—to a new heightened level of existence. Further, in this chapter I identify Christian spirituality as comprising awareness, response and participation in the Christo-centric redemptive drama played out in the biblical narratives. First, Christian spirituality is a deep awareness of the direct relevance to their own lives of the transformative potential found in the Christian story. Second, it is a response to the supernatural world-picture found in the biblical records—records that are understood to be historically accurate and existentially true. Third, it is a participation in the relational, redemptive and restorative drama that brings together Christ's multi-faceted healing potential with critical human need.

HUMAN FLOURISHING AS WELLBEING AND WHOLENESS

Descriptors associated with human flourishing include things such as happiness, wellbeing, coping, health, wholeness, healing, salutogenesis, resilience, felicity, serenity, integration, contentment, pleasure, altruism, ecstasy, elevation, euphoria, delight, and even love (Vernon, 2008). A person who is *flourishing* can be described as someone engaged in the process of living vigorously, and whose biological, psychological, emotional, intellectual, social, economic and political parts are integrated into a functioning whole. Each component part works cooperatively to produce a convivial, self-aware, productive individual.

According to Aristotle, the chief contributor to human happiness and the "good life" is *eudaimonia*, which refers to the realization of one's true potential (Shults & Sandage, 2006). Further, Aristotle argued that *eudaimonia* contributes positively both to individual wellbeing and to the whole *polis* and society. By contrast, the *hedonic* pattern prioritizes personal enjoyment and pleasure. The eudaimonic form refers to the human's full functioning when an inherent virtuous potential is realized, whereas the hedonic form relates to a momentary and personal choice in favor of subjective wellbeing (Deci & Ryan, 2008).

THE MEDICAL TRADITIONS

In 1946 through 1948 the World Health Organization defined wellbeing as a "state of complete physical, mental, and social wellbeing and not merely the absence of disease or infirmity" (Shults & Sandage, 2006, p. 190). Three medical traditions commonly operate in the Western world. Each in their own way wrestles with the WHO definition of health and tries to deliver health outcomes that are consistent with their understanding of the human being.

First, traditional Western medicine, represented by such activities as surgery, oncology and general practice, treats the symptoms and perceived root causes of disease through the application of curative technologies such as surgical intervention, chemical remedies or physical therapies. Its practitioners have received appropriate training in the philosophy and practice of this curative tradition. Guided by the "do no harm" code of the Hippocratic Oath, medical practitioners seek to heal the malfunctioning body. It adopts a "repair shop" approach to human wholeness. Individual patients' therapeutic needs are addressed by reading and responding to the physical symptoms. Various international and national healthcare frameworks and strategies have been developed in order to prevent the problem of specific symptoms (Ryff & Singer, 1998). Diagnosticians universally accept that symptoms represent a physical deficit in an individual or a population. They are limited to the bio-physical dimension, which excludes non-material causes. Such one-dimensionality largely ignores the growing body of literature connecting religion and spirituality to physical health (Hill & Pargament, 2003).

Secondly, so-called complementary medicine, expressed through such disparate practices as reiki, pranic healing and homoeopathy, represents a counterpoint to conventional Western medicine. Complementary medicine is strongly committed to a holistic approach to human wellbeing, and values extra-somatic elements in its therapeutic regime in order to restore harmony among perceived nervous, psychic and spiritual energies within the body. Although largely marginalized by traditional Western medicine, holistic and complementary medicines are increasingly welcomed by the general population and invited into the medical mainstream by limited numbers of medical practitioners and health insurance agencies. Although there is as yet no identifiable spiritual core to its therapeutic practice, complementary medicine pays particular attention to multiple dimensions of human wellbeing, and its genius is to harmonize the life-forces that belong to each dimension—physical, nervous, emotional, mental, cosmic and spiritual.

Thirdly, psycho-therapeutic medicine addresses pathology in the human psyche through a range of practices focused around psychology, psychiatry and psychotherapy. Although Sigmund Freud defined religion using terms such as neurosis and delusion, attitudes about religion and spirituality in contemporary psycho-therapeutic medicine are undergoing significant change. Willingness to renegotiate previous statements about the place of religion and spirituality in its psycho-therapeutic regimes is demonstrated by the American Psychiatric Association's *Diagnostic and Statistical Manual of Mental Disorders* (DSM-IV-TR, 2001). This has reversed its earlier policy of identifying religion and spirituality as pathogenic factors in diagnosis, and has now identified these as important contributors to positive human wellbeing (Oman & Thoresen, 2005).

THEOLOGY AND HUMAN HEALTH AND WELLBEING

This chapter argues that Christianity can also be called a healing tradition alongside the three identified above because of its historical and contemporary commitment to healing, and its preoccupation with restoring personal and cosmic wholeness. So what does Christian theology have to say concerning the project of human health, wholeness and wellbeing? Theology, as the "science of God," focuses on identifying the *theocentric* attributes of God. At first glance, it may seem that theology is preoccupied with other-worldly, metaphysical concerns that have little to do with the human project. But theology also has an *anthropocentric* aspect to it, which is concerned with the human reception of the divine life and its resources, resulting in the restoration of the broken *imago Dei* (image of God) post-creation.

Because humankind is created in the image of God, the categories of God's personhood (e.g., goodness, relational harmony, justice and peace) are understood to be primary categories of the godly life: "Your kingdom come, your will be done on earth as it is in heaven" (Matthew 6:10; unless stated otherwise all biblical references are New International Version— NIV). Augustine's question, "What, then, am I, O my God? Of what nature am I?" (Augustine, 1999, p. 219), represents an early "turn to the subject" in Christianity that has continued to the present time. Such willingness to explore human experience and its role in the interior life reflects Christianity's desire to draw from the overflow of divine superabundance in order to identify resources that contribute to the life of the human person. The biblical narratives are replete with stories of healing from sickness, restoration to wholeness, and resurrection to life—all of which have their origin in the divine life and will. Healing and wholeness are also intrinsic categories within Christian *soteriology* and represent a considerable component of the Christian understanding of human wellbeing. This is expressed in Christians' earthly existence as well as in a future eschatological fulfillment of Jesus' teachings. In short: salvation will not be fulfilled in an indefinite future, but has direct application to the current existential and historical moment.

Jesus came healing, and the narrative accounts of his interactions with people repeatedly express his concern for their physical, social, and spiritual wellbeing. Jesus' description of his own ministry was that "the blind receive their sight, the lame walk, those who have leprosy are cured, the deaf hear, [and] the dead are raised" (Matthew 11:5). The book of Revelation depicts the end of history as a time and place when "He [God] will wipe away every tear from their eyes. There will be no more death or mourning or crying or pain, for the old order of things has passed away" (Revelation 21:4). Such descriptors of the superabundance of the divine resources made available to human creatures and the restoration to wholeness it brings demonstrate the New Testament's vital interest in human health and wellbeing in the here and now. Yet Christianity's therapeutic domain is not limited to private self-interest, but extends to incorporate a cosmic dimension. In order to understand this we must proceed to discuss the categories of creation and redemption that form the Christian paradigm.

CREATION AND REDEMPTION

In order to arrive at a better understanding of Christianity's commitment to human health and wellbeing, we now turn to the *a priori* question of "What is the human person?"

In contrast to general conceptualizations of the human person, Christianity conceives of mankind in exalted terms, as being "created in the image of God" (Genesis 1:27). Along with the rest of creation, God also identifies humanity as intrinsically "good" (Genesis 1:31). Thus Calvin can argue that if God is the glory of man, then it can also be said that "man is the glory of God" (Vaux, 1997, p. 119). Therefore, humanity is more than simply a conscious and self-referential being capable of deliberative action, but a creature who exhibits God-like qualities and whose mind is synchronously engaged with both this-worldly and other-worldly concerns. Humanity is a divine project, undertaken by God in His own name, created in His likeness, made for His glory, and endowed with God-like qualities and gifts.

The doctrines of the *creation, fall* and *redemption* provide a firm theological foundation for Christianity's commitment to human wellbeing. In Genesis 1:27, humanity is created *imago Dei*—in the image of God. Immediately there follows God's command to "be fruitful and increase in number; [to] fill the earth and subdue it" (Genesis 1:28). This command represents a divine manifesto that directly mandates human flourishing. The three jussive imperatives, "be fruitful" (Hebrew, *pharu*, to be many, literally to flourish), "increase" (Hebrew, *rav*, to become a multitude), and "fill" (Hebrew, *malah*, to be fertile), occur in the context of God's blessing upon humanity (Westermann, 1984, pp. 140–141). Moreover, in Christian thought, human flourishing is dependent upon a harmonious balance among environmental, social, and spiritual relationships.

Later biblical narratives are filled with stories of healing from sickness, restoration to wholeness, and resurrection to life. Members of the early church shared their lives and possessions in a form of egalitarian socialism based on Jesus' teaching concerning the coming of the kingdom. The apostle John greeted his readers, "I pray that you may enjoy good health and that all may go well with you, even as your soul is getting along well" (3 John 1:2).

Despite the divine intention that humanity should flourish, Hobbes' characterization of life as "solitary, poor, nasty, brutish and short" is not entirely inaccurate. Humankind may have achieved numerical flourishing—to the extent that its rampant fruitfulness now threatens the very sustainability of the ecological system that sustains our species and others (Swedish, 2008)—but it has not achieved a corresponding *social, psychological* or *physiological* flourishing. Higher-than-acceptable rates of depression, anxiety, suicide and other mental health problems indicate a lack of human wellbeing. From the perspective of Christian theology, this lack of wellbeing is the result of sin. Johannes Metz (1971) stated: "Sin has something violent about it. It forces on the world something other than its own worldly being. Sin does not tolerate and let things be themselves . . . It over paints, distorts, forces, destroys things" (p. 49).

Similarly, Augustine's understanding of the concept of *concupiscentia* (perverted self-love) depicts humankind as a tragically flawed creature. In Augustine's terms, original sin (leading to *concupiscentia*) was thought to be transmitted biologically through sexual procreation. Such an understanding might cause us to suspect God of mis-creating humankind as a ontological defective beings. Such a view is exactly opposite to the biblical account of creation. In Christian theology, redemption is the process by which God takes the initiative to restore a dehumanized humanity to its original design and status. Mircea Eliade wrote, "Life cannot be repaired; it can only be recreated" (LaChance, 2006, p. 2). According to the biblical story, the end-product of sin's entrance into the world is pain, injustice, unhappiness, fragmentation and death. Any return to an Edenic state requires a comprehensive, cosmic solution. The redemption that God effected is represented by the statement, "God was in Christ, reconciling the world to himself" (2 Corinthians 5:19, New American Standard Bible—NASB). The nature of this redemption was concerned with suffering; God is willing to take human suffering into himself (Fiddes, 1992) by sending Christ to the cross in order to bring about a second or *re*-creation. Christ, as the second Adam, did what the first Adam could not, by dying in humanity's stead and so making possible the resurrection to a "new life" (Romans 6:4). Thus he repairs the cosmological breach and restores to life those who have experienced suffering and death through sin.

According to the Christian account of history, Jesus' crucifixion, resurrection and ascension *effected* the necessary reconciliation between God and his broken creation, restoring it to its original creative design. On these terms then, Christianity is as much a healing tradition as it is a religious tradition. Within this tradition, redemption does not simply atone for personal sin and resolve internal problems; it brings about the cosmic and ontological restoration of the whole order of creation. Christian theology claims that *creation* anticipates a harmonious existence for humans, comprised of physical wellbeing, social wellbeing and spiritual wellbeing. *Redemption* effects a *re*-creation in order to correct the Fall, linking physical and existential *wholeness* with spiritual, ethical and relational *holiness*.

As a healing tradition Christianity can be compared with other healing traditions according to their method, modes and outcomes (see Table 3.1).

TABLE 3.1   A Comparison of Models of Healing

Healing tradition	Method	Mode	Outcomes
(1) Western medicine	naturalistic	biological	curative
(2) Alternative therapies	holistic	systemic	harmonizing
(3) Psycho-therapeutic	developmental	psycho-somatic	integrative
(4) Christian "wholeness"	ontological	restorative	redemptive

This is not to say that Christianity ought to be seen in competition with the other healing traditions. On the contrary, there is the potential for a harmonizing of the healing traditions. More will be said about this harmonization in the closing sections of this chapter that address Christianity as a healing tradition and a proposed outline of a theology of wholeness, health and healing.

SPIRITUALITY AND ITS THERAPIES

Vernon (2008, pp. 6 & 102) borrows the philosopher Charles Taylor's terms "lower flourishing" and "higher flourishing" to represent the multi-level nature of human wellbeing. "Lower flourishing" relates to a "thriving in the everyday" pattern of living, which includes belonging to a happy and supportive family, participating in fulfilling employment, having good friends, and enjoying good physical and emotional health. "Higher flourishing" refers to the existence of intrinsic meaning and the ability to make sense of one's life. This arises from a clear understanding of one's purpose in the world, reason-for-being, and being right with God. The domains of religion, spirituality and morality provide access to this higher level of human wellbeing that other medical/healing traditions do not.

Some of the major "therapies" that belong to Christian spirituality can be described as follows. *Prayer* provides a psycho-spiritual means of "release" of emotional pressure through the confession of sin, the reception of forgiveness, and a return to a harmonious state of healing and wellbeing, the supernatural dimension as a major source of guidance and consolation. *Worship* delivers worshippers into the presence of God, giving them access to the divine Other who is the object of their affections and allegiance. Feelings of awe, mystery, wonder, ecstasy and delight are commonly experienced by worshippers who are actively engaged with God as their attachment-object. *Faith* provides the fierce conviction that, no matter what happens, God will "never leave . . . nor forsake" the community of believers (Deuteronomy 31:6). Faith also provides a perceptive factor, commonly referred to as *conation* (Groome, 1991) in which the "eye" of faith sees transcendent realities and appropriates heavenly resources for living the earthly life. Finally, hungering and thirsting after righteousness indicates that *holy living* is a divinely-mandated, intrinsically-felt activity that receives God's approval and benefits the worshipper in both this life and the next.

These spiritual "therapies" build up a resilience that enables persons to face the challenges posed by this life out of the resources provided by the next life. Such things as *christotherapy* (Tyrrell, 1975), consolation, reassurance, the "cure" of souls, and "deliverance from evil" (Matthew 6:13) indicate the outcomes of spiritual therapy undertaken within the Christian spiritual tradition. Biblical verses such as "Comfort, comfort my people says your God" (Isaiah 40:1) and "Do not let your hearts be troubled" (John 14:1) cannot be underestimated as sources of comfort and encouragement in the lives of believers as they cope with life's uncertainties and the exigencies of sickness, isolation, despair and death.

EXCURSIS: "WEAKNESS" IN CHRISTIAN SPIRITUALITY

There is, however, a counterpoint within the Christian spiritual tradition that must be discussed, although this counterpoint may *at first* appear to contradict the principles of health, wellbeing and wholeness we have been exploring. That counterpoint can be described in terms of the themes of "weakness" and "suffering." To ignore the themes of weakness and suffering in Christian theology would be to misrepresent a core element within Christian teaching. God's embrace of humanity, Jesus' embrace of the cross, and Paul's boasting of his suffering all represent a "special case" within the Christian spiritual tradition. At the heart of this special case is the principle of "voluntary vulnerability" in which those who possess wholeness, health and wellbeing voluntarily relinquish any claims to their own comfort in order to act in the interests of others whose lives are defined by limit-conditions of despair, marginalization, sickness and imprisonment.

Christian theology generally accepts the notion of the *passibility* of God—in other words, His voluntary choice to subject Himself to human limitation, including suffering, pain and change. Although such *passibility* does not belong to His essentially inviolable and immutable nature, nevertheless God's compassion for His suffering human creatures causes Him to choose to suffer with them, among them, because of them and for them. God's suffering is a "creative" suffering (Fiddes, 1992) insofar as it confronts the presence of evil, addresses the juridical problem of sin, and works towards the redemptive restoration and re-creation of fallen humanity. God's "self-immolation" is seen most clearly in Christ, whose crucifixion and suffering at the hands of the Roman authorities was not a passive resignation to Roman brutality but a strategic choice: "When I am lifted up from the earth, [I] will draw all men to myself" (John 12:32). Kenotic theology identifies Jesus as the "Suffering Servant" (Isaiah 53) who "lay down his life for his friends" (John 15:13). It is in the Son that the Father becomes the "crucified God" (Moltmann, 1974).

The principle of voluntary vulnerability works itself out most acutely in Christian discipleship, and can be clearly seen in the life of the apostle Paul. During his ministry to Jews and Gentiles, Paul was persecuted, beaten, imprisoned, shipwrecked, made homeless, naked, poor, hungry, and abandoned (2 Corinthians 11:23–27). In the face of the false apostles and his own "thorn in the flesh," Paul boasted of his weaknesses, suggesting that weakness, suffering and oppression were formidable tools for conveying the power of God, the truthfulness of the gospel, and the value of living the spiritual life to the minds and hearts of his human hearers. If the Christian gospel visibly exceeds and overcomes those most fearful limit-conditions, then it must of necessity be a force for good that is worth embracing. Paul conveyed his conception of the crucified life in his declaration, "I have been crucified with Christ and I no longer live, but Christ lives in me. The life I live in the body, I live by faith in the Son of God, who loved me and gave himself for me" (Galatians 2:20). This was not simply a description of his singular experience but the universal experience of all those who identify themselves as Christ's disciples. Subsequently, the notion of redemptive suffering has become a recurring theme in the lives of those exemplars who best represent the ideals of the Christian faith, such as Justin Martyr, Teresa of Avila, St. John of the Cross, Amy Carmichael and Mother Theresa. Like their Master Jesus, they willingly gave up themselves and their self-interest in order to benefit the needs of others who are suffering.

The principle of voluntary vulnerability paradoxically implies an obligation on the part of the strong to act in costly service on behalf of the weak. God suffers; Jesus suffers; the apostles suffer; and those subsequent disciples who are called to be leaders and exemplars in the church and world are likewise called to suffer: "If anyone would come after me, he must deny himself and take up his cross and follow me" (Mark 8: 34). Voluntary vulnerability is the *standard* for all those who would be disciples of Jesus.

> Every Christian generation has produced two kinds of Christians: the common, ordinary garden variety, and those who have discovered the deeper life. Some call this deeper life entire sanctification. Others call it the baptism with the Spirit, Christian perfection, perfect love, or holiness of heart and life. Whatever the label, it reflects a deep experience of Christ-likeness . . . reflected in a Spirit-directed, disciplined lifestyle, and *demonstrated in redemptive action in our world.* (Callen, 2002, pp. 189–90; emphasis added)

Walter Wink (1992) describes such martyrs in this way: "Martyrs are not victims, overtaken by evil, but hunters who stalk evil into the open by offering as bait their own bodies. Those who are willing to sacrifice nothing or very little, offer nothing or very little to history. It must be said that they offer little or nothing to their own soul" (p. 161). The voluntary humiliation of the righteous and their willingness to "lay down their lives for their friends" through costly service, replicates Jesus' archetypal self-abasement and fulfils the law of heaven to "love one another as I have loved you" (John 13:34). If such costly service means a painful interval in the ecstatic state experienced by those who dwell in the divine presence, it is for the benefit of others and only represents a temporary delay in their personal wellbeing and flourishing. John Donne (1990) makes the statement, "That I may rise and stand, o'rthrow me, and bend, your force to break, blow, burn and make me new" (p. 177).

JOHN WESLEY'S *PRIMITIV PHYSIC*

In discussing the therapeutic nature of the Christian tradition, it is important to acknowledge Christian spirituality's holistic contribution to human wellbeing. It is both unwise and unnecessary to pit the interests of the body against the wellbeing of the soul. The picture of the human agent divided into an outside and an inside—such a "true self" is a corrupted understanding of a self, "which is hidden, buried, to be excavated by one or another kind of therapy" (Williams, 1997, p. 29) and is inconsistent with the Christian understanding of humanity.

John Wesley's *Primitiv Physic* (Wesley, 1858), for example, represents an early conceptual model of holistic medicine. It expressed an effective concern for "both inward and outward health" (Madden, 2008, p. 6), and reflects the broader biblical concern for both spiritual and physical wellbeing. Wesley begins by suggesting that Methodists shared an interest in both the bodies *and* the souls of those to whom they sought to minister. Wesley's doctrine of entire sanctification is effectively a re-statement of the conviction of the Church Fathers that salvation is cosmic in scope, restoring not only the body and the soul, but generating a renewal of the created order in its entirety. Such is the efficacy of its transformative and re-creating power.

The *Primitiv Physic* is a prime example of Christianity's desire to address both physical and spiritual needs, in an attempt to generate human flourishing from the resources of the earthly and heavenly, physical and spiritual dimensions.

CHRISTIANITY AS A HEALING TRADITION

Despite the analyses above, Christianity's contribution to human wellbeing and flourishing has not been well understood by medical science. The regnant logical-positivist epistemological paradigm has displaced supernaturalist Christianity from its previously central role in delivering sustainable and holistic care. Subsequently Christian pastoral practice *vis-à-vis* healthcare has been restricted to the roles of chaplaincy, hospice-care, and palliative care. Christian "care," it would seem, is allowed in the preparation of the soul for the after-life in the transitional process from illness to death, but no more. Similarly, complementary medicine has been wary of Christian healthcare, mostly because of differences in their respective philosophies of the human person and disagreements concerning the source of the life-force or spiritual "power" that energizes the somatic body. On the strength of professional and epistemological concerns, the psycho-therapeutic tradition has also placed significant limits on the role of Christian practitioners. The question of what contribution Christianity might usefully make to research and healthcare practice in the Western world awaits a satisfactory answer, a small part of which will be answered by the present enquiry.

It is clear that Christianity's redemptive and restorative approach to human wellbeing need not necessarily exclude it from participating in either the naturalistic-biological-curative, the holistic-systemic-harmonizing, or the developmental-psycho-somatic-integrative paradigms of healthcare. The many medical doctors and health practitioners who hold Christian beliefs; the widespread existence of Christian hospitals, health clinics, research centers and the like; and the large number of patients who hold Christian beliefs suggest that we must consider the potential for inter-relationships among these contrasting medical traditions into the future.

A THEOLOGY OF WHOLENESS, HEALTH AND HEALING

This closing section of the chapter offers a theology of wholeness, health and healing from a Christian perspective. This is merely a pioneer exploration of an important topic, moving *towards* the rudiments of a Christian theology of wholeness, health and healing. Further reflection, development and elucidation is needed from healthcare workers from each of the healing traditions. Equally necessary is active and intentional engagement from spiritual practitioners such as priests and chaplains, who are frequently excluded from participating in the delivery of healthcare (even to members of their own faith-communities) by professional medical workers. Given that Christianity is as much a healing tradition as it is a religious tradition, spiritual practitioners operating within the Christian tradition are obligated to become more deeply involved in the delivery of healthcare that works towards human wellbeing in the name of Christ. On what grounds might they proceed?

First, secular modernity's ideal of producing an autonomously thinking and acting person, conceived of as: "a vigorous and self-conscious personality," "strong in body and mind," "free and independent," "spontaneous and creative," "capable of standing up for him- or herself," and "independent of others" (Waaijman, 2002, pp. 103–104) remains largely unfulfilled. Humanity's "Babylonian captivity" to illness, despair, oppression, injustice, violence, exclusion, poverty, terror, tears and finally death is surely not its intended state. Alienated humanity awaits the arrival of a higher state of happiness and wellbeing. The Christian gospel proclaims the arrival of the new life, which Christ came to bring.

Second, human flourishing expressed through wholeness, health and wellbeing, is a multi-dimensional phenomenon. Flourishing refers to the whole person, including the spiritual dimension. On the one hand, physically whole people can suffer from diseases of the "soul" such as depression, despair and hopelessness. On the other hand, people diagnosed with even life-threatening illnesses such as cancer can process their mortality and make their peace with God, so expressing healthy attitudes in their outlook on both life and death. Manifestly then, human health and wellbeing is *trans*-somatic and requires a balance among the elements of self-transcendence, relational wholeness, physical wellbeing, and community integration. Therapeutic interventions of any kind should address the multiple dimensions of human wholeness by taking trans-material dimensions of the human person, such as the spiritual, seriously.

Third, the primary impulse of the Christian faith is always towards healing and restoration. God's initiative in sending Christ to the cross is the reconciling act ("God was in Christ, reconciling the world to himself," 2 Corinthians 5:17, NASB) that has healed the wound. The gospel goes beyond individual reconciliation to provide cosmic restoration and healing. Thus Christianity can claim to be a therapeutic tradition at its root, by offering a healing and wholeness which is ontological, redemptive and restorative in nature—even as it awaits the complete realization of the coming of the kingdom of God and the "end" of history in terms of the anticipated "Behold, I make all things new!" (Revelation 21:5).

Fourth, the present crises wracking the human family (social, psychological, political, ecological, economic and military) invite us to consider the systemic nature of "health" as something that extends beyond the limited confines of individual human wellbeing to the systemic wellbeing of our social, psychological, ecological and economic systems. These systems are not dead, but are living systems with which we continuously interact. With respect to nature: "Dust we are, humus, cells and molecules, energy and matter—and unto death we shall return—what forms us, creates us, takes us back again. Our surroundings, this natural world, is us, the womb that births us and holds us" (Swedish, 2008, p. 184). Our definitions of health and wellbeing must expand to include a systemic understanding of human health that is organically sustainable and requires significant attention by future individuals, communities, multinationals and governments.

Fifth, spirituality represents a primary category in our understanding of human flourishing and wellbeing and has much to contribute to the achievement of personal and communal goals. It is defined variously as: meaning-making, the experience of being loved, the identification of core values, the encounter with God, answered prayer, personal self-transcendence, or a resource for coping with the stresses of illness, the modern world, financial problems, family relationships or the fear of death. Spirituality grounds the human person in a transcendent reality and provides them with resources for overcoming fears and anxieties. While spirituality is often understood as a metaphysical category, it manifests itself as a category of fundamental importance to the health and wellbeing of the embodied human person in search of flourishing, both in this world and the next.

CONCLUSION

This chapter has put forward three basic theses; first, that spirituality is a primary category in contributing to human health and wellbeing; second, that Christian spirituality can provide an especially strong resource for nurturing human wellbeing; and third, that as well as being a religious tradition, Christianity can be understood as a healing tradition, which offers various practical, theological and existential "therapies." Spirituality, and in this case *Christian* spirituality, provides a proper framework and environment for nurturing damaged human persons back to wellbeing and wholeness, physically, mentally and spiritually. The chapter has also argued that Christian contributions to health, wholeness and flourishing ought not to be seen as competing with other medical and wellness traditions. Rather, a growing accommodation and partnership among Christian spirituality and other therapeutic traditions is not only entirely possible, but in the face of the urgency and extent of the need, is advisable.

Throughout this chapter I have provided a series of arguments that support these three theses. Briefly, these are: (1) existing medical traditions in the form of Western medicine, complementary medicine and the psychotherapeutic traditions are increasingly keen to incorporate spirituality into their repertoire of therapies, but have been slow to recognize the healing resources within the Christian faith; (2) elements within Christianity have been resistant to defining the Christian gospel in anything other than forensic and propitiatory terms, despite the enduring presence of the healing and health metaphor in theology; (3) historical examples such as John Wesley's *Primitiv Physic* demonstrate Christian theology's concern for the human person as an integrated self created in the image of God, body, soul and spirit; (4) the principle of "voluntary vulnerability" found in the self-giving of God, of Jesus, and of those in Christian ministry, sometimes requires that healthy and free "agents" put their own health and happiness at risk in order to meet the needs for wellbeing and wholeness of the poor, sick and oppressed; and (5) a theology of wholeness, health and healing must go beyond theoretical analysis to the level of practice, and to incorporate the total human person—body, mind, soul, and spirit—into a flourishing *center,* which is inseparable from the full range of available physical, social, spiritual and intellectual resources available.

REFERENCES

American Psychiatric Association. (2001). *Diagnostic and statistical manual of mental disorders* (4th ed., text revision). Washington, DC: Author.

Augustine. (1999). *Confessions.* Nashville, TN: Thomas Nelson.

Callen, B. L. (2002). *Authentic spirituality: Moving beyond mere religion.* Grand Rapids, MI: Baker Books.

Deci, E. L & Ryan, R. M. (2008). Hedonia, eudaemonia, and well-being: An introduction, *Journal of Happiness Studies, 9,* 1–11.

Donne, J. (1990). *Holy sonnet 14: John Donne, major works.* (Oxford World Classics Series). Oxford: Oxford University Press.

Fiddes, P. S. (1992). *The creative suffering of God* (2nd ed.). Oxford: Clarendon Press.

Groome, T. H. (1991). *Sharing faith: A comprehensive approach to religious education & pastoral ministry.* New York: Harper.

Hill, P. C., & Pargament, K. I. (2003). Advances in the conceptualization and measurement of religion and spirituality: Implications for physical and mental health research. *American Psychologist, 58*(1), 64–74.

Hobbes, T. (1651). *Leviathan: Or the matter, forme, and power of a commonwealth ecclesiastical and civill.* London: Thomas Crooke.

LaChance, A. J. (2006). *The architecture of the soul: A unitive model of the human person.* Berkeley, CA: North Atlantic Books.

Madden, D. (Ed.). (2008). *'Inward and outward health': John Wesley's holistic concept of medical science, the environment, and holy living.* London: Epworth.

Metz, J. B. (1971). *Theology of the world.* New York: Herder & Herder.

Moltmann, J. (1974). *The crucified God.* London: SCM Press.

Oman, D., & Thoresen C. E. (2005). Do religion and spirituality influence health? In R. F. Paloutzian & C. L. Park, (Eds.), *Handbook of the psychology of religion and spirituality* (pp. 435–459). New York: the Guilford Press.

Peplau, L. A., & Perlman, D. (1982). *Loneliness: A sourcebook for current theory, research and practice.* New York: Wiley.

Ryff, C., & Singer, B. (1998). The contours of positive human health. *Psychological Enquiry, 9*(1), 1–28.

Shults, F. L.& Sandage, S. J. (2006). *Transforming spirituality: Integrating theology and psychology.* Grand Rapids, MI: Baker Books.

Swedish, M. (2008). *Living beyond the "end of the world": A spirituality of hope.* Maryknoll, NY: Orbis Books.

Tyrrell, B. J. (1975). *Christotherapy: Healing through enlightenment.* New York: Seabury Press.

Vaux, K. L. (1997). *Being well.* Nashville, TN: Abingdon Press.

Vernon, M. (2008). *Well-being.* (Art of Living Series). Stocksfield: Acumen Press.

Waaijman, K. (2002). *Spirituality: Forms, foundations, methods.* Leuven, Belgium: Peeters.

Wesley, J. (1858). *Primitive physic, or an essay and natural method of curing most diseases.* Boston, MA: Cyrus Stone.

Westermann, C. (1984). *Genesis 1–11: A Commentary.* London: SPCK.

Williams, R. D. (1997). Interiority and epiphany: A reading in New Testament ethics. *Modern Theology, 13*(1), 29–51.

Wink, W. (1992). *Engaging the powers: Discernment and resistance in a world of domination.* Minneapolis, MN: Fortress Press.

CHAPTER 4

THEOLOGY AND HUMAN FLOURISHING

The Benefits of Being "Known by God"

Brian S. Rosner
Moore Theological College and Macquarie University

Loyola M. McLean
University of Sydney

ABSTRACT

This chapter considers the psycho-spiritual benefits of being known by God. Biblical-theological investigation of the notion is supported by attachment theory and a psychological understanding of the self. It concludes that secure attachment to the Transcendent One, being known by God as His child, supplies a strong sense of a valuable and lovable self. Similar to the human parent-child relationship, such attachment can lead to a healthy sense of significance, offer an effective source of comfort in dispiriting circumstances, and give moral direction. Receiving one's identity as a relational gift, rather than solely striving for it as an individual achievement, is an attractive alternative to the identity angst of a postmodern world where a stable and secure sense of self can be so elusive.

Beyond Well-Being: Spirituality and Human Flourishing, pages 65–83
Copyright © 2012 by Information Age Publishing
All rights of reproduction in any form reserved.

The study of Christian theology and spirituality regularly concentrates on the human side of the divine–human relationship. Participation in a community of faith, acts of piety, prayer, giving, and the like are investigated. Often, their positive outcomes for the worshipper and tangible psychological benefits are proposed (see Paloutzian & Park, 2005). Not surprisingly, "the knowledge of God" is a phrase taken to mean our knowledge of Him, rather than His knowledge of us. However, like every relationship, any relationship with God has two sides.

This chapter considers the other, God-ward side, or God's knowledge of us. Whereas human activity in relation to God is accorded much space in the Bible, the accent is in fact on the divine initiative on every page. We love God because he first loved us (1 John 4:19—where not indicated the translations of the Bible are by the author, B. S. Rosner). The same goes for a host of other verbs: we call upon, seek, choose and serve God, because he first called, sought, chose and served us. This is "the syntax of salvation," to quote one biblical scholar (Hays, 1997, p. 138). In grammatical terms, when it comes to God and us, the passive voice takes precedence over the active.

In this connection, we consider the theme of being *known by God* in the Bible and theology. Countless publications focus on knowing God. What does it mean to be known by God? With respect to spirituality and human flourishing, what psycho-spiritual benefits does being known by God bring along with it? (For articles on being known by God in literature and in biblical theology respectively, see Rosner, 2005, 2008). In order to answer these questions this chapter primarily proceeds theologically, but with auxiliary assistance from the experience of believers and psychological theories of attachment and self. It is hoped that a contribution will be made to the broad subject of human flourishing by clarifying the nature and theological basis of a secure attachment to God and its potential positive effects on the believer.

To set the stage brief consideration will be given to the subject of personal identity and self in contemporary psychotherapeutic thought and the world. Being known by God assumes a person who is the object of this knowing. A brief review of the ways in which a person's sense of self is supported by attachment relationships and the health benefits that are associated with a strong and secure sense of self and attachment security are outlined below.

PERSONAL IDENTITY AND A SENSE OF SELF

A Stable Self

There has been much recent interest in developmental psychology and psychiatry in concepts of self and the benefits of a strong and stable sense of self. The major themes are that: 1) the self is an organizing system, organizing our experience; 2) a healthy self is conscious of itself and others, able to respond flexibly and in an integrated way, to self, others and the world; and 3) the self forms within and through relationships and in particular attachment relationships (Lee & Martin, 1991; Meares, 2005; Wallin, 2007).

Modern thinking has grappled with notions of self for some time. Descartes thought of mind as the defining issue ("I think, therefore I am"), seeking to prove that one knew at least that oneself existed but with ensuing problems in establishing that others existed too (Meares & Graham, 2008). Early notions of two aspects to self are implicit in Kant's thinking of a phenomenal and noumenal self (Lee & Martin, 1991). However, modern definitions of the self in psychology begin with William James, who emphasized this dual quality, describing an "I and me" (Meares, 2005; Meares & Graham, 2008), but both aspects are nevertheless experienced as connected. In this dual relationship one is aware of one's personal existence and is the known and knower simultaneously.

The contextuality of self has also been an important theme of postmodern thought. Relational theorists point out that we feel and behave very differently in different relationships and that over a lifetime the self is in transition and responds to an interactive, interpersonal field (Mitchell, 1988; Stolorow, Brandschaft, & Atwood, 1987; Tolpin, 1986). Seen by many strands of developmental psychology, the healthy self is that which develops as a cohesive whole, becomes conscious of itself as it matures, and emerges from a matrix of supportive and enhancing experiences. A stable self-system is not an unchanging one, but one that regulates and integrates new experiences through feedback systems and is able to think about self and others (Basch, 1988; Choi-Kain & Gunderson, 2008; Fonagy & Target, 1997; Meares & Graham, 2008). Stability lies less in the self being unchanging and more in the flow of self-reflection being free or playful (Meares, 2005), continuous and integrative (Fonagy & Target, 1997), and collaborative and cohesive (Main, Goldwyn, & Hesse, 2002).

Consciousness, representations of the self and others, and interactions between minds become the key issues. In attachment theory our early attachment relationships foster the development of our representations of self and other. Modern theory and much research now demonstrate that it is secure attachment relationships or an internalized secure attachment state of mind that gives rise to a positive sense of self and other (Bowlby, 1973, 1988; Lee & Martin, 1991; Main et al., 2002; Stern, 1985). Bowlby proposed that each person interprets his or her early experience to form "internal working models" of the self and others (Bowlby, 1973, 1988).

These working models predict the lovability of oneself and the usefulness and helpfulness of others. Further, they can be carried forward beyond the relationship in which they were formed and become predictive schema (for a "map" of these schema see Chapter Twelve of this volume). If one experiences the parent as safe, comforting, responsive, and validating of one's thoughts and feelings, one feels good about oneself and valuable as a person; hence, the attachment is secure. One may hope, based on experience, that others can be helpful. Furthermore, one values what one thinks and feels and the capacity to think and act openly and flexibly. One can value such open and flexible thinking and action in others and appreciate that they have minds of their own. This gives our selves the most flexible capacity to respond to others and even modify our representations in the light of new experience. Conversely, if the experiences with the parent are uncomforting or unsafe, one can experience oneself or others or both negatively, and these three attachment relationships are then insecure. We cannot safely or comfortably be open, direct and in need, and so we must constrict ourselves and our communications to manage the lack of safety and comfort. We develop more extreme strategies to manage this discomfort (Crittenden, 2006; Main et al., 2002).

In his studies of infants, Stern (1985) observed the self emerging from the earliest days of life with aspects that grew in developmental sequence over the first few years of life in interaction with the carer. The infant, regulated by the carer, experiences sensations, affects, and the separateness from the mother and begins to organize these experiences in more complex ways as the mental apparatus becomes capable of speech and memory and the telling of one's own story. The self experiences agency (a sense of control and the ability to act), coherence, affectivity (emotion), and history (continuity/memory/narrative) (Stern, 1985; Lee & Martin, 1991). Each of these aspects is essential to a healthy self, and we continue to experience ourselves somatically, emotionally, representationally and reflectively (Meares, 2005; Wallin, 2007). A secure state of mind gives us more flexible access to all these aspects of experience (Main et al., 2002; Slade, 1999).

The adult self that we become can then tell the story of who we are and where we came from. Mary Main and her colleagues have been able to show in their work on adult attachment that the way we speak about our childhood experiences in our narrative reveals our internal representations of ourselves and others. Her work on metacognition found evidence that thinking about one's own mind and about another's was associated with a secure state of mind (Main et al., 2002). Peter Fonagy and colleagues have furthered this work and found that the ability to reflect on one's own and other's thinking is protective and develops from the caregiver's ability to communicate understanding of the child's intentional stance. This kind of reflective thinking protects the parents from transmitting disorganizing effects of their own early experience onto their children. Such reflective thinking is deficient in significant personality dysfunction (Fonagy & Target, 1997; Fonagy & Bateman, 2008). Early security or later acquired security and reflectivity foster a stable self (Fonagy & Target, 1997; Fonagy & Bateman, 2008) and a coherent narrative about oneself (Main et al., 2002).

The Benefits of a Stable Self

A relatively coherent and stable personal identity underpinned by a strong and secure sense of self is now being shown to be critical to psychological health and well-being. Research into both risk factors and protective factors for psychological and physical illness suggest that personality disorders and dysfunctional coping are risk factors for illness, comorbidity and poorer recovery from illness (Fava & Sonino, 2000; Lawrence & Fauerbach, 2003; Maunder & Hunter, 2001; Parker et al., 1998; Tyrer, Seivewright, & Johnson, 2004), whereas positive aspects of self functioning are protective (Vaillant, 1977, 2008). The effects impact on important health outcomes such as mortality rates (Surtees, Wainwright, & Luben, 2006), effective adjustment to serious injury such as burns (Kildal, Willebrand, Andersson, Gerdin, & Ekselius, 2005), and prognosis in serious illnesses such as cardiac disease (Denollet et al., 1996). In the domain of cardiac research in particular, "Type D (distressed) personality," characterized as a joint tendency to experience negative emotions and to socially inhibit expression of them, has been linked with poor prognosis (Denollet et al., 1996).

Theory and research also support an association between attachment states of mind and wellbeing (Maunder & Hunter, 2001). Attachment contributes to the way an individual responds psychologically and physically to stress. Attachment insecurity can lead to risk of disease through several mechanisms: increased susceptibility to stress, altered physiology (Picardi et al., 2007), increased use of external regulators of affect (such as drugs and alcohol), and altered help-seeking behavior (such as less adherence to treatment). Furthermore, the health benefits of social support derive more from attachment relationships than non-attachment relationships and are therefore more accessible to those who are securely attached (Maunder & Hunter, 2001).

Losing Your Self

The postmodern world puts great stock in answering the question of personal identity; authenticity is the ideal. Reality show contestants audition for such television programs in order to "find themselves" and the ultimate postmodern advice is to "be true to yourself." Yet, ironically, it is arguably harder to know oneself than at any other time in history and true authenticity may be elusive.

In the past an individual's identity was much more stable and predictable. Many of the big questions in life were settled before one's birth: where one would live, what one would do, whom one would marry, one's basic beliefs, and so on. The shape of life was molded by constraints that limited choices. Today, the multicultural pluralism found in most Western nations presents considerable challenges to those seeking to define themselves, as it throws up an overabundance of alternative lifestyles and choices. Polish sociologist Zygmunt Bauman explains:

> Traditional communities are rivers, while modern societies are oceans. A river has a direction and carries you along with the current, just as traditional societies direct their members in a particular way. In modern societies there is no current; we can choose to go any direction, no direction, or to shift direction with every change of winds. (Bauman, 2005, p. 33)

In addition to the obvious midlife crisis, social commentators claim that you can have a crisis of identity at many points in life. These include the "thrisis" in your thirties and "cuspiety," where people feel anxious about turning the "big one" (30, 40, 50, 60, etc.), not to mention big life changes like redundancy, marital breakdown, serious illness, death of parents, and so on. The self in the modern world seems at risk of being less stable, often in transition, with an associated stress or "angst" surrounding identity.

In addition to greater instability of the self, many versions of the modern self are less than secure. There are widespread challenges to a sense of identity such as the modern focus on body image, the internet as a platform for life, and relationship problems. All these challenges potentially render a secure self, positive and confident of itself and others, difficult to attain and sustain. Even when a strong sense of self is forged, the urge to redefine oneself can be irresistible. Sociologists Anthony Elliot and Charles Lemert suggest that we respond to the instability of globalization by reinventing ourselves (Elliot & Lemert, 2006). If the self is formed and sustained in a matrix of relationships, then the tumultuous flow of the matrix of modern life may place huge demands on our sense of stable identity and may offer little support to ease the ensuing "angst."

The Need for Transcendence

In view of the high incidence of "identity angst" in society at large, it is apt to consider theologian Peter Leithart's (2008) assertion that "[p]ersonal identity cannot be anchored convincingly without transcendence" (p. 131). Initially each of us receives our identity from outside of ourselves—namely, from our parents. As infants our parents give us not only our genes, but also our names and earliest experiences. They reflect back to us, hopefully with pleasure and a "gleam in the mother's eye" (Kohut, 1971, p. 116) who we are and that we are loved. In a million tiny moments our parents validate (or not) our needs and our very selves. Adolescence is then experienced as a time of testing, owning or disowning this inherited identity and reshaping a new identity for ourselves. As young adults, and again at other times of change, we need to tell afresh the story of who we are and how we became, to claim our agency and coherency in the adult world and move the story on. This new identity may be close to or far removed from the one given to us in childhood.

It is this chapter's contention that theology has something important to contribute to the discussion of personal identity and sense of self in the postmodern world. In short, the Transcendent One, "the Most High God," to use a biblical title, (e.g., Daniel 5:18) may be thought of as offering believers a secure identity, residing in a secure relationship between God and the individual and God and His family. This chapter seeks to answer the following questions: How does the divine-human relationship affect our sense of self? In particular, from the God-ward side, does our Heavenly Father function similarly to our earthly parents vis-à-vis our identities? Does this attachment relationship with God help foster a sense of self that aids our personal and communal flourishing?

BEING KNOWN BY GOD

Knowing in the Bible is a deeply personal and relational notion. Frequently it involves the will and the emotions, as well as the intellect. Famously, "Adam knew Eve," a reference to sexual relations (Gen. 4:1; cf. the term "carnal knowledge"). Similarly, childlessness (Isaiah 47:8), disease (Isaiah 3:3), and divine punishment (Jeremiah 16:21) can be described as objects of knowledge. This is not simply Hebrew idiom, but reveals a concept of knowledge that goes beyond abstract cognition and involves an experiential component.

References to knowing God, and being known by Him, must be read in this fuller sense. For the Bible to say that God knows someone is a reference to personal relationship of some sort. In terms of the divine attributes, it refers not so much to His omniscience as to His love. This distinction will be significant when it comes to considering the benefits of being known by God.

Although less frequent than themes of knowing God, references to being known by God appear at critical points in the biblical narrative: in the Old Testament, Abraham (Genesis 18:19), Moses (Exodus 33:12), David (2 Samuel 7:20), Jeremiah (Jeremiah 1:5), and the nation Israel (Amos 3:2; Hosea 13:5) are all known by God; and in the New Testament being known by God defines Christian existence (Galatians 4:8–9; 1 Corinthians 8:3), is a criterion of the last judgment (Matthew 7:23 ["I never knew you"]; 25:12; cf. Luke 13:27) and is a measure of eschatological glory (1 Corinthians 13:12 ["then I shall know, even as I have been fully known"]).

The Definition of Being Known by God

Since "being known," by God no less, is such an intimate and emotive concept, not unlike a metaphor, it is capable of varied and flexible application. Hence, we should not expect a neat and even definition that fits every instance.

A survey of the twenty or so occurrences of being known by God in the Bible reveals three interrelated meanings (see Rosner, 2008). First, to be known by God is to *belong to God*. In John's Gospel Jesus reassures His disciples: "I know my sheep;" and he claims that His sheep "listen to my voice" (John 10:14 & 16). The ones who "hear what God says" are "those who belong to God" (John 8:47). This conjunction suggests that being known by God and belonging to God can function synonymously. The relationship implied here is based in intimate knowledge and conversation. We know from psychodynamic psychotherapy that a sense of belonging in relationship is one of the basic nurturing experiences of self and is often mediated by recognition: "Recognition...underpins the state of mind James called self" (Meares & Graham, 2008, p. 433).

Second, there is a link between being known by God and being *chosen or loved by God*. In certain texts the verb "to know" is actually translated in English versions with the verb "to choose." For example, God's choice of Abraham for extraordinary blessing is explained with the words, "for I have chosen him" (Revised Standard Version—RSV, New International Version—NIV), which in Hebrew is literally, "for I have known him." Likewise in the New Testament, a synonym for God's election is His foreknowledge: "those God fore*knew* he also predestined" (Romans 8:29). Foreknowledge in biblical parlance is not about knowing something presciently, so much as it connotes the setting of God's love upon someone in advance. The benefits of knowing that one is loved are profound: a clear sense of being loved and lovable is core to the secure state of mind (Main et al., 2002). As noted above, modern research suggests that knowing that one is loved and lovable underlies the secure state of mind that promotes well-being and protects against illness (Maunder & Hunter, 2001; Proctor & McLean, 2009; Proctor, Miner, McLean, Devenish, & Ghobary Bonab, 2009).

Third, a range of biblical and early Jewish texts support a link between being known by God and being a *child of God*. Galatians 4:8–9 contains a self-conscious reference to being known by God: "Formerly, when you did not know God... But now that you know God—*or rather are known by God*." The broader context makes Paul's preference for being known by God over knowing God clear. The subject of Galatians 3:26 through 4:7 concerns divine adoption of believers as God's sons: "You are all sons of God through faith in Christ Jesus" (Galatians 3:26). As several Jewish texts make clear, to be known by God is to be His child, for example: Psalms of Solomon 17:27b:

"he [i.e., the Messiah] shall know them, that they are all sons of their God," and Odes of Solomon 41:2: "And *his children* shall be known by him."

Compared to the first two definitions, the definition of being known by God in the way a parent knows his or her child deepens our grasp of the concept. In attachment terms, it is the nub of it. The association of being known by God through divine adoption marks the belonging of the one who is known as carrying a filial sense rather than a nuptial or some less personal sense. Even the idea of being chosen by God is non-specific and less personal in comparison with adoption and the intimacy of a parent-child relationship. The intimacy of the knowledge of God, and particularly being known through the father-creator or the mother-nurturer aspect of God, extends even beyond the intimacy of a parental bond, and is shown in, for example, Jeremiah 1:5 (NIV) "Before I formed you in the womb I knew you, before you were born I set you apart," and Isaiah 49:15 (NIV) "Can a mother forget the baby at her breast and have no compassion on the child she has borne? Though she may forget, I will not forget you!"

Further, being known by God as His child makes good sense in the light of personal experience. Involved, loving parents know their children intimately. This includes their child's personality, likes and dislikes, physical capabilities, needs and desires. Indeed, a child's well-being appears initially to depend less on knowing their parents than on being known by them. The child is born seeking companionship in knowledge and skills and meaning (Trevarthen, 2001) but requires that a parent will "attune to" these early strivings and engage in the earliest dialogues, termed "proto-conversations" (for summary see Trevarthen, 1974, 2001). Even before true verbal conversations, all "communications" from the child are examined by an attentive parent and responded to. Attachment bonds are vital in both directions, but the caregiver is critical. As we shall see below, to feel oneself uniquely known by God as His child may be of immense practical value to the one who is part of God's family.

Attachment theory and a related body of psychodynamic literature attest to the primacy of the caregiver in establishing a loving and secure relationship with the child. Winnicott, a significant psychoanalyst and pediatrician, famously noted that "there is no such thing as baby," referring to the situation that an infant is unable to survive without the physical, but also the emotional, care of the parent (Winnicott, 1947/1964, p. 88). It became clear in observational studies of children that unattached infants, even if fed and kept sheltered would often die or become grossly impaired: a condition termed "non-organic failure to thrive" (Krugman & Dubowitz, 2003). Modern science now understands this as the very organic consequences of no bond with a carer. However, the nature of the bond is also crucial. In the scoring of an attachment measure called the Adult Attachment Interview (AAI), whereby the participant recounts events from his or her youth, the parent receives little credit for "loving" behavior that would promote security by simply providing the basics of life, such as food and shelter, and even basic comfort. Instead they are only considered loving when they demonstrate "personal interest and dedication to the child as an individual." Higher levels are scored when "the parent consistently treasured the child and found pleasure in them" (Main et al., 2002, p. 20).

Inherent in parent-child attachments are opportunities for the rich relational diet that grows selves. Given that the presence of one loving parent is often enough to gift a child with a sufficient experience of security to carry an internal idea of the lovability of themselves and others into adulthood, the potential value of "being known" as a beloved child of God may be invaluable and protective if it functions in this attachment sense. Certainly research is beginning to suggest that for some, this experience of security is demonstrable in their attachment to God, whether that experience is founded on early or later experience (Granqvist & Kirkpatrick, 2008; Proctor & McLean, 2009; Proctor et al., 2009). For some there is the possibility that the experience of a secure experience in the relationship with God can help shift an insecure state of mind (Granqvist & Kirkpatrick, 2008).

Major Benefits of Being Known by God

Significance

The theme of being known by God offers something in response to the most basic question of all, namely, who am I? What does it mean to be a human being? Personal identity in a postmodern context is determined solely by one's place within a local culture and by its particular story (Leithart, 2008). This leads to a confusing plethora of answers about a person's essential identity. Being known by God offers a different answer to this age-old question. Instead of the Enlightenment dictum of "I think, therefore I am," or "I know, therefore I am," it suggests a different tack: "I am known, therefore I am" (Meares & Graham, 2008). Such a definition of personhood gives an individual a secure identity, not based on achievement or even capacity, but on the gracious beholding of another. It gives another position to the inevitable solipsism of the Cartesian "I" (Meares & Graham, 2008) and puts the self in relationship to others.

In child development this aspect of being seen by another is crucial to a sense of value or worth. This "gleam in the mother's eye" (Kohut, 1971, p. 116) also involves the interactional recognition of the child, as early as from birth, when the mother "doubles" for her infant in the earliest of playful conversations (Meares, 2005). The mother reflects back to the baby in important ways who they are (Meares & Graham, 2008). This coupling behavior involves a resonant matching that evokes a feeling of well-being and promotes a sense of value. One's reality is made up of "meaning" and "value," one giving "truth" and the other the "good" of one's being (Meares & Graham, 2008), and establishing that one is significant. Recognition is fundamental to self-consciousness and relies on internal and external mediating forms of consciousness (Meares & Graham, 2008). To be known by God may function as an external consciousness of our being.

If being human means having the capacity to know, then the embryo, the severely mentally-disabled and the person in a persistent vegetative state, for example, may fail the test. Gilbert Meilaender is typical of a growing number of Christian ethicists who lament the modern tendency to define personhood solely in terms of consciousness and self-awareness (Meilaender, 2005, p. 5). If being human is fundamentally to be known, a case for the human status of the aforementioned may be more readily mounted.

To illustrate, consider the following case of a twelve-year old boy who is profoundly disabled. The boy is deaf and blind and severely cognitively impaired and, to put it bluntly, by Descartes' standard we can only make a marginal case for his status as a person. To those who have met him, however, it is obvious that his being depends not on what he knows, but rather on the fact that he is known by his parents. Their loving interactions with him, attending to his needs and drawing out his responses, give him a secure and meaningful identity. Their loving, knowing relationship also offers him a better chance of developing his own sense of self.

To cite a further example, the need to be known was set in sharp relief in the early twentieth century in a different context. In the First World War, Britain was faced with the dilemma of how to mark the remains of soldiers whose identity had been lost. At the suggestion of Rudyard Kipling, who was a member of the Imperial War Graves Commission, every grave of an unidentified British Empire soldier was marked with the words "Known unto God." Officially adopted in World War One, this practice was also used in subsequent conflicts. This poignant inscription gave the person buried therein a significance and identity they would otherwise have been denied.

Comfort

Another potential benefit of being known by God in an attachment-like relationship is the provision of comfort that ensues in such a bond or from such a state of mind. In her discussion of attachment to God, Miner writes that "God theoretically functions as an attachment figure because monotheistic religions hold to belief in a personal God whose loving qualities are similar to the ideal parent" (Miner, 2007, pp. 112–113). She explains further that "one's relationship with God serves many of the functions of [parental] attachment, such as providing a safe haven and secure base." Recent work shows that for some, this theoretical possibility is borne out, with some believers able to describe these functions in their relationships with God (Granqvist & Kirkpatrick, 2008; Proctor et al., 2009): comfort and protection that form a "secure base" from which to engage with the world. The theological theme of being known by God as His child is supported by the experience of believers that a secure relationship with God, like a good parent, provides comfort and protection.

In a wide range of biblical texts, being known by God appears in contexts offering reassurance and consolation to people who find themselves in extreme difficulties. The most obvious examples are those where the verb "to know" is translated by most English Bible versions as "be concerned about," "care for" or "protect." Note the following three examples: "God heard their [the Israelites'] groaning [in bondage in Egypt] . . . looked on the Israelites and was concerned about (literally, "knew") them" (Exodus 2:23–24, NIV); "I cared for (literally, "knew") you in the desert, in the land of burning heat" (Hosea 13:5, NIV); "The LORD is good, a stronghold in a day of trouble; he protects (literally, "knows") those who take refuge in him" (Nahum 1:7, NRSV).

Other biblical texts demonstrate that God affords comfort. First, 2 Timothy 2:19 introduces a quotation of Numbers 16:5 with a solemn pronouncement making explicit the consolatory effect of being known by God: "God's solid foundation stands firm, sealed with this inscription: 'The Lord knows those who are his.'" Secondly, in Exodus 33:12 God reassures Moses in two complementary ways: "I know you by name and you have found favor with me" (NIV).

A third and interesting example appears in Revelation 2:17, where two words of encouragement are offered to the persecuted church at Pergamum. One is "hidden manna," the other is a puzzling reference to "a white stone with a new name written on it, known only to him who receives it." The consensus among biblical commentators is that "[w]e simply do not know what the white stone signified, though clearly it did convey some assurance of blessing" (Morris, 1987, p. 69). Whatever else the "new name" reference denotes, its hidden nature, known only to God and its bearer, speaks of an intimate, interpersonal relationship, a knowledge that would encourage the one "who overcomes" to persevere. Being given a secret name by God is another way of affirming that a person is known by God.

The comfort offered in being known by God in these biblical and Jewish texts ranges from God's knowing (in the sense of his specific and active care) to a more general notion of consolation simply because of being known by Him as a parent knows his child, a knowledge that survives hardship and even death of the child. In terms of the latter, it seems that being known by God within a secure attachment relationship can offer a stable and secure identity, not unlike that which parents hope to provide for their young children. This can be the case irrespective of practical assistance. When a young child stubs his or her toe, the wound needs to be cleaned as well as covered. But the child also needs the reassuring embrace of a caregiver. When confronted with uncertainty and hardship, being known by God can be of genuine consolation. The benefits of consolation also extend psychologically to the affirmation of one's lovability, value and belonging to someone that can be internalized in a positive schema of self and potentially accessed at times of challenge. Perhaps most clearly Isaiah 66:13 describes this parental aspect of God's comfort: "As a mother comforts her child, so will I comfort you."

Although we cannot be sure of its meaning, it may be worthwhile to speculate on a "reading" of the white stone mentioned above. The image may speak to our need to be "cleansed" or "reborn" after traumatic suffering, which can attack and "destroy" the old self. Herman (1992) writes that: "Having come to terms with the traumatic past, the survivor faces the task of creating a future. She has mourned the old self that the trauma destroyed; now she must develop a new self" (p. 196). The white stone mentioned here is not a *tabula rasa*, but a stone cleansed by the surmounting of suffering, ready for a new self. In psychological terms the resolution of suffering has the opportunity to bring about a re-organization of the self after the disorganizing consequences of trauma or loss. The secret name may affirm that our deepest identity is known and protected and celebrated for the day of our transformation. In modern psychoanalytic thinking, this transformation is the fruit of a particular kind of intimate relationship and conversation that supports the "dissolution" of trauma (Bowlby, 1980; Herman, 1992; Meares, 2005). In this context the relationship with God affirms the sufferer's significance, and supports his or her identity through recognition and relationship during a period of transformation.

Dietrich Bonhoeffer, German pastor and conspirator against Adolf Hitler, exemplifies this notion of comfort that actually protects our identity and sense of self in one of his prison poems. Former Australian Prime Minister, Kevin Rudd, described Bonhoeffer as the man he most admired from the twentieth century, in part for his robust commitment to following the implications of his faith in public life. Incarcerated for two years, Bonhoeffer also offers profound reflections on the subject of anguish and suffering. His poem, "Who am I?" was written as a kind of self-analysis in 1944, the year before his execution. It concludes with a powerful affirmation of the existential value of being known by God.

The question contained in the title occurs five times in the body of the poem. The opening three stanzas report how the guards view Bonhoeffer as "composed, contented and sure." Bonhoeffer's view of himself in the next stanza is less positive and more anguished. The final lines of the poem voice further his frustration, but close with a simple but powerful affirmation:

Who am I? Lonely questions mock me.
Who I really am, *you know me*, I am yours, O God! (Robertson, 1998, p. 38)

The experience of not being abandoned in our suffering, the sense that two are present in the terror or the pain, that one is not forgotten but is instead held in mind, appears to be one of the quintessential requirements for the resolution of loss and trauma and for the reestablishment of a strong self. If the "lonely questions" are answered with an experience of presence of the other "synchronously" sharing the experience, hearing the story transform, affirming our value and identity, then suffering is bearable and transmutable (Bowlby, 1980; Herman, 1992; Meares, 2005; Neimeyer, 2006; Stern et al.,1998) and our sense of self is affirmed.

Direction

The moral life, by definition imbued with values, is often excluded from psychological discussions of human flourishing. This may seem consistent with the pluralistic nature of Western societies, but it is naïve to think that flourishing can be divorced from character and ethics. As it turns out, positive psychology increasingly advocates strategies such as acts of altruism and attitudes of forgiveness and thankfulness (e.g., Seligman, 2002; Vaillant, 2008), which clearly overlap with ethical and spiritual concerns. The third note-worthy psycho-spiritual benefit of being known by God is the moral direction it supplies.

Being known by God as His child includes the believer in the family history of God's people. Two great moments of divine adoption in the Old Testament define the people of God and sum up God's purposes for the world. First, God adopts Israel as His son at the time of the Exodus (Exodus 4:22; Deuteronomy 32:10; Hosea 11:1; cf. Romans 9:4). Secondly, God adopts the king of Israel as His son in the Davidic covenant (2 Samuel 7:14; 1 Chronicles 17:13; cf. 1 Chronicles 28:6 [of Solomon]; Psalms 2:7). In the New Testament, we see both Old Testament moments of adoption coalesce: the sonship of God's new people is by virtue of God's unique Son. As Ephesians 1:5 puts it, "he destined us for adoption as his children *through Jesus Christ.*" Of interest here is the fact that Romans 8:29 juxtaposes being known by God with being adopted by God: "those God foreknew he also predestined to be conformed to the likeness of his Son, that he might be the firstborn among many brothers."

Being a child of God carries with it a moral identity and agendum. To cite just two examples, notice first how the identity of the people of God is meant to inform their behavior in Colossians 3:12–14:

> Therefore, as God's chosen people, holy and dearly loved, clothe yourselves with compassion, kindness, humility, gentleness and patience. Bear with each other and forgive whatever grievances you may have against one another. For-

give as the Lord forgave you. And over all these virtues put on love, which binds them all together in perfect unity.

Jesus' words in the Sermon on the Mount are just as clear in establishing a link between being a child of God and being like God:

> But I tell you: Love your enemies and pray for those who persecute you, that you may be sons of your Father in heaven. He causes his sun to rise on the evil and the good, and sends rain on the righteous and the unrighteous . . . Be perfect, therefore, as your heavenly Father is perfect. (Matthew 5:44–45, 48, NIV)

To be known by God is to be included in His story. That story concerns His determination to redeem the world in the election of Abraham and David, the exodus from Egypt, and ultimately in the sending of His Son. In theological terms it is to identify with this history of salvation. In a different context, Alasdair MacIntyre has reflected on the role of stories for the moral life. He writes: "Deprive children of stories and you leave them unscripted, anxious stutterers in their actions as in their words" (MacIntyre, 1981, p. 216). Such a story, if McIntyre is correct, is eminently practical for, "I can only answer the question 'What am I to do?' if I can answer the prior question 'Of what story or stories do I find myself a part?'" (MacIntyre, 1981, p. 217).

Modern psychodynamic thinking suggests that in the kind of relationship where a person is supported to come to know himself or herself, a deep and playful conversation can take place. This particular kind of conversation enables a person to shift from more rigid forms of discourse into telling his or her story as a narrative, with an unfolding and creative structure that mirrors and arises from the unfolding self (Meares, 2005). Similarly, the need to reconstruct the narrative self after trauma underpins many contemporary psychotherapeutic approaches (Herman, 1992; Meares, 2005; Niemeyer, 2006; Wallin, 2007). Secure attachment to God may help us develop ourselves and our stories. To be known by God in this intimate way thus offers the possibility of a profound buffer against the vicissitudes of life and a strong support to our sense of security and direction in the world.

At the simplest construction, being known by God as His child defines the individual as a member of God's family with responsibilities to other brothers and sisters in Christ. The sense of kinship with others is fostered within the Christian family. However, in more complex ways than this, secure attachments foster moral development and a direction towards others that is characterized by a propensity for forgiveness and a more humble understanding of one's own and other's frailties.

Research has shown that a secure state of mind is associated with certain capacities that aid the ethical and moral life, including: a) a capacity for implicit and explicit forgiveness; b) a capacity to acknowledge with "rueful regret" that one does not always do as one wills or plans and often repeats the mistakes of one's parents; and c) a metacognitive capacity, which entails the ability to observe one's own and others' thinking (Main et al., 2002). This latter capacity for reflective functioning, or mindfulness (Fonagy & Target, 1997; Fonagy & Bateman, 2008; Main et al., 2002), allows us to frame those Appearance and Reality Distinctions (ARDs) that more mature ethical thought and a tolerance of difference and paradox often requires, such as: Things are not always as they seem; What I thought today I may not think tomorrow; There can be different views of the same story. The formation of ARDs constitutes higher-order abstract thinking and seems to be conducive to integration and the ability to hold things in tension, inherent in such paradoxes as "whoever loses his life will preserve it" (Luke 17:33, NIV). This thinking, fostered by security in God, helps us behold and know ourselves and others with more flexibility, tolerance and humility: we are disposed to forgive.

CONCLUSION

According to the data thrown up by our biblical-theological investigation, and supported by attachment theory and psychological understanding of the self, being known by God as His child has distinct psycho-spiritual benefits. These benefits are based upon the firm foundation of a strong sense of a valuable and lovable self, a knowledge anchored in secure attachment to the Transcendent One. Similar to the human parent-child relationship, when such an attachment is based in a lived experience of being known and loved, it can lead to a healthy sense of significance that is internalized beyond the context of the attachment relationship and is an effective source of comfort in response to dispiriting difficulties. Research into attachment to God supports this proposition. Being known by God, who is holy and gracious, also offers moral direction, as the child of God seeks to take on the family likeness, and the mental benefits that foster forgiveness and self-reflection that are associated with a secure state of mind. In a nutshell, rather than finding one's self, Christian faith offers the alternative of being found. In the paradoxical words of Jesus: "Those who find their life will lose it, and those who lose their life for my sake will find it" (Matthew 10:39, NRSV). Receiving one's identity as a relational gift, rather than solely striving for it as an individual achievement, is an attractive answer to the "lonely questions" (to recall Bonhoeffer's phrase) of a postmodern world where a stable and secure sense of self can be so elusive.

REFERENCES

Basch, M. (1988). *Understanding psychotherapy.* New York: Basic.

Bauman, Z. (2005). *Liquid life.* Cambridge: Polity.

Bowlby, J. (1973). *Attachment and loss: Vol. 2. Separation: anxiety and anger.* New York: Basic Books.

Bowlby, J. (1980). *Attachment and loss. Vol 3. Loss: Sadness and depression.* New York: Basic Books.

Bowlby, J. (1988). *A secure base: Parent-child attachment and healthy human development.* London: Basic Books.

Choi-Kain, L. W., &. Gunderson, J. G. (2008). Mentalization: Ontogeny, assessment, and application in the treatment of borderline personality disorder. *American Journal of Psychiatry, 165,* 1127–1135.

Crittenden, P. M. (2006). A dynamic-maturational model of attachment. *Australian and New Zealand Journal of Family Therapy, 27,* 105–115.

Denollet, J., Stanislas, S., Stroobant, N., Rombouts, H., Gillebert, T. C., & Brutsaert, D. L. (1996). Personality as independent predictor of long-term mortality in patients with coronary heart disease. *Lancet, 347,* 417–421.

Elliot, A., & Lemert, C. (2006). *The new individualism: The emotional costs of globalization.* London: Routledge.

Fava, G. A., & Sonino, N. (2000). Psychosomatic medicine: Emerging trends and perspectives. *Psychotherapy and Psychosomatics, 69,* 184–197.

Fonagy, P., & Target, M. (1997). Attachment and reflective functioning: Their role in self-organization. *Development and Psychopathology, 9,* 679–700.

Fonagy, P., & Bateman, A. (2008). The development of borderline personality disorder: A mentalizing model. *Journal of Personality Disorders, 22*(1), 4–18.

Granqvist, P., & Kirkpatrick, K. (2008). Attachment and religious representations and behaviour. In J. Cassidy & P. R. Shaver (Eds.), *Handbook of attachment: Theory, research, and clinical applications* (2nd ed., pp. 906–933). New York: The Guilford Press.

Hays, R. B. (1997). *First Corinthians: Interpretation.* Louisville, KY: John Knox Press.

Herman, J. (1992). *Trauma and recovery.* New York: Basic Books.

Kildal, M., Willebrand, M., Andersson G., Gerdin B., & Ekselius L. (2005). Coping strategies, injury characteristics and long term outcome after burn injury. *Injury, 36,* 511–518.

Kohut, H. (1971). *The analysis of the self.* New York: International Universities Press.

Krugman, S., & Dubowitz, H. (2003) Failure to thrive. *American Family Physician, 68*(5), 879–884.

Lawrence, J. W., & Fauerbach, J. A. (2003). Personality, coping, chronic stress, social support and PTSD symptoms among adult burn survivors: A path analysis. *Journal of Burn Care and Rehabilitation, 24*(1), 63–72.

Lee, R. R., & Martin, J. C. (1991). *Psychotherapy after Kohut: A textbook of self psychology.* Hillsdale, NJ: The Analytic Press.

Leithart, P. J. (2008). *Solomon among the postmoderns.* Grand Rapids, MI: Brazos Press.

MacIntyre, A. (1981). *After virtue: A study in moral theory.* Notre Dame, IN: Notre Dame.

Main, M., Goldwyn, R., & Hesse, E. (2002). *Adult attachment scoring and classification systems.* Unpublished manuscript: University of California at Berkeley.

Maunder, R., & Hunter, J. (2001). Attachment and psychosomatic medicine: developmental contributions to stress and disease. *Psychosomatic Medicine, 63,* 556–567.

Meares, R. (2005). *The metaphor of play: Origin and breakdown of personal being* (3rd edition). New York: Routledge.

Meares, R., & Graham, P. (2008). Recognition and the duality of self. *International Journal of Psychoanalytic Self Psychology, 3,* 432–446.

Meilaender, G. (2005). *Bioethics: A primer for Christians.* Grand Rapids, MI: Eerdmans.

Miner, M. (2007). Back to the basics in attachment to God: Revisiting theory in light of theology. *Journal of Psychology and Theology, 35*(2), 112–122.

Mitchell, S. (1988). *Relational concepts in psychoanalysis: An integration.* Cambridge, MA: Harvard University Press.

Morris, L. (1987). *The Revelation of St John.* Tyndale New Testament Commentaries series. Grand Rapids MI: Eerdmans.

Neimeyer, R. A. (2006). Complicated grief and the reconstruction of meaning: Conceptual and empirical contributions to a cognitive-constructivist model. *Clinical Psychology: Science and Practice, 13*(2), 141–145.

Paloutzian, R. F., & Park, C. L. (Eds.). (2005). *Handbook of the psychology of religion and spirituality.* New York: The Guilford Press.

Parker, G., Hadzi-Pavlovic, D., Roussos, J., Wilhelm, K., Mitchell, P., Austin, M., et al. (1998). Non-melancholic depression: The contribution of personality, anxiety and life events to subclassification. *Psychological Medicine, 28,* 1209–1219.

Proctor, M-T., & McLean, L. (2009). Reviewing the place of the spiritual domain in the clinical and psychotherapeutic setting: Framing and assessing issues within an attachment perspective. In M. Miner, M-T. Proctor & M. Dowson (Eds.). *Spirituality in Australia, Volume 2: Directions and Applications* (pp. 90–110). Sydney: ACSS/CHILD.

Proctor, M-T., Miner, M., McLean, L., Devenish, S., & Ghobary Bonab, B. (2009). Exploring Christians' explicit attachment to God representations: The development of a template for assessing attachment to God experiences. *Journal of Psychology and Theology, 4*(37), 245–264.

Picardi, A., Battisti, F., Tarsitani, L., Baldassari, M., Copertaro, A.. Mocchegiani, E., et al. (2007). Attachment security and immunity in healthy women. *Psychosomatic Medicine, 69,* 40–46.

Robertson, E. (1998). *The prison poems of Dietrich Bonhoeffer: A new translation with commentary.* Guildford, Surrey: Eagle.

Rosner, B. S. (2005). Known by God: C.S. Lewis and Dietrich Bonhoeffer. *The Evangelical Quarterly, 77*(4), 343–352.

Rosner, B. S. (2008). Known by God: The meaning and value of a neglected biblical concept. *The Tyndale Bulletin, 59*(2), 207–230.

Seligman, M. E. P. (2002). *Authentic happiness: Using the new positive psychology to realize your potential for lasting fulfillment.* New York: Free Press.

Slade, A. (1999). Attachment theory and research: Implications for the theory and practice of individual psychotherapy with adults. In J. Cassidy & P.

Shaver (Eds.), *Handbook of attachment: Theory, research and clinical applications* (pp. 575–594). New York: The Guilford Press.

Stern, D. (1985). *The interpersonal world of the infant.* New York: Basic.

Stern, D. N., Sandler, L. W., Nahum, J. P., Harrison, A. M., Lyons-Ruth, K., Morgan, A. C., Bruschweiler-Stern, N., & Tronick, E. Z. (The Process of Change Study Group). (1998). Non-interpretative mechanisms in psychoanalytic therapy: The 'something more' than interpretation. *International Journal of Psychoanalysis, 79,* 903–921.

Stolorow, R. D., Brandschaft, B., & Atwood, G. E. (1987). *Psychoanalytic treatment: An intersubjective approach.* Hillsdale, NJ: The Analytic Press.

Surtees, P. G., Wainwright, N. W. J., & Luben, R. (2006). Mastery, sense of coherence, and mortality: Evidence of independent associations from the EPIC-Norfolk Prospective Cohort Study. *Health Psychology, 25*(1), 102–110.

Tolpin, M. (1986). The self and its self-objects: A different baby. In A. Goldberg (Ed.), *Progress in self psychology, Vol. 2,* (pp. 115–128). New York: Guilford.

Trevarthen, C. (1974). Conversations with a two-month-old. *New Scientist, 62,* 230–235.

Trevarthen, C. (2001). Intrinsic motives for companionship in understanding: Their origin, development, and significance for infant mental health. *Infant Mental Health Journal, 22*(1–2), 95–131.

Tyrer, P., Seivewright, H., & Johnson, T. (2004). The Nottingham study of neurotic disorder: Predictors of 12-year outcome of dysthymic, panic and generalized anxiety disorder. *Psychological Medicine, 34,* 1385–1394.

Vaillant, G. E. (1977). *Adaptation to life.* Boston, MA: Little, Brown.

Vaillant, G. E. (2008). *Spiritual evolution: A scientific defense of faith.* New York: Broadway Books.

Wallin, D. J. (2007). *Attachment in psychotherapy.* New York: The Guilford Press.

Winnicott, D. (1964). Further thoughts on babies as persons. In D. Winnicott, *The child, the family, and the outside world* (pp. 85–92). Harmondsworth, England: Penguin Books. (Original work published 1947)

SECTION II

RESOURCING HUMAN FLOURISHING

Preface

Section I of this volume considered *why* Christian spirituality and theology provide important resources for human flourishing. Section II examines in more detail *how* spiritual resources can be accessed and used in different life contexts. The authors contributing to this section of the volume discuss contexts such as Australian society and Australian people in general, schools and educational organizations, and the church as a social organization. The material is derived from either deep theoretical reflection or empirical studies analyzed in new ways that capture the use of these spiritual resources. These chapters develop the claim that spirituality is a unique and important resource for human flourishing.

ORIENTATIONS TO SPIRITUALITY

In Chapter 5 Peter Kaldor, Alan Black, and Philip Hughes present findings from social research spanning a decade, discussing how spirituality is understood and how it can promote community engagement. Their research investigates relationships between Australians' broad spiritual orientations and empirical indicators of personal and social well-being. Through analyzing how Australians make sense of life, the authors develop a typology of spiritual orientations, including religion-based spirituality (Christian, Buddhist and other), nature-based spirituality (spirituality oriented to the land, or nature,

Beyond Well-Being: Spirituality and Human Flourishing, pages 85–88
Copyright © 2012 by Information Age Publishing
85

as in Aboriginal spirituality), non-specific transcendent spirituality (belief in something beyond material existence without further specification of the nature of the "something beyond"), spiritual uncertainty, and non-belief. They found gender and age differences among these orientations in ways that are generally consistent with other sociological studies of Western spirituality and religion. However, of central interest was whether the type of spiritual orientation affected personal and community flourishing.

People classified according to Kaldor et al.'s spiritual typologies differed with respect to their reported personal and social well-being. Spiritual orientation significantly affected measures related to flourishing such as purpose in life, openness to personal growth, optimism, attitudes to money, and altruism. No single spiritual orientation constituted the "best" spiritual orientation in terms of flourishing, and no one type of spirituality was uniformly beneficial across all indicators of personal and social well-being. However, when the Christian orientation was divided into "reflectively Christian" and "uncritically Christian" groups, the reflectively Christian group scored higher on all indicators than the uncritically Christian group. Further, the reflectively Christian group demonstrated high levels of well-being across all indicators of flourishing. As a result of their work, Kaldor et al. advocate the development of reflective spirituality (forged and maintained through community engagement) to increase flourishing.

EDUCATION FOR FLOURISHING

Education has been considered as an important means of promoting human flourishing since philosophers in Ancient Greece contemplated training in virtue (e.g., Plato in *The Republic* of 385 BCE). In Chapter 6 Tony George, Maureen Miner and Martin Dowson discuss the role of the teacher as a spiritual, as well as academic and social, mentor. In doing so, the authors of this chapter consider how teachers in particular, and the education system more generally, can promote human flourishing.

In contrast with recent exclusive emphases on the academic development of students through curriculum standardization and delivery, George et al. argue that the focus of schooling should shift to the holistic development of students, including spiritual development, as a means of promoting student flourishing. Two dimensions of spirituality with particular relevance to spiritual development are discussed: meaning and connectedness. Specifically, George and colleagues show how secure interpersonal attachments can promote meaning-making and self-control in ways that enhance student flourishing. Yet much of the theory and research associated with issues of meaning-making and connectedness is limited to secular issues. However, some attention has been paid to spiritual extensions and applications of theories relating to meaning-making (e.g., attribution theory) and connectedness (e.g., attachment theory). George et al. use spiritual extensions of secular arguments to demonstrate the role of spiritual attributions and connectedness as routes to flourishing. The authors also discuss practical ways in which teachers, as attachment figures and spiritual mentors, can promote secure attachment, healthy attributions, and appropriate self-regulation.

MATURITY AND FLOURISHING

The implications of spirituality for core psychological processes leading towards maturity and flourishing are considered in Chapter 7. Here Martin Dowson and Maureen Miner demonstrate that psycho-spiritual maturity is a unique dimension of personal maturity. They also argue that various dimensions of maturity contribute to human flourishing, and human flourishing in turn contributes to further maturation of self and others. In doing so, the authors of this chapter make important distinctions between maturity and flourishing, while tracing relationships between spiritual forms of maturity and flourishing.

Further, Chapter 7 points to flourishing as a component of personal development at all phases of life rather than flourishing being an end in itself. In this manner, the chapter provides a dynamic account of flourishing, consistent with accounts that emphasize the contributions of ongoing relationships to flourishing. Moreover, maturation that is uneven across the psychological and spiritual dimensions of maturity is not conducive to flourishing. The authors emphasize the importance of taking a developmental perspective on flourishing. Such a perspective takes seriously the flourishing of those who are very young and very old, psychiatrically struggling, physically incapacitated, developmentally challenged, or environmentally traumatized. The chapter considers states that impede and facilitate maturation across the lifespan, based on the argument that maturity is a functional as well as a developmental construct. Finally, Dowson and Miner suggest ways in which services directed to the psychological, social, intellectual and spiritual development of individuals can promote synchronous development across domains of maturation. However, the main purpose of the chapter is to provide a conceptual and theoretical account of maturation from which empirical studies of maturation and flourishing can be further developed.

SPIRITUALITY AND ORGANIZATIONAL FLOURISHING

In addition to the role of spirituality in providing resources for flourishing through community engagement, education, and personal maturity, spirituality can also support organizational flourishing. In Chapter 8, Stephen Smith discusses an action research project within the Churches of Christ in NSW, Australia. The aim of this project was to identify contextually relevant means of developing and maintaining healthy leaders (with holistic physical, mental, spiritual and social well-being), and thus foster healthy Christian communities. The project method involved describing and analyzing leaders' experiences and personal theories of ministry practice, with the explicit goal of facilitating positive change at individual and community levels. Participants provided rich accounts of the wounded leader: a common theme variously described by participants' use of adjectives such as *drained, derailed, driven* and *defeated.* Their accounts typically show a pathway from a sense of struggling in ministry to eventual ministry derailment. On the other hand, the optimally functioning leader responds adaptively to struggle. The adaptive process critically involves spiritual transformation indicated by awakening, cleansing, and illuminating and resulting in the savoring of life. Savoring as an outcome is itself marked by engagement and pursuit of a meaningful life, or flourishing. Smith concludes by charting the typical life patterns of leaders who flourish in ministry as proposed by study participants. By drawing on these implicitly-known life patterns and processes, individual ministers are able to make changes conducive to flourishing, and organizations are able to promote practices that encourage flourishing.

CHAPTER 5

HOW AUSTRALIAN PEOPLE MAKE SENSE OF LIFE AND ASSESS ITS ULTIMATE SIGNIFICANCE—AND THE DIFFERENCE IT MIGHT MAKE

Peter Kaldor
Leadership Institute, Uniting Church NSW, and
New River Leadership Institute

Alan Black
Edith Cowan University

Philip Hughes
Edith Cowan University

ABSTRACT

Australians make sense of life and assess its ultimate significance in various ways. In a research project stretching over the decade 2001 through 2010, these patterns of responding about life and its significance have been explored and mapped. Based on comprehensive Australian data collected in

Beyond Well-Being: Spirituality and Human Flourishing, pages 89–108
Copyright © 2012 by Information Age Publishing
All rights of reproduction in any form reserved.

2002, and some summary measures in 2009, this chapter distinguishes those making use of religious frameworks, alternative spiritualities, and largely secular approaches. Demographic characteristics of those making sense of life in different ways are discussed, with particular reference to age groups. The chapter also pinpoints ways in which these different approaches affect personal wellbeing and the common good. With respect to personal wellbeing, different approaches to making sense of life affect a sense of purpose in life, openness to personal growth, optimism and attitudes towards financial wellbeing. With respect to communal wellbeing, these different approaches affect other centered values and lived concern for others. Hence, some approaches appear to be more beneficial than others. In particular, embracing spirituality in reflective ways appears to enhance individual and community wellbeing and flourishing.

Winds of change are blowing across the spiritual landscape in Australia and elsewhere. Changes are occurring in how people make sense of life, their values, beliefs and frameworks for living. Historically, civilizations have applied a variety of spiritual and religious beliefs in order to help them make sense of life.

Sometimes beliefs have been translated into ethical, moral, and legal codes, in part intended to protect and sustain the civilization and its way of life. In some cultures, the way of life has been supported and sanctioned by one religion to which everybody belongs. By contrast, in post-white settlement Australia, the story has been one of appropriating a range of religions and traditions, often reflecting underlying ethnic and communal loyalties.

Yet the story in Australia goes back much further than white settlement, right back into the Aboriginal dreamtime. At the risk of over-simplification, Australia has had three distinct movements in relation to the ways her people see the world and approach life. Each has played a major role in shaping our contemporary culture. The first was the *spirituality of indigenous people* (Edwards, 2010) whose occupation of the land spanned tens of thousands of years (Swain, 1991). The second, a *traditional religious orientation* to life (Hughes, 2010), commenced with the coming of Europeans, who brought with them approaches to life rooted in various religions, mainly Christian but also including some Jews, and Chinese miners, Afghan camel-drivers and Indian hawkers bringing with them Buddhist, Islamic and Hindu ways of making sense of life.

The third movement, towards an *increasingly individualistic orientation* (Luckmann, 1967; Wuthnow, 2000), occurred in conjunction with major changes in culture that have occurred across the Western world since the 1960s. Globalization and technology have increased our awareness of the diversity of philosophies, religions, spiritualities and approaches to life across the globe, and multiculturalism has brought these to our shores. People began to see their approach to life and the world as personal, something they chose, rather than something that was given to them as part of their ethnic and cultural heritage. Some maintained religious commitments, while others looked for meaning and hope in alternative spiritualities of various kinds. Still others chose a non-religious way of seeing life (Bouma, 2006). However, a key feature of all contemporary approaches to making sense of life is that it is seen as a personal decision. Understanding one's place in the universe has shifted from a question related to ethnic and community loyalties—something inherited and passed on from one generation to the next, provided by authority or tradition—to one of individual choice and construction.

Australians are increasingly being invited to select from a supermarket of meaning-options available on our doorstep. Churches sit alongside mosques and other places of worship, increasingly augmented by other types of religious life and an array of alternative spiritualities, communicated and/or marketed to us in many ways. Moreover, there is much in our society that encourages Australians to live for the here-and-now, without regard to religion or spirituality, and to focus on whatever is seen to make up the "good life."

HOW WE MAKE SENSE OF LIFE, AND DOES IT MATTER?

A first key goal of the project informing this chapter was to explore and map how people in contemporary Australia make sense of life and assess its ultimate significance. This is the focus of the first half of this chapter. The 2002 Wellbeing and Security Survey was designed to explore the breadth of ways Australians make sense of life, and some more recent survey work in 2009 indicates the extent to which these ways might be changing. Mapping these diverse ways might be interesting, but does it matter—especially, in the current context—for human flourishing?

A second key purpose of this project was to see whether and how those different approaches to making sense of life impact our personal and communal wellbeing. We examine these questions in the second half of this chapter. Further detail of results reported here can be found in *Spirit Matters* (Kaldor, Hughes & Black, 2010). We invite you to join with us in this exploration of the human spirit.

HOW WE MAKE SENSE OF LIFE: EXPLORING
THE CONTOURS

The first goal of this project was to explore and map how people in contemporary Australia make sense of life. The 2002 Wellbeing and Security

Survey included approximately 80 questions covering different aspects of religion, spirituality and perspectives on life and their importance in people's lives. The survey provides a rich picture of the diversity of ways Australians approach making sense of life. Detailed exploratory analysis was carried out using a range of statistical techniques. Various models were investigated, particularly using factor analysis, and scales were developed to measure each of the following underlying dimensions of how we make sense of life:

- A belief that there is something beyond this life that makes sense of it all, that there is more to it than the "here and now"
- An orientation to a particular religious or philosophical approach: Christian or other religions, Buddhism and/or New Age philosophies, a spiritual connection with the land or nature
- An uncritical approach, feeling that it is important to believe and not question one's beliefs
- An eclectic approach that draws meaning from any (or many) philosophies that might be helpful
- Involvement in religious, eastern, New Age or other reflective groups or practices

Scales based on these dimensions formed the backbone of more detailed analysis throughout the project (see Figures 5.1 and 5.2).

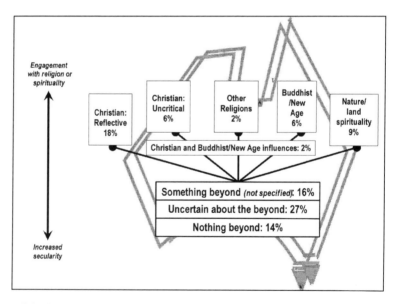

Figure 5.1 How Australians make sense of life. *Source:* Wellbeing and Security Survey.

The following system of classification of the various ways Australians make sense of life was developed as part of this research project:

1. *Those who professed an active Christian religious orientation:* people who affirmed as definitely or probably true of themselves that "God, the creator or life-force, has a big influence on how I live," and who also attended a church or a Christian group at least once a year.
   These people were divided into two categories according to whether they felt it right to question one's beliefs (*reflectively Christian*) or not to do so (*uncritically Christian*).

2. *Those strongly influenced by **Buddhist and/or New Age thinking:*** people who affirmed as definitely or probably true that they were strongly influenced by Buddhist and/or New Age thought and were involved, at least occasionally, in Buddhist or New Age practices.
   Some people (around 2% of Australians) felt they were significantly influenced by both Christian and Buddhist/New Age thinking. For more detailed analysis these people were included in the Buddhist/New Age group.

3. *Those identifying with **other major world religions:*** people connected with other religions and involved, at least occasionally, in related religious or spiritual practices.

4. *Those with **a strong spiritual connection with the land:*** people who said they felt a strong spiritual connection with the land but who did not fit into any of the previous categories.

5. *People falling into other categories.* The rest of the population was divided into three groups based on their beliefs about whether "there is something beyond this life that makes sense of it all." Those agreeing with this, but not fitting into any previous categories, made up the *something beyond* group. Those uncertain were included in the *uncertain about the beyond* group, while those who disagreed were included in the *nothing beyond* group.

Figure 5.2 How we make sense of life—the typology developed in this study

So How Do Australians Make Sense of Life?

While there are many ways in which a summary typology could be constructed, the map shown in Figure 5.1 is a useful starting point for discussion about religion, spirituality and secularity in contemporary Australia. It provides a pictorial representation of both the religious beliefs and values people subscribe to, but also other competing religious views of life. It is these counter-views of life that frequently lead people either to adopt nominal religious affiliations, or to abandon religious convictions altogether. By including several categories of those more secular in orientation, it is more truly reflective of the range of pathways for making sense of life that exist among Australians.

Those influenced by particular religious or spiritual traditions, and involved in activities at least yearly, were identified first. Then those not indicating such influences and involvement were categorized according to whether or not they agree that *there is something beyond this life that makes sense of it all.* More detailed classifications were made according to the definitions summarized in Figure 5.2.

Religious and Spiritual Ways of Making Sense of Life

Three out of ten Australians (30%) are influenced by religious thinking about how to make sense of life. Despite what some commentators may wish us to think, religious ways of making sense of life are far from dead in contemporary Australia. Around 8% of Australians are significantly influenced by Buddhist or New Age spiritualities. Some may be surprised that the percentage is not higher given the publicity these spiritualities often receive in discussions of health and wellbeing in both intellectual and popular circles. Perhaps they generate curiosity and interest due to their freethinking and exploratory nature, rather than building more extensive commitment and belonging.

A similar percentage (9%) expressed a strong spiritual connection to the land but do not fall into any of the other categories. Taking those influenced by "land spiritualities" and those influenced by Buddhism or the New Age movement together as a group, we can suggest that around 17% of Australians intentionally seek to make sense of life via such alternative spiritualities. Sixty-five per cent of people interviewed report that they appropriated alternative spiritualities in an eclectic fashion. That is to say, they affirmed and embraced them for what they contributed to their everyday lives rather than their apparent "truthfulness." Such truthfulness might be understood as more related to religious belief than to spiritual practice.

BEYOND THE CONTENT: HOW WE APPROACH MAKING SENSE OF LIFE

Regardless of the content of belief, our research also identifies two very different approaches to making sense of life among believers of various sorts. First, some hold to their beliefs or perspectives in a very clear-cut but uncritical way. They feel it is important to believe but do not reflect on or question those beliefs. Some within this first group hold their views in an inflexible and authoritarian way that resists change or variation. Others (the second sub-group) simply accept the necessity for holding religious beliefs, but do so uncritically. Immigrants tend to bring their religious identities with them and associate personal identity with a particular, religiously validated way of being in the world—for example, Italian Catholics and Orthodox Greeks, or Vietnamese Buddhists and Hindu Indians. The second sub-group form a minority of 20–25% of those who self-identified as having a religious orientation to life.

Second, the majority of those with a religious orientation think it is appropriate (or important) to question and to explore different approaches to life, coming to their eventual understandings through some form of reflective journey or assessment.

These two different groups (the uncritical and the questioning religious groups) differ in their approaches, but not necessarily the content of their beliefs. Two people may arrive at the same religious beliefs, one in a reflective way, and the other in an uncritical or dogmatic manner.

By contrast, those making sense of life via other alternative spiritualities tend to do so in highly eclectic ways: 65% of those embracing alternative spiritualities affirmed that *the best way to develop spirituality these days is to take on board whatever is helpful from different spiritualities or religions.*

More Secular Approaches

The results also indicate that around 16% of Australians agree that *there is something beyond this life that makes sense of it all* but do not acknowledge any more definite spiritual influences, 27% are uncertain, and 14% disagree with this proposition.

For most in these categories, religious and/or spiritual approaches are not so much rejected as ignored as irrelevant or unknowable. Life is lived in the present, in the world of the here-and-now. Religion or spirituality is just not seen to matter. Thus, many feel they can live their daily lives without religion or spirituality troubling them. Secularization in Australia, then, seems to have more to do with a distancing from the categories of religion/spirituality than a massive rejection of these categories.

Making Sense of Life—What Do We See?

The results reported here suggest that in contemporary Australia people are choosing, sometimes carefully, sometimes eclectically, to explore meaning in very different ways. Some believe they have found means of discerning absolute truth; others are engaged in spiritual journeying, valuing the search, the complexity and even the potential paradoxes involved in making sense of life. In addition, many take a secular "here-and-now" approach, not seeing spirituality as important at all.

Gender and Age Differences

Over many years researchers into religion have found that women are more likely to be religious or attend religious services (e.g., Kaldor, 1987). Our research into how Australians make sense of life suggests that the same is true of alternative spiritualities as well.

There are also some significant age differences in how people choose to make sense of life. According to our survey, those with a religious orientation tend to be older. By way of example, nearly one third of all people over 60 attend church at least monthly, compared with half that among 40 to 60 year olds, 14% of those in their 30s, and 10% of those 18 through 29 years of age. Among those who feel there is something beyond this life that makes sense of it all, younger respondents are more likely to be eclectic in their approach, compared to those who are older, who are more likely to feel that we should just believe and not question our beliefs.

For older Australians, religiosity and spirituality tend to be much the same thing. And, while some younger people see themselves as religious, there is also a significant group of younger people that prefer to use the word "spiritual" in a way not connected with organized religion.

Turning to alternative spiritualities, people aged between 40 and 60 years are proportionately over-represented in the New Age/Buddhist group. Those under 40 are no more highly-represented in this group, and are proportionately under-represented in the land/nature spiritualities group. Those who are younger are over-represented in the "something beyond" and "uncertain" categories (but not in the "nothing beyond" group). While some younger adults may become more able to articulate their religious or spiritual positions clearly as they get older, these results suggest there is no particular way to predict in what directions they may turn.

To what extent do these results identify important shifts in the Australian population and their attitudes to meaning-making? Are these age differences simply to do with a stage in life, changing as people get older, or are they due to generational shifts? To get some insights into these questions we can turn to more recent data.

A Changing Picture?

Unfortunately no parallel data are available since this survey was carried out in 2002/2003, though there is data from 2009 that explores similar territory. The Australian Survey of Social Attitudes (Evans, 2009) contained one core item from our typology concerning whether people believed there was *something beyond this life that makes sense of it all?* The comparative results from the two surveys are shown in Table 5.1 below.

TABLE 5.1   There is Something Beyond that Makes Sense of It All (2002 and 2009)

	2002 Wellbeing and Security Survey	2009 Australian Survey of Social Attitudes	Difference
Strongly agree	17.9	16.6	−1.3
Agree	28.0	28.1	0.1
Neither agree nor disagree	35.8	33.5	−2.3
Disagree	10.8	14.2	3.4
Strongly disagree	7.5	7.6	0.1

As can be seen from Table 5.1, in 2009 slightly fewer agreed with the statement, and there was a shift from uncertainty to disagreement (though not in "strong disagreement"). Given likely measurement errors, these results suggest only small changes in a predominantly stable picture over the six to seven years between surveys. While at the time of writing detailed work on the 2009 database was still to take place, initial examination of other items reinforces such conclusions.

The 2009 survey also enables the construction of a *How we make sense of life* map similar to that in Figure 5.1. While question and wording differences limit what can be drawn from it, using parallel assumptions a parallel typology to that from 2002 was created. The two maps of how Australians make sense of life are shown in Figure 5.3. Details of discrepancies can be found in *Spirit Matters* (Kaldor, Hughes & Black, 2010).

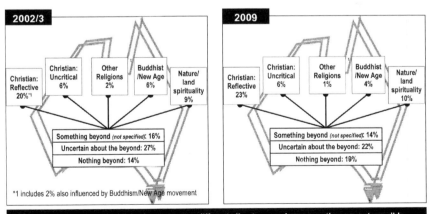

Figure 5.3   How Australians make sense of life (2002–2003 and 2009).

While wording or structural changes in the items used in the two surveys prevent direct comparison, at the same time the two surveys produce similar maps, with possibly some moderate shifts from uncertainty to a lack of belief in anything beyond this life that makes sense of it all. The similarity of the two maps suggests stability and reliability to the map and the distribution that emerges.

WHAT DIFFERENCE MIGHT IT MAKE?

Mapping how we make sense of life might be interesting, but does it matter—in particular for human flourishing? Though underneath the surface of our lives, to what extent might making sense of our lives affect our wellbeing, both personally and in terms of the wellbeing of our society as a whole? Intuitively, how we make sense of life should affect how we live it. It should affect our values, how we live them out, and how we cope. When problems arise, many reach deep into the spiritual dimension of their lives to find optimism, hope, self-reliance and determination. Some turn to spiritual resources outside of themselves, to their belief in a God who is loving and powerful, or perhaps to a belief in the natural outworking of fate. Some people find a spiritual connection with nature, finding peace and wholeness within the natural world by seeking ways of living in ecological harmony. There are also many who cope with problematic experiences without reference to spiritual resources.

What kinds of links are there between how we make sense of life and our personal wellbeing? Or with wider community wellbeing? To explore these questions, the Wellbeing and Security Survey utilized a wide range of measures of both personal and community wellbeing, as summarized in Figure 5.4.

Detailed multivariate examinations of the links between these wellbeing measures and how people make sense of life were conducted using the spirituality scales developed at the outset of the project. Then differences in wellbeing among the various groupings were also explored. This research suggests, not surprisingly, that how people make sense of life shapes their individual wellbeing in only relatively small ways. Far more significant can be their personal make up, and the life experiences they face. However, several key channels were identified through which how we make sense of life was linked with personal and communal wellbeing, as discussed below and detailed in Table 5.2.

Measures of personal wellbeing

1. **Standard of living:** personal and family income, the importance of wealth and satisfaction with standards of living.
2. **Health:** physical and mental, alcohol consumption and exercise.
3. **Psychological wellbeing:** personal optimism, self-esteem, sense of control, purpose in life and openness to personal growth.
4. **Feelings about life:** satisfaction with life as a whole and with different aspects of life.
5. **Coping with difficult experiences:** adverse experiences people had recently encountered.
6. **Safety and security—present and future:** insecurity due to too little choice, stress created by too much choice, fears about future personal security (employment, financial, relational), concerns about the future of our society and planet.
7. **Relational wellbeing:** satisfaction with and quality of relationships with others, (partners, children and friends).

Measures of community wellbeing

8. **Trust in others:** the extent to which people trust various groups of people, particularly those who are different, levels of confidence in various types of organizations or institutions.
9. **Core values:** the relative importance of enjoying life, an exciting life, being successful, broadmindedness, being helpful to others, concern for social justice and the environment, and the relative importance of individual rights and the needs of others.
10. **Contributing to others:** ways people contribute to the lives and wellbeing of others including volunteering, giving to charity and informal caring in daily life.

Figure 5.4 Measures of wellbeing included in the survey.

Channel 1: Sense of Purpose in Life

The results of the present study indicate that how people make sense of life is closely related to their sense of purpose in life. Those with a spiritual orientation of some sort, particularly a reflective religious orientation, are likely to have a stronger sense of purpose in life, while those with a more secular here-and-now mindset recorded less strength of purpose in life. The two Christian groups averaged higher purposefulness scores than the sample as a whole, with lowest scores found among the three secular groups. The two alternative spirituality groups reported levels of purposefulness in between the Christian and secular groups.

TABLE 5.2 How We Make Sense of Life and Selected Measures of Wellbeing

	Reflectively Christian	Uncritically Christian	New Age and/or Buddhist	Land/nature spirituality	Something beyond	Uncertain about the beyond	Nothing beyond	Total population	Strength of Relationship Variance Able to be Predicted (%)
Optimism									
Optimism (scale score out of 100)	65	66	64	65	62	61	59	63	Strong (5.3%)
Values									
Enjoying life (enjoying food, sex, leisure—scale score)	72	68	80	81	80	80	80	78	Strong (5.7%)
Having an exciting life (stimulating experiences)	60	54	71	68	69	69	68	66	Moderate (3.4%)
Being successful (achieving goals)	67	65	74	69	72	73	71	71	Weak (2.7%)
Broadmindedness (tolerance of different ideas and beliefs)	73	66	85	81	76	73	74	75	Very Strong (15.7%)
Being helpful (working for the welfare of others)	74	69	75	70	68	65	66	69	Strong (6.4%)
Being concerned for social justice and the environment	73	69	79	79	70	67	69	71	Very Strong (10.3%)

Individual Rights or Needs of Others

Indicator									
It is more important to act on your individual rights than to look to the needs of others. (% agree or strongly agree)	**8%**	**23%**	8%	17%	14%	**20%**	16%	15%	Very Strong (**14.5%**)

Contributing to Others

Indicator									
Hours of voluntary help per week (average number of hours)	**2.2**	1.5	1.5	**2.0**	**0.9**	**1.0**	1.1	1.4	Strong (**7.9%**)
Donating to charities in past 12 months (% donated several times)	**74%**	**68%**	61%	63%	53%	**52%**	**51%**	59%	

Trust in Others

Indicator									
People in neighborhood	66	62	64	**70**	62	63	61	64	Weak (**1.5%**)
People with whom work/study	71	65	67	72	**65**	68	69	68	Weak (**1.2%**)
Other races	63	63	65	65	**58**	**58**	59	61	Moderate (**4.6%**)
Other religions	66	64	65	68	61	**60**	59	63	Moderate (**3.5%**)

Standard of Living

Indicator									
Household gross annual income ($)	$59,589	**$39,988**	$61,371	$65,137	$57,272	$66,340	**$72,445**	$62,583	Moderate (**3.2%**)
Satisfaction with standard of living (score out of 100)	76	**79**	71	74	**70**	74	74	74	Weak (**0.9%**)
Importance accorded to wealth (score out of 100)	**52**	**50**	56	56	**61**	**62**	61	58	Strong (**5.5%**)

Source: Wellbeing and Security Survey
Notes: 1. Cell entries in bold indicate significant differences from the total population at a 95% level of confidence.
2. Last column indicates amount of variance able to be predicted from scales measuring people's religious or spiritual beliefs and practices, if any, after taking account of age and gender.

Intentionally exploring how we make sense of life can plausibly generate greater clarity of purpose that in turn can help us make healthy and directed life decisions, keep us on course when circumstances become difficult, and provide us with meaning and significance beyond ourselves. Such a pathway from reflection on life to clear purposes and thence to personal meaning, significance, and fulfillment echoes claims of positive psychologists who argue that personal fulfillment will be found by using strengths we have towards wider purposes that matter to us (e.g., Seligman, 2002).

Channel 2: Openness to Personal Growth

In our detailed research strong links were found between openness to personal growth and a general spiritual orientation, particularly among those embracing alternative spiritualities. Those with a more here-and-now mindset and those with an uncritical religious orientation recorded less openness to personal growth.

The New Age/Buddhist group recorded the highest average scores on openness to personal growth. After accounting for age and gender differences in the make-up of groups, the Reflectively Christian group also recorded high openness to personal growth. By contrast, the Uncritically Christian group had the lowest levels of openness to personal growth. In between was the openness of those in the "nothing beyond" and "uncertain about the beyond" groups.

How we make sense of life is linked with a more general openness to personal growth, which in turn can generate greater self-understanding and sense of self, increasing our ability to make wise decisions about how we live our lives. A carefully developed sense of meaning in life can also be a fruit of a desire for personal growth.

Channel 3: Optimism

How people make sense of life may build or diminish their optimism and the value they place on themselves. By way of example, to believe we are created in God's image or that God has a plan for our lives may generate optimism and place value on who we are. To see ourselves as functioning within the complex ecosystems of the planet, or as having an unbreakable connection with the land may also instill a positive sense of optimism and place. On the other hand, an emphasis on human sinfulness or on rampant and inevitable destruction of the land or those ecosystems may possibly reduce optimism.

As can be seen in Table 5.2, our research suggests that higher levels of optimism are found among those with a religious or spiritual orientation. On balance, a carefully-developed religious or spiritual way of making sense of life appears more likely to be linked with greater optimism than are more secular perspectives.

Channel 4: Other-Centered Values

A fourth major connection is in the area of espoused values. How we make sense of life may result in us adopting different core values. The survey invited people to rate the importance of various values, including enjoying life, being successful, being helpful to others, leading an exciting life, concern for social justice and the environment, and broadmindedness. As can be seen in Table 5.2, there are links between how we make sense of life and the values we hold.

As part of exploring these differences, the top three values were identified for each grouping. People in the more secular categories most valued enjoyment of life, then broadmindedness and success. Those in the Christian groups most valued helping others, then concern for social justice and the environment. The alternative spirituality groups most valued broadmindedness, followed by enjoyment of life and concern for social justice and the environment (Kaldor, Hughes & Black, 2010, p. 132).

As can be seen in Table 5.2, the majority in all groups valued concern for others over individual rights. However, twice as many of those in the more secular groupings agreed that individual rights were more important than a focus on helping others, compared to the Reflectively Christian or those embracing Buddhist/New age spiritualities.

Religious and spiritual groups may therefore make a significant contribution to community social capital by generating a greater willingness to strive for justice, equity, or the needs of others. With occasional exceptions, most such groups encourage these values, reinforcing them at communal events or gatherings. If lived out, these differences in espoused values could make a difference to the wellbeing of individuals and communities.

Channel 5: Lived Concern for Others

Our research suggests that the other-centered values described above are lived out in terms of action, at least as measured by contributions to charities, volunteering, and attitudes towards other races or religions. Those with a more secular here-and-now mindset are less likely to spend time in volunteer activities or in giving to charities. Even after accounting for age and gender differences, the Reflectively Christian and those exploring some form of alternative spirituality tend to be more involved in volunteering or giving. They are also more trusting of those from different racial or religious backgrounds than are people with a predominantly secular orientation.

This does not mean that the spiritual or religious people have a monopoly on altruism. However, it does highlight the important overall contribution of religious and spiritual organizations to social capital and communal wellbeing.

Channel 6: Attitudes Towards Financial Wellbeing

Even after accounting for age and gender differences among the groups, the religious groups tended to earn the least; and those in the "nothing beyond" group tended to have the highest incomes. The Reflectively Christian also appeared more likely to choose people-focused professions than technically-focused ones, while the reverse is true for those taking more secular perspectives (Kaldor, Hughes & Black, 2010). Thus, how people make sense of life may result in different priorities in choosing a career, resulting in different financial outcomes.

Perhaps more significantly, how we make sense of life may also result in a different value placed on wealth itself. As noted above, people with a predominantly secular orientation are more likely to emphasize material success. Those influenced by religious beliefs, though they tend to earn less, report being somewhat happier with what they earn, whilst placing significantly less importance on wealth.

HOW WE MAKE SENSE OF LIFE—IT DOES MATTER

It does matter—how people make sense of life can affect their personal wellbeing and the wider wellbeing of the communities in which they live. The links summarized in Figure 5.5 represent hypotheses for how this effect may occur.

While there are no doubt complex questions of cause and effect, at few points do those making sense of life in purely secular ways appear to experience higher personal wellbeing or contribute to greater community wellbeing than do those who have worked at reflectively exploring their place in the universe.

Our research also suggests that how we make sense of life may have implications for the wider community as well: to the way we relate to and trust

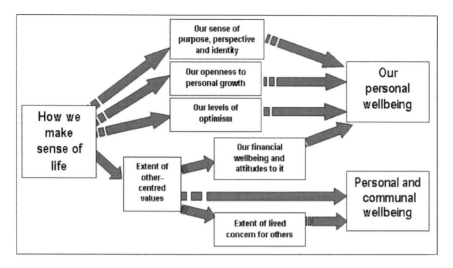

Figure 5.5 Life orientations and wellbeing.

each other, to the priority we place on concern for others, and to living out such a wider concern in the form of altruism and generosity, for example.

These results, and the potential generational shifts identified earlier, suggest some potential wider social challenges. Given the higher wellbeing of those who are Reflectively Christian and the significant contribution this group makes to voluntary activities, to social trust and giving in a range of areas, lower levels of this group in society may have a negative impact on the wellbeing and resilience of the community at large.

Spirit matters, then, not just to the individual, but to the whole community, in ways that are often subtle yet pervasive. The forms of spiritual life and pursuit of meaning that are encouraged in our society have implications for the quality of life of our community—presumably not just for our own generation, but for the generations to come. There are implications here for those concerned about social policy, personal or community wellbeing, health education, and personal development. Obviously, there is much here of relevance to churches, religious and other groups concerned with spirituality and meaning.

Approaches to Meaning

The results of this research also suggest that, whatever religious, spiritual or secular avenues people may choose in exploring their place in the universe, how they approach the journey is also important. A reflective, thoughtful approach appears more helpful than an unquestioning or dogmatic one. It appears to be beneficial to engage with questions of meaning and explore them with integrity, recognizing our human limitations in the process, piecing together our understandings over a lifetime. It may be easier to accept beliefs uncritically, or to seek to reduce reality to a simplistic formula of one sort or another. The research here, however, suggests that there can be limitations in doing so.

Additionally, the research reported here suggests that, as a society, we may benefit from promoting reflection on belief. Clarity about our place in the scheme of things can generate values, purposes and priorities that take account of the needs of others as well as our own. Encouraging such a reflective journey can build altruism and concern for others in both informal and more organized ways.

At least for some people, a communal dimension is important in developing, maintaining or refining their life orientation. Through communal activities in which beliefs and values are expressed, and maybe even challenged, a way of life is consolidated or modified. Through group discussion and action, the nuances of a way of life can be explored, and chosen values can be applied to the practicalities of life.

We do not need all the answers to begin to engage the questions. Making sense of life and nurturing our inner spirit is neither easy nor instant. Nevertheless, time spent alone in personal reflection has a long history in many religious and spiritual traditions. It has also come to be important in various leadership development and capacity building programs. The Outward Bound program, for instance, develops personal resilience, not only by pushing people to their limits on rock faces, but also by requiring participants to spend several nights and days on their own, not traveling anywhere but spending time in a relatively isolated location engaging the experience. This strategy creates space for deeper reflection on life, and a refining of purposes. Such time spent alone may allow many to know better their own inner resources.

We hope that our research helps to start discussion on the importance of making sense of life, for its findings have implications for those who are concerned about personal and community wellbeing, and for individuals seeking a flourishing life.

A RESEARCH AGENDA FOR THE FUTURE

It is important to acknowledge some limitations of survey research in such complex areas as life orientations and wellbeing. A broad-brush survey is by its nature a blunt instrument needing to be augmented by more nuanced case studies or longitudinal research. Unless they are very large-scale, general social surveys cannot provide detailed analysis of every variety of religion or spirituality. Reliable analysis of, for instance, the impacts of Hinduism, Islam, or Judaism would require a much larger sample size or a series of more targeted surveys.

Nor did the survey examine in detail the often significant roles played by religious and non-religious institutions in important areas such as politics, education and social welfare.

Nevertheless, the mapping carried out does suggest a research agenda for the future. International comparisons would obviously be useful, as would be more detailed mapping of sub-communities in Australia. Nuanced methodologies including case studies and longitudinal analyses would also be helpful. More extensive research with specific subgroups such as cancer sufferers, prison inmates or people coping with the death of a partner might uncover some of the mechanisms whereby how people make sense of life affects their wellbeing, and the ways people cope with difficult experiences.

ACKNOWLEDGEMENTS

The *Wellbeing and Security Survey* was undertaken in 2002 by Edith Cowan University, Deakin University, NCLS Research and Anglicare (Sydney), with funding from these organizations and the Australian Research Council. It was completed by a random sample of approximately 1500 adults selected from Australian electoral rolls.

The 2009 data comes from the 2009 Australian Survey of Social Attitudes (Evans, 2009). The survey was completed by 1718 adults randomly selected from across Australia. Access to the data has been provided by NCLS Research, which was a partner in the consortium that commissioned the survey. Further details of both the 2002 and 2009 research can be found in Kaldor, Hughes & Black (2010).

REFERENCES

Bouma, G. (2006). *Australian Soul.* Melbourne: Cambridge University Press.

Edwards, W. (2010). Aboriginal. In P. Hughes (Ed.), *Australia's religious communities: A multimedia exploration* (3rd ed.). Melbourne: Christian Research Association.

Evans, A. (2009). *AuSSA_A_religiosity.sav,* The Australian Survey of Social Attitudes, Australian Social Science Data Archives [computer file]. Canberra: Australian National University.

Hughes, P. (Ed.). (2010). *Australia's religious communities: A multimedia exploration (3rd ed.).* Nunawading, Victoria, Australia: Christian Research Association.

Kaldor, P. (1987). *Who goes where? Who doesn't care? Going to church in Australia.* Sydney: Lancer Books.

Kaldor, P., Hughes, P., & Black, A. (2010). *Spirit matters: How making sense of life affects wellbeing.* Preston, Victoria, Australia: Mosaic Press.

Luckmann, T. (1967). *The invisible religion.* New York, NY: Macmillan.

Seligman, M. E. P. (2002). *Authentic happiness: Using positive psychology to realise your potential for lasting fulfilment.* Sydney: Random House.

Swain, T. (1991). Aboriginal religions in time and space. In A. Black (Ed.), *Religion in Australia: Sociological perspectives* (pp. 151–165). Sydney: Allen and Unwin.

Wuthnow, M. (2000). *After heaven: Spirituality in America since the 1950s.* Berkeley, CA: University of California Press.

CHAPTER 6

HUMAN FLOURISHING IN EDUCATION

The Relationships Among Student Attachments, Attributions and Self-Regulation

Tony George
St. John's University, Tanzania

Maureen Miner
Australasian Centre for Studies in Spirituality

Martin Dowson
Australasian Centre for Studies in Spirituality

ABSTRACT

This chapter explores the contribution that classroom teachers can make to the lives of their students, causing them to flourish. While emphasis has been given historically to curriculum development and the intellectual development of students, more thought is needed in considering the roles of the

Beyond Well-Being: Spirituality and Human Flourishing, pages 109–126
Copyright © 2012 by Information Age Publishing

teacher and their students as whole people. This chapter considers human flourishing in education by examining the relationships among student attachments, student attributions and student self-regulation in the intellectual, emotional, social and spiritual development of students. The research gives rise to important implications for further consideration of the teacher as role model, life coach and spiritual guide.

Over the past 50 years Australian school education has emphasized curriculum development, delivery and outcomes. This emphasis has culminated in strong recent interest by Australian governments and parents in making comparisons across school communities based on the average performance of students undertaking national literacy and numeracy tests. While the interest in improving Australian school education is encouraging for educationalists, a reductionist approach to evaluating and comparing schools on the basis of average literacy or numeracy results may be overly simplistic. The simplistic equating of education with academic achievement leads to an assumption that students will flourish if they actualize their academic potential. This conclusion is questionable: some students who develop academic gifts nonetheless experience serious emotional and relational problems, whereas others who do not fully actualize their academic potential flourish in other areas of life. Flourishing is not just actualizing potential for academic activities, although academic achievement may be one indicator of flourishing.

There is more to education in schools than simply the intellectual development and comparative achievement of students. While intellectual development is a significant part of school life, education also includes the emotional, social, and spiritual development of students. Based on the argument that flourishing involves more than actualizing academic potential, we propose that flourishing students also actualize their social, emotional and spiritual potential in addition to their intellectual potential. Psychological theories explain how such multi-focused development produces flourishing. In particular, theories associated with attachment have rich applications to student flourishing. Attachment theories, together with cognitive-emotional-social theories of attributions and self-regulation, also suggest what teachers need to do to produce flourishing students. Hence, this chapter considers how teachers may encourage students to flourish through paying specific attention to attachment relationships and associated attributions and student self-regulation. We explore the role of the classroom teacher beyond that of delivering the formal curriculum, to that of being a role model, life coach and spiritual guide for students under their tutelage and care.

In this chapter we draw upon a number of significant psychological theories to advance a perspective of education that includes consideration of the intellectual, emotional, social, and spiritual development of students and the role of educators in positively and actively contributing to the flourishing of their students. In short, we explore how educators as significant attachment figures can contribute to student well-being and achievement, especially through encouraging and enabling the development of appropriate student attributions and self-regulation.

HUMAN FLOURISHING AND EDUCATION

Psychology has recently refocused on positive notions of mental health (Seligman & Csikszentmihalyi, 2000; Seligman, Steen, Park & Peterson, 2005). These notions of mental health are not articulated merely as the absence of mental illness but in terms of human flourishing. Surprisingly, while educational success has often been attributed to teacher capability and student intellectual ability, relatively little reference has been made to student mental health, or to human (student) flourishing. This situation, however, is beginning to change as demonstrated by increased interest in the relationship between positive psychology and education, for example, with respect to resilience and student engagement as positive characteristics contributing to success (Reschly, Huebner, Appleton & Antaramian, 2008).

Human flourishing is described by Nakamura and Csikszentmihalyi (2002) as "finding meaning and enjoyment in one's relationship with the world" (p. 83). Thus, human flourishing implies social, religious and spiritual connectivity and engagement (Eaude, 2009; Greenfield, Vaillant, & Marks, 2009; Vaillant, Templeton, Ardelt, & Meyer, 2008). Further, Emmons (2002) observes that, "as far as we know humans are the only meaning-seeking species on the planet. Meaning-making is an activity that is distinctly human, a function of how the human brain is organized" (p. 105).

In terms of the discussion above, schools as educational communities may be considered as places where students in relationship with others, especially their teachers, seek to make sense of themselves and the world in which they live. To the extent to which meaning is found, effective schools are places characterized by human flourishing. Schools, however, are complex social environments. For example, in a secondary educational school context, it is not uncommon for an adolescent student to have as many as ten different teachers in as many different classes. This number of relationships alone contributes to a complex social environment that many mature adults would find challenging. Consequently, we propose that in such an environment, a consideration of student flourishing ought not only to take into account the influence of relationships and the importance of meaning making, but also the development of pro-social cognition and behavior. In doing so, we suggest that well-established psychological theories will enhance our understanding of student flourishing in educational contexts. Specifically, Attachment Theory (e.g., Bowlby, 1969,) is well-positioned for understanding the influence of relationships, Attribution Theory (e.g., Spilka, Shaver, & Kirkpatrick, 1985) is well-positioned for understanding the importance of meaning-making, and Self-Regulation Theory (e.g., Baumeister & Vohs, 2004) is well-positioned for understanding the development of pro-social behavior and restraint. Together, these theories contribute to a more comprehensive understanding of the intellectual, emotional, social and spiritual well-being of students. The following sections explore the contributions of these three psychological theories to understanding student flourishing.

ATTACHMENT AND HUMAN FLOURISHING

Connected people are happy people. More formally, healthy relationships and positive affect are critical to human flourishing. As Vaillant (2008) observes, "human relationships and positive emotions are critical" (p. 12) to human development. Attachment theory provides important insights into the development of human relationships, and hence flourishing.

Attachment theory, as proposed by Bowlby (1969, 1988), postulates that humans have a unique and innate need for relatedness with others. It is in the context of relatedness that children develop expectations concerning self, others, and self-in-relation-to-others. These expectations form the basis of a child's internal working models (cognitive representations of how relating-to-others works). Attachment theory thus provides a basis for considering the roles that parents, teachers and significant others play in the cognitive development of a child's mental representations, or working models, of the relational world.

Attachment theory is not only a well-researched psychological theory (Cassidy & Shaver, 2008), but it also has spiritual implications. Miner (2007) draws on Christian Trinitarian theology to argue that this innate need for relatedness within humans is due to humans being a) creations of a relational God, who b) embody and reflect God's relational and spiritual nature and, thus, c) whose relationality and spirituality are intrinsic, purposive and holistic aspects of their created status. Thus, rather than spirituality being an evolved quality in humans, Miner posits that our spiritual capacity is due to the existence of a creator God who has created humanity with a spirit for the purpose of relationship with Him and with their fellow humans. She further argues that human relationships are enhanced by attachment to God. This argument is significant in its identification of God as a relational being with whom humans may form an attachment. Consequently, spirituality is not merely a psychological condition as demonstrated in some kind of metaphysical yearning, but it is an authentic means of relating that finds its expression in attachment to a relational God who is Spirit and who created humans with spirit of their own.

The primary significance of Miner's argument is in her acknowledgement that human spirituality may be incorporated into our understanding of student flourishing by including God as a significant "other" with whom students (including, but not limited to, those learning in a Christian school context) may form an attachment. Thus, God may be included alongside mother, father, friends and teachers when considering a student's attachments and attributions. In contrast to the attempt to incorporate a sophisticated psychology of spirituality or religion with attachment theory, the simple inclusion of God as a significant other maintains the integrity of attachment theory as it currently stands while at the same time recognizes human spirituality.

Attachment may be understood in terms of two dimensions and four resulting styles (Bartholemew & Horowitz, 1991). The first dimension posits a binary, positive or negative, model of the self: the self as worthy of love and support, or not. The second dimension proposes a similar binary model of the significant other: the other as trustworthy and available, or not. From these two dimensions, four styles or types of attachment may be considered: the first is the person who is secure (positive sense of self, positive sense of other); the second is the person who is pre-occupied (negative self, positive other); the third is the person who is dismissive-avoidant (positive self, negative other); and the fourth is the person who is fearful-avoidant (negative self, negative other). These dimensions, and derived styles or types, determine our cognitions, affect and behavior in relationships. Further, secure attachments directly impact human flourishing through the guiding influence of positive (self and other) internal working models on emotion regulation and subsequent well-being (Bretherton & Munholland, 1999; Gross & John, 2003).

In school settings, students with a secure attachment style are likely to be less anxious and more confident in engaging with others and their learning environment. Consequently, they are likely to be more engaged in their studies and to perform better academically. A study by Allen, Moore, Kuperminc, and Bell (1998) found attachment security predicts peer acceptance in academically at-risk adolescents. Securely attached individuals are viewed by their friends as warm, caring and dependable; hence, they develop positive social networks that can counteract the effects of poorer academic performance. Students with a secure attachment style can also be expected to be more involved in the life and culture of the school, particularly sporting and other extracurricular activities. In short, secure students tend to be happier and flourish in school. Insecure students, on the other hand, can be more anxious or removed from the learning environment, with the result of being less engaged in learning. In more extreme cases, they may become depressed, self-sabotage, or engage in bullying behavior towards other students (Allen et al., 1998; Rosenstein & Horowitz, 1996).

While parents, especially mothers, have the most significant attachment relationship with students, there is evidence to suggest other relationships contribute significantly to the development of a student's attachment style (Markiewicz, Lawford, Doyle, & Haggart, 2006). In particular, teachers and peers can influence a student's attachment style (La Guardia, Ryan, Couchman & Deci, 2000).

Teachers can contribute to more secure attachment styles among their students in two main ways. First, a teacher can encourage secure attachment bonds with students, thus becoming a secure attachment figure. The means of encouraging secure attachment bonds is by emotional attunement with students, or cognitive-emotional awareness of students' needs and feelings, and provision of care that is consistent with such awareness—in other words, good care giving. If a teacher is a good caregiver, students are more likely to use the teacher as an attachment figure in times of distress and to seek out the teacher as a "safe haven" amidst emotional turmoil and a secure base from which to re-engage with their own learning processes and the school community. As an effective safe haven, a teacher is able to soothe a student's unstable emotions and calm an angry, anxious or depressed student by a) correctly identifying the emotion; b) accepting the emotion as a valid expression of the student's current state without denying it or suppressing it; c) providing a calm "space" in which the emotional intensity can be reduced; and d) actively helping the student to calm herself by appropriate tone of voice, words and actions—including expressions marked by gentleness, empathy and attunement.

Second, a spiritually attuned teacher can also point students to God as the Ultimate Attachment Figure. A student will be more likely to seek God as a spiritual safe haven and secure base if a caring teacher demonstrates through word and action how God is loving, nurturing, and responsive. Third, a teacher can talk informally about how to pray in times of great distress, such as by using familiar prayers and psalms, and how prayer is an immediate, available resource. In short, a teacher who is a secure attachment figure can directly improve student flourishing, help students achieve more secure attachment styles through other secure attachment relationships, and encourage the use of helpful resources. Each of these activities leads directly and indirectly to the enhancement of student flourishing.

ATTRIBUTIONS AND HUMAN FLOURISHING

Meaning-making, or making sense of one's relationship with the world and other people, is an important aspect of human flourishing (Emmons, 2002). For example, it is generally recognized that people who do not blame others are less angry and happier than people who are vitriolic. One's inclination to attribute blame to others or not depends in large part on one's attributional style. Attribution style has been associated with hope, self-esteem, trust, emotional, and spiritual well-being (Ciarrochi, Heaven, & Davies, 2007; VonDras, Schmitt, & Marx, 2007). Conversely, attributional style has also been associated with hurt feelings, anger, guilt, and depression (Calvete, Villardon, & Estevez, 2008; Hareli & Hess, 2008; Sanjuan & Magallares, 2009).

The language of attribution theory includes terms such as intentionality, beliefs, values, causes, meaning and so on (e.g., Fincham, Diener, & Hokoda, 1987; Graham, & Juvonen, 1998; Hong, Chiu, Dweck, Lin, & Wan, 1999; Orobio De Castro, Veermen, Koops, Bosch, & Monshouwer, 2002; Robins & Pals, 2002). These terms imply that attributions are nested within a reasonably stable and, at least somewhat, organized set of cognitions that may be said to constitute a person's worldview (Spilka, Shaver, & Kirkpatrick, 1985). Here, we define a worldview as a core set of beliefs, values and attributions that enables a person to make sense of themselves and the world in which they live. The notion of worldview from a psychological perspective always included metaphysical elements (James, 1890/1963) and has recently reclaimed a focus on religious concepts and cognitive representations of the practices associated with religion (Hall, 2004; Hill & Pargament, 2003; Kirkpatrick, 1997a, 1997b). By understanding worldview in this way, we are able to consider a person's beliefs and values as seeking to make sense of self, the world (including others), and of the meta-physical world (e.g., Miller & Thoresen, 2003). Further, in making sense of self, the world, and the meta-physical world, a person makes causal explanations (attributions) with respect to each of these core constituents, including the interaction or relationships among these attributions.

Attribution theory, as it is classically formulated, considers how people conceptualize the causes of events and processes in the world. Classically, these attributions are classified into two major types: internal (personal) attributions and external (situational) attributions. Internal attributions assign causality to the individual, while external attributions assign causality to factors outside the person. For example, if a student fails an examination, an internal attribution (causal explanation) would be that he or she did not study enough, while an external attribution would be that the examination was too hard. Further, distinction between positive and negative attributions has been made to distinguish further among causal explanations (Ickes, 1988). For example, a student sitting a difficult examination having made an external attribution (the examination was too hard) may form a further negative external attribution (the teacher wants to fail me) or a positive external attribution (the teacher wants to challenge me). An example of a positive internal attribution would be if a student who studied hard and did well attributed success to his or her own effort. Generally speaking, students who make positive internal attributions will flourish more than students who make negative external attributions.

Classical presentations of attribution theory place an emphasis on learning through individual experience, to the exclusion of learning through attachments (e.g., learning from the history of interactions with others, and even in interaction with the self, see Gergen, 1987). However, a great deal of what we hold to be true about ourselves and the world, often expressed in our causal explanations, is further internalized in the context of relationships with others whom we trust (Brewer, 1991; Leary, 2002; Granqvist & Hagekull, 1999, 2001; Kirkpatrick, 1994). Moreover, it appears that the greater the trust, the greater the significance and influence of "the other" on our causal constructions and attributions (Kirkpatrick & Shaver, 1992). Thus, attributions arise from experiences in the context of relationships. Further, a significant limitation of attribution theory as it is classically conceptualized is its omission of attributions to the meta-physical, to God. Following recent advances in the psychology of religion, however (e.g., Hall, Halcrow, Hill, & Delaney, 2005; Kirkpatrick, 1999; Spilka, Shaver, & Kirkpatrick, 1985), we assert that attributions to God are an important missing set of attributions in attribution theory. Applying these dimensions of attribution theory in the context of each attachment relationship may help us to understand the impact of different attachment figures on a student's causal explanations concerning self and others. The inclusion of God as an attachment figure allows us to introduce meta-physical attributions and acknowledge the place of a person's spirituality in making causal explanations.

Some of the antecedents of attributions have been explored—the classic one being feedback from others. However, also neglected in the educational psychology literature are the relational antecedents of attributions—or the relationships which predate, and lead to, our system of attributions. From attachment theory we know that the quality of attachment relationships is critical to the development of internal working models which, in turn, influence a range of cognitive processes such as attributions. So there is good reason to consider the role of attachments in the development and operation of attributions. This exploration is important in schools as we consider the role of teachers in helping students to take responsibility for themselves, rather than simply blaming others for their mistakes. Further, as students develop positive internal attributions they are more likely to engage in the learning environment and respond positively to the challenges of learning.

Teachers who are secure attachment figures can help students develop more positive internal attributions and apply appropriate causal attributions to God. They can foster more positive attributions through modeling, reinforcement, direct suggestion and attributional "pep talks." As an example of modeling, teachers can correctly acknowledge responsibility for their own mistakes or failures in minor matters (such as not returning marked assignments on time). To develop more positive, internal, stable attributions, teachers can reinforce small achievements and attribute students' small successes to effort, ability and other stable, internal qualities. The teacher can also attribute unexpected lack of success to external causes (any relevant feature of the situation) as appropriate. Through classroom pep talks the teacher can draw explicit links between effort and achievement and praise the class as a whole for good work.

Since attributions are also components of one's global worldview, secure attachment figures can affect others' worldviews. Working at the level of a global worldview, a teacher can discuss causes of major world events—acknowledging human and spiritual causes. It may be helpful to distinguish between God directly causing an event, God allowing an event to happen, and God working through people to cause an event, since spiritual attributions (a) predict coping behaviors beyond the effects of material attributions, and (b) contribute to longer term psychological adjustment and other indicators of flourishing (Miner & McKnight, 1999).

SELF-REGULATION AND HUMAN FLOURISHING

Self-regulation refers to a person's ability to control the self in terms of cognitions, behaviors, and motivations (Zimmerman, 1989). While there is difference of opinion within the literature as to whether or not this regulation is only conscious or unconscious as well, there is certainly an emphasis on the conscious, intentional, deliberate efforts at self-regulation (Baumeister & Vohs, 2004).

Self-regulation has been shown to be an important variable with respect to many kinds of outcomes consistent with human flourishing (e.g., academic success, pro-social behavior, mental health, relationship stability and development) (Baumeister & Vohs, 2004). However, models of self-regulation have often focused on only one or two aspects of self-regulation such as cognitive or meta-cognitive self-regulation, or emotional or motivational self-regulation. Consequently, more broadly-based models of self-regulation are required in order to explain adaptive human functioning with respect to a range of important outcomes. In a school setting, the more broadly-based model of self-regulation is essential as schools are concerned with a whole range of self-regulatory cognitions and behaviors. These lead to adaptive behavior not just in the academic domain but also in the relational and social domains (New South Wales Department of Education & Training, 2003). Further, the relationally complex nature of schools requires that students self-regulate in order to flourish. For example, a student who lacks self-regulation is more inclined to be disruptive, misbehave, lose focus, or procrastinate. These behaviors in turn may not only have a detrimental effect on the individual student, but may also affect others around the student.

Teachers can enhance student self-regulation through their role as attachment figures. This work of promoting self-regulation will be discussed further below as the relationships among attachment, attributions and self-regulation are explored.

THE RELATIONSHIP BETWEEN ATTACHMENTS AND ATTRIBUTIONS

Attachment theory has been used to explain both the child's development of an internalized understanding of the social world, and the child's motivation to act in accordance with that understanding (Kirkpatrick & Shaver, 1990; cf. Markus & Nurius, 1987). Attachments, then, influence both the formation of a person's attributions (as a specific set of mental representations about social causes operating in the world) and the motivation to act in keeping with those attributions (Spilka et al., 1985). Moreover, attachment theory suggests that as the salience of any attachment increases, the likelihood of mental representations of the world associated with that attachment being internalized by the child also increases (Hall, 2004). Thus, it is reasonable to assume that the security of an attachment correlates with the likelihood of more positive attributions salient to that relationship becoming internalized by the child. For example, a teacher may develop a positive attachment relationship with a student that extends beyond the giving of instruction to involve elements of mutual trust and respect. In the context of such a relationship it is more likely that attributions held by the teacher (e.g., that cleaning up litter represents a commitment to good citizenship and/or to environmental concerns) will be internalized by the student than otherwise. On this basis, it would be expected that the student will actually do something about litter in response to his or her relationally-affected and internalized citizenship/environmental attributions.

More generally, we suggest that the process of teaching works through, or at least takes place in the context of, attachments and that these attachments are particularly significant in the formulation of attributions relating to schooling and learning (Dowson, Richards, Johnson, & Ross, 2005). Thus, to limit the causes of attributional development to personal experience alone is to neglect the role that parents and others (especially teachers) can have in the development of attributions. In addition, the attributional influence of others becomes more significant the more the child trusts the other. This trust, in turn, is significantly influenced by the child's perception of the other's concern for the child's wellbeing (Granqvist &

Hagekull, 2001; Kobak, 1999; cf. Selman, 1980). Consequently, as a teacher develops a relationship of trust with a student, the teacher is more able to influence the positive development of the student's attributional style, and so contribute positively and actively to his or her human flourishing.

THE RELATIONSHIP BETWEEN ATTRIBUTIONS AND SELF-REGULATION

We suggest that internal working models guiding self-regulation are essentially attributional in nature (i.e., causal attributions guide and direct self-regulation). Attribution theory has identified some types of attributions (e.g., attributions to luck, task difficulty, effort and ability) and has identified some causes of these attributions, namely, people's success and failure experiences, and the relationship of these experiences to self-worth and other psychological variables. More recent research has identified a link among attachments, negative attributions and behavioral intent in romantic partners (Collins, Ford, & Guichard, 2006) and among attachments, negative attributions and depression in adolescent girls (Margolese, Markiewicz & Doyle, 2005). Such research suggests there is merit in exploring the role of different attachment figures in adolescent adjustment. While negative attributions have been linked to depression in girls, it is also suggested that the impact of negative attributions in boys may lead more to inappropriate behavior such as acting out or anger in which there is a failure of self-regulation (Margolese, Markiewicz & Doyle, 2005).

Thus, within the school context, students with positive attributional styles are more inclined to engage positively and actively with the learning environment as they tend to view the role of the teacher and the purpose of education more positively. Such an inclination is more conducive to self-regulation such as increased effort and sustained concentration, as well as less disruptive and anti-social behaviors. Self-regulated students, then, would be expected not only to exhibit human flourishing, but in so doing encourage and contribute to wider human flourishing in school.

THE RELATIONSHIP BETWEEN ATTACHMENTS AND SELF-REGULATION

Attachment theory suggests strong biological-relational foundations of emotional and cognitive self-regulation. Previous research has identified direct effects of attachment bonds on self-regulation via the internalization of emotional regulation by the caregiver (Schore, 2003b). Security of attachment allows the infant to develop self-regulation because the parent is a source of external regulation for the child. For example, when the child is distressed, the parent gives the child physical comfort in response. These external functions become internalized by the child both emotionally and cognitively, allowing the child to develop and deploy his own self-soothing (emotionally regulating) thoughts and behaviors. While it is first held as an implicit (yet-to-be-articulated) emotional working model, as the child develops the capacity for language, the verbal narrative surrounding the relationship informs the development of an explicit cognitive working model. Moreover, especially where a secure attachment is salient (Schore, 2003a), normal brain development allows for the development of increasingly sophisticated working models of relationship between self and other.

While there is no direct empirical evidence that secure attachments lead to emotional self-regulation in adolescents, secure attachments have been shown to impact behavior that is consistent with self-regulation of mood, thought and behavior in children, pre-adolescents, adolescents and young adults. For example, parental qualities of sensitivity (associated with attachment attunement) and autonomy support (associated with the secure base function of attachment) are associated with the development of cognitive processing in young children, including impulse control (Bernier, Carlson, & Whipple, 2010). Attachment style in pre-adolescents has been shown to predict increases in self-disclosure, productive client behavior, and responsiveness to others (Shechtman & Dvir, 2006). Secure attachments have also been associated with reduced antisocial behavior in young adolescents (Eamon & Mulder, 2005), and positive parent and peer attachments are associated with lower depressive symptoms in college students (Ying, Lee & Tsai, 2007). Further, increased security of parent attachment is associated with decreased levels of adolescent gambling (Magoon & Ingersoll, 2006), and secure adolescents show more constructive motivational strategies and fewer disorganized strategies when compared to insecure adolescents (Soares, Lemos & Almeida, 2005). This evidence highlights the value in further exploring pathways by which attachments influence behavior in adolescents. It also justifies researching the theoretical model proposed here since attachment to parents serves as a paradigm for attachment to both teachers and God.

In short, secure attachment to the parent contributes to the development of internal working models, which in turn influence emotional, cognitive and behavioral self-regulation in infants. In the same way secure attachments will contribute to elaborated internal working models in adolescents—models that influence emotional, cognitive, and behavioral self-regulation in adolescents. Further, we also posit that if secure attachments to parents influence self-regulation in adolescents, then so too will attachment to significant others, such as teachers and God, since attachment to parents serves as a paradigm for attachment to teachers and God.

In particular, teachers can help students to self-regulate, and thence flourish, by using the attachment relationship in several ways. First, if the attachment relationship is secure, students are likely to seek emotional support and soothing (external emotional regulation) from a teacher as needed. This support is a direct contribution to students' emotional regulation. Second, a teacher can model self-regulation in the classroom. For example, a teacher can show some (moderate) levels of emotional intensity in the classroom but firmly control expression of higher levels (whether anger, euphoria or depression). Students with secure attachment to the teacher are more likely to learn vicariously from the teacher's example than those with insecure attachments. Third, teachers can use classroom management that moves from external regulation of behavior to self-regulation (e.g., from teacher-imposed time out for anger, to student-chosen time out; from teacher-initiated coping with stress and anxiety to self-talk to counter stress or anxiety, etc.). Fourth, when teachers point to God as a fully sufficient attachment figure, students are more likely to develop a secure relationship with God and the capacity to use spiritual resources for self-regulation if the teacher-student attachment relationship is secure. In these four ways a secure attachment relationship directly or indirectly promotes emotional/behavioral regulation and thence flourishing.

CONCLUSION

In this chapter we have argued that any consideration of the effectiveness of schools ought to take into account the intellectual, emotional, social *and* spiritual development of students and the role of educators in positively and actively contributing to the flourishing of their students. Rather than focusing on the average literacy and numeracy performance of students, we ought to consider their performance more broadly in terms of human flourishing. In doing so, we will be concerned with student attachments, student attributions, and student self-regulation, and we will be more widely concerned with student well-being and achievement emotionally, socially and spiritually, as well as intellectually. Further, given the primary importance of a student's attachments for human flourishing in school, we should not underestimate the significance of the teacher as an attachment figure. Thus, in addition to curriculum development and delivery, we ought to consider carefully the role of the teacher as a role model, life coach and spiritual guide for the students in their care. We should also seek to understand further the positive and active influence teachers can have as attachment figures in the learning environment of schools. Whether teachers are conscious of their influence as attachment figures or not, their influence is still significant and may even be detrimental to student flourishing, including learning, if not considered and intentional. Our hope is that we will see renewed interest in the role and significance of teachers not only in the teaching of information (curriculum), but in the formation of our students as whole people: humans who flourish.

REFERENCES

Allen, J. P., Moore, C., Kuperminc, G., & Bell, K. (1998). Attachment and adolescent psychosocial functioning. *Child Development, 69*, 1406–1419.

Bartholomew, K., & Horowitz, L. M. (1991). Attachment styles among young adults: a test of a four-category model. *Journal of Personality and Social Psychology, 61*, 226–244.

Baumeister, R. F., & Vohs, K. D. (Eds.). (2004). *Handbook of self-regulation: Research, theory, and applications.* New York: Guilford.

Bernier, A., Carlson, S., & Whipple, N. (2010). From external regulation to self-regulation: Early parenting precursors of young children's executive functioning. *Child Development, 81*(1), 326–339.

Bowlby, J. (1969). *Attachment. Vol. 1 of Attachment and loss.* New York: Basic Books.

Bowlby, J. (1988). *A secure base: Parent-child attachment and healthy human development.* New York: Basic Books.

Bretherton, I., & Munholland, K. A. (1999). Internal working models in attachment relationships: A construct revisited. In J. Cassidy & P. R. Shaver (Eds.), *Handbook of attachment: Theory, research, and clinical applications* (pp. 89–111). New York: Guilford.

Brewer, M. B. (1991). The social self: On being the same and different at the same time. *Personality and Social Psychology Bulletin, 17*, 4750–4782.

Calvete, E., Villardon, L., & Estevez, A. (2008). Attributional style and depressive symptoms in adolescents: An examination of the role of various indicators of cognitive vulnerability. *Behaviour Research and Therapy, 46*, 944–953.

Cassidy, J., & Shaver. P. (Eds.). (2008). *Handbook of attachment: Theory, research, and clinical applications.* New York: Guilford.

Ciarrochi, J., Heaven, P., & Davies, F. (2007). The impact of hope, self-esteem, and attributional style on adolescents' school grades and emotional well-being: A longitudinal study. *Journal of Research in Personality, 41*, 1161–1178.

Collins, N. L., Ford, M. B., & Guichard, A. C. (2006). Working models of attachment and attribution processes in intimate relationships. *Personality and Social Psychology Bulletin, 32*, 201–219.

Dowson, M., Richards, G. E., Johnson, K., & Ross, M. (2005). The current state of middle schooling: A review of the literature. Proceedings of the combined AARE/NZARE biennial conference. Melbourne: AARE.

Eamon, M. K., & Mulder, C. (2005). Predicting anti-social behavior among Latino young adolescents: an ecological systems analysis. *American Journal of Orthopsychiatry, 75*, 117–127.

Eaude, T. (2009). Happiness, emotional well-being and mental health—what has children's spirituality to offer? *International Journal of Children's Spirituality, 14*(3), 185–196.

Emmons, R. A. (2002). Personal goals, life meaning, and virtue: Wellsprings of a positive life. In C. L. M. Keyes (Ed.), *Flourishing* (pp. 105–128). Washington: American Psychological Association.

Fincham, F. D., Diener, C. I., & Hokoda, A. (1987). Attributional style and learned helplessness: Relationship to the use of causal schemata and depressive symptoms in children. *British Journal of Social Psychology, 26*, 1–7.

Gergen, K. J. (1987). Toward self as relationship. In K. Yardley & T. Honess (Eds.), *Self and identity: Psychosocial perspectives* (pp. 53–63). New York: John Wiley & Sons.

Graham, S., & Juvonen, J. (1998). Self-blame and peer victimization in middle school: An attributional analysis. *Developmental Psychology, 34*, 587–599.

Granqvist, P., & Hagekull, B. (2001). Seeking security in the new age: On attachment and emotional compensation. *Journal for the Scientific Study of Religion, 40*, 527–545.

Granqvist, P., & Hagekull, B. (1999). Religiousness and perceived childhood attachment: Profiling socialized correspondence and emotional compensation. *Journal for the Scientific Study of Religion, 38*, 254–273.

Greenfield, E. A., Vaillant, G. E., & Marks, N. F. (2009). Do formal religious participation and spiritual perceptions have independent linkages with diverse dimensions of psychological well-being? *Journal of Health and Social Behavior, 50*, 196–212.

Gross, J., & John, O. (2003). Individual differences in two emotion regulation processes: implications for affect, relationships, and well-being. *Journal of Personality and Social Psychology, 85*, 348–362.

Hall, T. W. (2004). Christian spirituality and mental health: A relational spirituality paradigm for empirical research. *Journal of Psychology and Christianity, 23*, 66–81.

Hall, T. W., Halcrow, S. R., Hill, P. C., & Delaney, H. (2005, April). Internal working model correspondence in implicit spiritual experiences. National Convention of the Christian Association for Psychological Studies, Dallas, TX.

Hareli, S., & Hess, U. (2008), When does feedback about success at school hurt? The role of causal attributions. *Social Psychology of Education, 11*, 259–272.

Hill, P. C., & Pargament, K. I. (2003). Advances in the conceptualization and measurement of religion and spirituality: Implications for physical and mental health research. *American Psychologist, 58*, 64–74.

Hong, Y. Y., Chiu, C., Dweck, C. S., Lin, D., & Wan, W. (1999). Implicit theories, attributions, and coping: A meaning system approach. *Journal of Personality and Social Psychology, 77*, 588–599.

Ickes, W. (1988). Attributional styles and the self-concept. In L. Abramson (Ed.), *Social cognition and clinical psychology: A synthesis* (pp. 66–97). New York, NY: Guilford.

James, W. (1963). *The principles of psychology.* New York: Holt, Rinehart & Winston (Original work published 1890)

Kirkpatrick, L. A. (1994). The role of attachment in religious belief and behavior. K. Bartholomew & D. Perlman (Eds.), *Attachment processes in adulthood. Advances in personal relationships, Vol. 5.* (pp. 239–265). London: Jessica Kingsley Publications.

Kirkpatrick, L. A. (1997a). An attachment-theory approach to the psychology of religion. In B. Spilka & D. N. McIntosh (Eds.), *The psychology of religion: Theoretical approaches* (pp. 114–133). Boulder, CO: Westview Press.

Kirkpatrick, L. A. (1997b). A longitudinal study of changes in religious belief and behavior as a function of individual differences in adult attachment style. *Journal for the Scientific Study of Religion, 36,* 207–217.

Kirkpatrick, L. A. (1999). Toward an evolutionary psychology of religion and personality. *Journal of Personality, 67*(6), 921–952.

Kirkpatrick, L. A., & Shaver P. R. (1990). Attachment theory and religion: Childhood attachments, religious beliefs, and conversion. *Journal for the Scientific Study of Religion, 29,* 315–334.

Kirkpatrick, L. A., & Shaver P. R. (1992). An attachment-theoretical approach to romantic love and religious belief. *Personality & Social Psychology Bulletin, 18,* 266–275.

Kobak, R. (1999). The emotional dynamics of disruptions in attachment relationships: Implications for theory, research, and clinical intervention. In J. Cassidy & P. R. Shaver (Eds.), *Handbook of attachment: Theory, research, and clinical applications* (pp. 21–43). New York: Guilford.

La Guardia, J. G., Ryan, R. M., Couchman, C. E., & Deci, E. L. (2000). Within-person variation in security of attachment: A self-determination theory perspective on attachment, need fulfillment, and well-being. *Journal of Personality and Social Psychology, 79*(3), 367–384.

Leary, M. R. (2002). When selves collide: The nature of the self and the dynamics of interpersonal relationships. In A. Tesser, D. A. Stapel, & J. V. Wood (Eds.), *Self and motivation: Emerging psychological perspectives* (pp. 119–145). Washington, DC: American Psychological Association.

Magoon, M. E., & Ingersoll, G. M. (2006). Parental modeling, attachment, and supervision as moderators of adolescent gambling. *Journal of Gambling Studies, 22,* 1–22.

Margolese, S. K., Markiewicz, D., & Doyle, A. B. (2005). Attachment to parents, best friend, and romantic partner: Predicting different pathways to depression in adolescence. *Journal of Youth and Adolescence, 34,* 637–650.

Markiewicz, D., Lawford, H., Doyle, A. B., & Haggart, N. (2006). Developmental differences in adolescents' and young adults' use of mothers, fathers, best friends, and romantic partners to fulfill attachment needs. *Journal of Youth and Adolescence, 35*(1), 127–140.

Markus, H. R., & Nurius, P. S. (1987). Possible selves: The interface between motivation and the self-concept. In K. Yardley & T. Honess (Eds.), *Self and identity: Psychosocial perspectives* (pp. 157–172). New York: John Wiley & Sons.

Miller, W. R., & Thoresen, C. E. (2003). Spirituality, religion, and health: An emerging research field. *American Psychologist, 58,* 24–35.

Miner, M. (2007). Back to the basics in attachment to God: Revisiting theory in light of theology. *Journal of Psychology and Theology, 35*(2), 112–122.

Miner, M. H., & McKnight, J. (1999). Religious attributions: Situational factors and effects on coping. *Journal for the Scientific Study of Religion, 38*(2), 273–285.

Nakamura, J., & Csikszentmihalyi, M. (2002). The construction of meaning through vital engagement. In C. L. M. Keyes (Ed.), *Flourishing* (pp. 83–104). Washington DC: American Psychological Association.

New South Wales Department of Education & Training. (2003). *Quality teaching in NSW public schools: A classroom practice guide.* Sydney: NSW Department of Education & Training.

Orobio De Castro, B., Veermen, J. W., Koops, W., Bosch, J. D., & Monshouwer, H. J. (2002). Hostile attributional intent and aggressive behavior: A meta-analysis. *Child Development, 73,* 916–934.

Reschly, A. L., Huebner, E. S., Appleton, J. J., & Antaramian, S. (2008). Engagement as flourishing: the contribution of positive emotions and coping to adolescents' engagement at school and with learning. *Psychology in the Schools, 45*(5), 419–431.

Robins, R. W., & Pals, J. L. (2002). Implicit self-theories in the academic domain: Implications for goal orientation, attributions, affect, and self-esteem change. *Self and Identity, 1,* 313–336.

Rosenstein, D. S., & Horowitz, H. A. (1996). Adolescent attachment and psychopathology. *Journal of Consulting and Clinical Psychology, 64*(2), 244–253.

Sanjuan, P., & Magallares, A. (2009). A longitudinal study of the negative explanatory style and attributions of uncontrollability as predictors of depressive symptoms. *Personality and Individual Differences, 46,* 714–718.

Schore, A. N. (2003a). *Affect dysregulation and disorders of the self.* New York: Norton.

Schore, A. N. (2003b). *Affect regulation and the repair of the self.* New York: Norton.

Seligman, M. E. P., & Csikszentmihalyi, M., (2000). Positive psychology: An introduction. *American Psychologist, 55*(1), 5–14.

Seligman, M. E. P., Steen, T. A., Park, N., & Peterson, C. (2005). Positive psychology progress: Empirical validation of interventions. *American Psychologist, 60*(5), 410–421.

Selman, R. L. (1980). *The growth of interpersonal understanding: Developmental and clinical analyses.* San Diego, CA: Academic Press.

Shechtman, Z & Dvir, V. (2006). Attachment style as a predictor of behavior in group counseling with preadolescents. *Group Dynamics: Theory, Research and Practice, 10,* 29–42.

Soares, I., Lemos, M. S., & Almeida, C. (2005). Attachment and motivational strategies in adolescence: exploring links. *Adolescence, 40,* 129–154.

Spilka, B., Shaver, P., & Kirkpatrick, L. A. (1985). A general attribution theory for the psychology of religion. *Journal for the Scientific Study of Religion, 24,* 1–20.

Vaillant, G. (2008). *Spiritual evolution: A scientific defense of faith.* New York: Broadway.

Vaillant, G., Templeton, J., Ardelt, M., & Meyer, S. E. (2008). The natural history of male mental health: Health and religious involvement. *Social Science & Medicine, 66,* 221–231.

VonDras, D., Schmitt, R., & Marx, D. (2007). Associations between aspects of spiritual well-being, alcohol use, and related social-cognitions in female college students. *Journal of Religious Health, 46,* 500–515.

Ying, Y. W., Lee, P. A., & Tsai, J. L. (2007). Predictors of depressive symptoms in Chinese American college students: parent and peer attachment, college challenges and sense of coherence. *American Journal of Orthopsychiatry, 77,* 316–323.

Zimmerman, B. J. (1989). A social cognitive view of self-regulated academic learning. *Journal of Educational Psychology, 81*(3), 329–339.

CHAPTER 7

TOWARDS A THEORY OF PERSONAL MATURITY

Links to Spirituality and Human Flourishing

Martin Dowson
*Wesley Institute and
Australasian Centre for Studies in Spirituality*

Maureen Miner
*University of Western Sydney
Australasian Centre for Studies in Spirituality*

This chapter seeks to provide some building blocks towards a theory of maturity, with an emphasis on an understanding of both spirituality and human flourishing from the perspective of maturation and maturity. In addressing this focus, the chapter provides a rationale for the study of personal maturity, and a definition of maturity in terms of human flourishing. The chapter also provides both a *structural* and a *causal* model of personal maturity, which together define personal maturity as a multidimensional, hierarchically-arranged and causally- specified construct. In building the models, the chapter identifies key functions of maturity, showing how asynchronous development with respect to these functions can lead to a variety of deleterious psychological, psychosocial and psychospiritual consequences. Finally, the chapter

Beyond Well-Being: Spirituality and Human Flourishing, pages 127–149
Copyright © 2012 by Information Age Publishing
All rights of reproduction in any form reserved.

outlines ways in which psychological, educational, social and spiritual services may promote synchronous maturation and, hence, human flourishing.

Maturity may be conceptualized as a particular way of being in, and relating to, the world. As such, maturity is typically (if anecdotally) considered to play a major role in influencing personal, social and occupational success—with age and maturity not necessarily developing or proceeding together. Maturity is thought to underpin a person's ability to make appropriate decisions, take appropriate action, and commit deeply and dependably to relationships. The emotional control and empathic reasoning associated with maturity can facilitate shared communication and enable interpersonal conflicts to be more respectfully understood and resolved. Maturity also enables individuals to explore and express their own uniqueness, but in ways that maintain the integrity of their relational, ethical and other commitments. Specific indicators or examples of maturity may include adapting positively to changing circumstances, solving problems promptly and transparently, coping with losses and setbacks, and displaying integrity despite inevitable compromises and conflicts. Conversely, immaturity may be marked by defensiveness and obfuscation, inability and/or unwillingness to accept responsibility or acknowledge appropriate authority, complacency towards the quality of personal work, impaired ability to compromise even in order to preserve relationships, and a tendency to resort or revert to argument rather than constructive communication.

Certain environmental conditions (such as attentive parenting) and experiences (such as opportunities for exploration) are apparently foundational to the maturation process (Bowlby, 1969: Piaget, 1970). However, mature responses may also be the product of individual biology and learning—perhaps especially as individuals consciously confront negative feelings and imperfections in themselves and others (e.g., Beck, Rush, Shaw, & Emery, 1979; Ellis, 1994). Critically, for the present context, maturity may also be structurally and developmentally related to flourishing to the extent that maturity is both an aspect of, and a contributor to, flourishing.

This chapter begins with two basic assumptions:

1. human flourishing is a desired state of human existence; and
2. human flourishing is supported and facilitated by maturity, but undermined and constrained by immaturity.

These assumptions will be explored later in the chapter. However, by acknowledging these assumptions, the chapter may be described as an attempt to conceptualize and theorize *personal maturity* in terms of human flourishing—thus showing how maturity and human flourishing are linked. This attempt seeks to provide a basis for:

- understanding personal maturity as a valid construct related to human development, but not synonymous with the culmination of human development;
- ongoing investigations into personal maturity as a construct distinct from development per se; and
- a life-span approach to informed practice in support of personal maturity.

HUMAN DEVELOPMENT, MATURITY, AND FLOURISHING

We begin with a brief orientation to the relationships among human development, maturity and flourishing. This orientation will guide the later development of a theory of maturity and its relationship to human flourishing.

From a psychological perspective (which is the overarching perspective taken in this chapter), human development involves related biological and psychological changes leading to increased personal capacity across key domains of functioning (e.g., emotional, intellectual, social, and spiritual). In the developmental psychology literature, maturity is usually defined as the end-point or end-state of some developmental process—for example, sexual maturity is the end point/state of the process of psychosexual development. In the sense that it is used in this chapter, however, maturity refers not to the culminating outcome of a developmental process, but to the deployment of either developed or developing capacities in ways that promote human flourishing. This definition of maturity (stated formally later) implies that maturity a) can be attainted at all points of development, not just at the end-point of development, and b) may not be (necessarily) attained at the end-point. In other words, the definition of maturity used in this chapter decouples maturity directly from development, while recognizing that maturity is always expressed in the context of development.

In a healthy state, human beings are essentially both developing and maturing beings (Helson & Wink, 1987; King, 2002) who develop and demonstrate maturity across physical, emotional, intellectual, social, and spiritual domains (Batson, Schoenrade, & Ventis, 1993; Bornstein & Lamb, 2005; Lerner, 2002). For these reasons, any understanding of human flourishing must necessarily take into account the developmental-maturing nature of human beings; in other words, human flourishing cannot be understood without recognizing the developing/maturing essence of human beings—evident across domains. Moreover, as these domains of development/maturation are interrelated (Lerner & Walls, 1999), development and maturation in one domain may affect development in other domains (e.g., Ozarak, 1989). Hence, any understanding of human flourishing must take into account the interaction of development and maturation across different domains.

Various factors may support or impede development and maturation (Brandtstadter & Lerner, 1999; Deci & Ryan, 2008) and, due to the relative influence of supporting or impeding factors over time, human development or maturation does not always occur at any given rate within or across domains (Arnett, 2000). So, any understanding of human flourishing must take into account the relative mix of attendant factors that may exist with respect to human development and maturation leading to variations in the point and rate of development and maturation within and across domains.

RATIONALE: THE IMPORTANCE OF INVESTIGATING PERSONAL MATURITY

Maturity (understood in terms of the deployment of capacities and not just the development of capacities) is a core concern across many fields including: religion (Sanders, 2005), psychology (Allport, 1960, 1961; Sheldon & Kasser, 2001), education (Adorno & Becker, 1999), and the law (Fagan, 2005). Hence, maturity has wide applicability and may act as a unifying construct across fields. Maturity is also intuitively and commonly understood to be an essential prerequisite for a productive life, and to be foundational to effectiveness in many endeavors, particularly the provision of human services such as leadership, teaching, counseling, and ministering. From a moral/ethical perspective, maturity has the potential to integrate notions of what is good for oneself and what is good for others (Kohlberg, 1969), thus integrating psychological and moral perspectives on human maturation and flourishing.

On the other hand, immaturity (in the sense of inadequate capacity-deployment or patterns of capacity-deployment that undermine flourishing) in both adults and children is both a significant personal problem for affected individuals and a wider problem for families, employers and communities. Immaturity may play an important role in the onset and continuance of psychological disorders (Cooper, 1984) and may even define certain disorders such as, for example, the "dramatic-erratic" personality disorders including narcissism and borderline, histrionic and antisocial personality disorders (e.g., Golomb, 1992). Immaturity may also be associated with substance abuse (Brook & Spitz, 2002) and other unproductive behaviors.

PREVIOUS RESEARCH

Maturation in developmental psychology (although not necessarily in other fields) is typically conceived of as a developmental construct, culminating in some level of maturity, that implies progression from simple to more complex understandings of, and reactions to, self and others. Initially (as far as we know from developmental psychology) the child is *embedded in his or her own subjective perspective; in other words,* the child is only capable of understanding the world from his or her own point of view (Damon & Hart, 1988; Piaget, 1970). As such, the child *cannot understand* how others might think and feel, or how others might view him. As the child grows and develops, however, he or she acquires an increasing ability to see the world from other people's perspectives (Youniss, 1980). This increasing ability to see self and others from the other's point of view is foundational to maturity. Maturation implies the acquisition of an increasingly wide social-relational perspective on the world. As the person grows in awareness of what others are thinking and feeling, he is able to *conceptualize* himself and others as embedded in a wider social-relational network (Bowlby, 1969). This conceptualization represents the emergence from embedded subjectivity toward some level of interpersonal objectivity. Part of this development includes a recognition that estimations of another's perspective are typically inaccurate (at least to some extent), and so should be treated as provisional and open to modification as more information becomes available.

Individual and Relational Conceptualizations of Maturity

Without necessarily using the term "maturity," most theories of personal or psychological development define maturity (i.e., as an end-state of some description) in individualistic terms. Thus, mature (fully-developed) people are said to be self-determined (Deci & Ryan, 2008), self-actualized (Maslow, 1968), self-developed (Brandtstadter, 1999) or similarly described in reflexive terms. Reflexive definitions of maturity, however, may fail to recognize appropriately the impact of others on maturation (e.g., Elliot, & Thrash, 2004) and the responsibility to others of the mature person (Rossi, 2001). In contrast, a relational conceptualization of maturity recognizes both the inherent relatedness of every human person and their individuality. More specifically, a relational conceptualization of maturity can lead to a balanced understanding of the individual's:

- inherent relatedness and his or her capacity to be alone;
- degree of integration into his or her social networks, while simultaneously maintaining a healthy sense of self;
- openness to critical feedback from others and acceptance of self;
- awareness of the interests of others and appropriate advancement of his or her own self-interest;
- commitment to social causes and a critical distance from those causes in order to maintain moral autonomy.

A relational definition of maturity is consistent with approaches to development that center on basic structures of personality, self, and mind *and* corresponding capacities for relatedness (e.g., Asendorpf & Wilpers, 1998), both of which influence levels of psychological and social (and perhaps spiritual) functioning (Hogan & Roberts, 2000). Within these approaches, representations of self and others and modes of relating to others are fundamental domains of concern. A relational perspective on maturity, then, involves realistic appraisals of self and others, leading to stable, enduring relationships (Roberts, Caspi, & Moffitt, 2001).

Theorizing Maturity

Theories of personality development have typically focused on either cognitive maturation *or* social-emotional maturation as end-points/states of development. Somewhat simplistically, cognitive maturity refers how the person *thinks* about himself, others and the world, while social-emotional maturity refers to how the person *feels* about himself, others and the world. Theories of cognitive development (e.g., Piaget, 1970; Vygotsky, 1978) describe the movement towards increasing cognitive complexity. Theories of social-emotional development describe the movement towards increasing awareness and control of emotions and self-in-relationships (e.g., Bowlby, 1969; Freud, 1953; Maslow,1968).

Cognitive Maturity. Theories of cognitive development focus on the individual's increasing ability to understand self, others and the world—with increasing cognitive complexity being demonstrated in, among other things, the problem-solving ability of the person. Theories of cognitive development may end at adolescence (e.g., Piaget, 1970) or extend into adulthood (e.g., John, Pals, & Westenberg, 1998). Recent research has shown that cognitive maturation may be related to growth in adaptive personality qualities such as responsibility, tolerance, independence, resilience, and interpersonal integrity (Helson & Roberts, 1994; Westenberg & Block, 1993).

Social-Emotional Maturity. Social-emotional theories of human development include some of the major theories in psychology such as psychoanalytic theory (Freud, 1953), object relations theory (Greenberg & Mitchell, 1983), attachment theory (Bowlby, 1969), Erikson's (1950/1994) theory of psychosocial development, and Maslow's (1968; see also Rogers, 1961) humanistic approach to development. These theories typically track quantitative and qualitative changes in the ability of the individual to adapt to the social and emotional demands of life, and to the challenges posed by ongoing personal development. In general, social-emotional maturity is seen as critical to the social integration (Harris, 1995) and well-being of the person

(Roberts & Chapman, 2000; Ryff & Keyes, 1995). Conversely, lack of social-emotional maturity may lead to social isolation and a variety of deleterious psychological impacts (Dodge, 2006).

Limitations of Previous Research

Despite the valuable contribution of previous research, some key limitations of this research are salient. As noted above, maturity (in psychology, if not in other fields) is typically defined and investigated in longitudinal terms—as the end point of a particular process of development (e.g., Eisenberg, Carlo, Murphy, & van Court, 1995; Jahnukainen, 2007). This perspective is certainly valid. However, it ignores the fact that maturity also has a cross-sectional dimension—for example, a "mature" seven year old *is* mature relative to her peers despite the fact that she may be immature relative to the person she may become further down the developmental pathway. Longitudinal investigations of human development have also been limited by stage-based approaches taken by various theorists (e.g., Fowler, 1981; Piaget, 1970; Kohberg, 1969). In contrast, non-stage based (continuous) approaches to development (e.g., Newman & Newman, 2006) are currently proving more fruitful.

For these reasons, a treatment of maturity that encompasses both cross-sectional and continuous aspects of maturity would probably be of most assistance to the advancement of maturity research. In particular, the lack of a cross-sectional (or relative i.e., relative to some developmentally appropriate standard) conceptualization of maturity may have hampered *analytical* research into maturity. If maturity is just the end-point/state of a developmental (maturation) process, then all that is necessarily required is a *description* of that end-point/state. Such a description may center on the process leading to maturity rather than on the mature-state itself. In contrast, defining maturity as related to, but distinct from, development enhances the scope to investigate maturity analytically as a construct in its own right (see Sheldon & Kasser, 2001 for an indicative approach).

Recent work in psychology (rediscovering the perspectives of James, 1902 and Allport, 1950) has seen the re-emergence of investigations of spirituality not only as an important domain of human *activity*, but also as a potentially important domain of human *development* (e.g., Emmons, 1999; Peidmont, 1997). As yet, however, there is no capacity-deployment (as opposed to capacity-development, e.g., Fowler, 1981) conceptualization of personal maturity in psychology that takes into account spirituality. Such a conceptualization might unify a psychological perspective with religious perspectives on maturity (e.g., Sanders, 2005), which similarly emphasize maturity in capacity-deployment terms. More generally, a capacity-deployment perspective on maturity may help reconcile psychological understandings of maturity with other capacity-deployment perspectives in, for example, education, law and moral philosophy.

Maturity is often discussed both as an outcome and a prerequisite of psychological health and well-being (Rask, Åstedt-Kurki, Tarkka, & Laippala, 2002; Ryan & Deci, 2000) or, in our terms, human flourishing. This implies that maturity and human flourishing are reciprocally related in some way. Yet definitions and examinations of maturity do not show why or how this reciprocity eventuates. This chapter, in contrast, specifically addresses the reciprocal relationship between maturity and flourishing.

Finally, the implications of an understanding of maturity for human services and interventions have not been explicated in a way that directly relates to the specification of maturity as a construct. Thus, recommendations for how to support and facilitate maturity tend to be general and atheoretical. More specific, theory-based recommendations, however, could result in improved service and intervention outcomes. These are framed at the end of this chapter.

Definitions

Taking into account the analyses above, this section provides key definitions for maturity and related constructs.

We define *personal maturity* as the willingness and ability to relate to self and others (human and divine) in ways that promote and support human flourishing in self and others (human not divine).

Immaturity implies a lack of willingness or ability to relate to self and others (human and divine) in ways that promote human flourishing, or relating to self and others (human and divine) in ways that actively undermine or suppress flourishing in self and/or others (human not divine).

Maturation refers to the ongoing development of attitudes and capacities that support the flourishing of self and others.

Flourishing denotes ongoing maturation which is consistent with the:

- unique developmental potential of each person, and
- coordination of individual developmental trajectories to the mutual benefit of all concerned.

The definitions above imply a reciprocal relationship between maturity and flourishing which will be detailed later in the chapter.

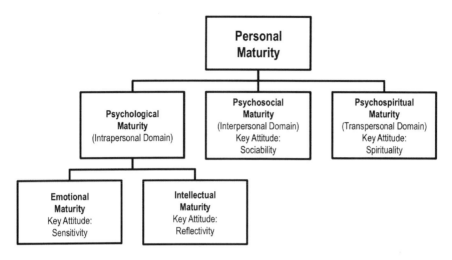

Figure 7.1 Structural model of maturity.

Model of Maturity

The literature reviewed previously suggests that maturity is not a unidimensional construct—but, at least, involves cognitive, emotional and social dimensions of development (cf. Deci & Ryan, 2008). In this chapter, we propose a multidimensional, hierarchically-arranged model of maturity that, crucially, incorporates a spiritual dimension of maturity. The model is presented in Figure 7.1 and explained in the next section.

EXPLANATION OF MODEL

From a personal maturity perspective, the model accepts the three domains of human existence: the intrapersonal (within person), the interpersonal (between persons), and the transpersonal (beyond (human) persons) domains. The first two of these domains are non-controversial. The third domain necessarily posits either the existence or, from a psychological point of view, the assumed existence of a reality beyond the person that the person can nevertheless access in some way. Consistent with James (1902), Allport (1950) and other luminaries, we do not seek to prove the existence of a transpersonal reality in ontological terms. We simply say that if a person attempts to relate to such a reality (whether this reality actually exists or not), the way in which the person seeks to relate to this reality can be evaluated in terms of their maturity or, at least, "healthiness" (Batson, Schoenrade, & Ventis, 1993; Eysenck, 1998; Roman & Lester, 1999). We disagree with classic (e.g., Freud, 1928) and contemporary (e.g., Hitchens, 2007) perspectives that suggest that attempting to relate to a transpersonal reality must, by definition, be regarded as immature.

Within our model, psychological maturity refers to maturity in the intrapersonal domain. Psychosocial maturity refers to maturity in the interpersonal domain. Psychospiritual maturity refers to maturity in the transpersonal domain. Each dimension of maturity in our model (emotional, intellectual, psychosocial and psychospiritual) is associated with certain functions (awareness, control and acceptance). Awareness (Duval, 2001; Smith, 2005) constitutes the *perceptive* function of maturity. Control (Carver & Scheier, 1999 ; Dodge, 2006) constitutes the *regulatory* function for maturity. Acceptance (Thompson & Waltz, 2008) constitutes the *integrative* function of maturity—allowing experiences and outcomes of self-awareness and control to become consciously accessible and controllable elements of the self-system without provoking ongoing emotional distress.

Awareness is conceptualized as one aspect of mature ability because awareness implies the perception (recognition and interpretation) of *intangible* realities such as the emotional states of self and others (Damon & Hart, 1988). This perception requires the development and deployment of complex (mature) cognitive and emotional processes, and is essential for effective self-control.

Self-control (which is typically referred to as self-regulation in psychological literature) involves the ability to subordinate and manage cognitions, emotions, motivation, and behavior (Ryan, Deci & Grolnick, 1995). The ability to subordinate and manage aspects of self plays a critical role in healthy emotional, cognitive, social, and spiritual functioning. Self-control, for example, is implicated in the ability to identify another's position, appropriately express concern for others, cooperate, offer assistance, and share. The development of this ability originates in early child-caregiver attachment, and self-control develops gradually in the context of ongoing social interactions (Barber, Stolz, Olsen & Maughan, 2005; Goldberg, 2003). Hence, self-control is properly conceived of as part of the overall maturation of the person. It is evident that as people age, they generally develop increased self-control. Essentially, they develop the understanding that it is beneficial to delay certain outcomes, and to weigh the consequences of presenting options. These abilities suggest the need for increased cognitive and emotional capacities—again implicating maturation.

Self-acceptance involves the conscious acknowledgement and recognition of self and different aspects of self—whether these aspects are liked or disliked by the person. Self- acceptance is related to the development of self-identity, feelings of confidence, and improved relationships (Erikson, 1968; McAdams, Reynolds, Lewis, Patten, & Bowman, 2001). Self-acceptance can provide a measure of independence from peer judgment, expectations, and affirmations, and so can enhance the capacity for independent decision making (the latter of which is related to mature conduct).

Like self-awareness and self-control, self-acceptance develops in infancy under the influence of parents and other important caregivers. For this reason, self-acceptance is rightly construed as a developmental (maturation-related) construct. The child's self-acceptance is shaped largely by his or her perception of how he or she is viewed by the parents (Bowlby, 1969). Inconsistent parental acceptance can leave the child feeling uncertain, inferior or inadequate. As a result, the child—and the emerging adolescent and adult—may have difficulty showing and accepting love. Conversely, they may demand love, but simultaneously seek to avoid any sign of needing love. Both of these consequences are evidence of immaturity. Mature individuals, on the other hand, understand the need for love in positive terms, and their inherent sense of security allows them to display both vulnerability and strength in expressing love and accepting expressions of love.

With an understanding of self-awareness, control and acceptance in mind, we move next to describe psychological, psychosocial and psychospiritual maturity as nested dimensions of overall personal maturity.

Psychological Maturity

Psychological maturity can be conceptualized as a subset of overall personal maturity, referring to the flourishing quality of the psyche (the inner person). Psychological maturity is comprised of two sub-domains: emotional and intellectual maturity.

Emotional maturity. Emotional maturity refers to the flourishing quality of the person's inner emotional world:

1. Sensitivity operationalizes the desire (willingness) to explore emotions, and implies increasing ability to understand emotions over time.
2. Emotional-self-awareness (awareness of emotions), emotional self-control (monitoring and controlling emotions), and emotional acceptance (acknowledging the emotional characteristics of self) operationalize the ability to explore emotions.
3. Emotional integration (experienced as sense of emotional stability, harmony or completeness) is the immediate intrapersonal result of mature (i.e., emotionally aware, regulated and accepting) emotional self-exploration.
4. Emotional integration provides a stable basis for ongoing emotional maturation.

5. Ongoing emotional maturation partially (see also comments on intellectual maturation below) operationalizes human flourishing in the intrapersonal domain.

Intellectual maturity. Intellectual maturity refers to the flourishing quality of the person's inner cognitive world:

1. Reflectivity operationalizes the desire (willingness) to explore thoughts and thought-processes, and implies increasing ability to understand thoughts and thought processes over time.
2. Intellectual-self-awareness (awareness of thoughts/thinking), intellectual self-control (monitoring and controlling thoughts/thinking), and intellectual acceptance (acknowledging the intellectual characteristics of self) operationalize the ability to explore thoughts and thinking.
3. Intellectual integration (experienced as a sense of intellectual stability, harmony, or completeness) is the immediate intrapersonal result of mature (i.e., intellectually aware, regulated, and accepting) intellectual self-exploration.
4. Intellectual integration provides a stable basis for ongoing intellectual maturation.
5. Ongoing intellectual maturation partially (see also comments on emotional maturation above) operationalizes human flourishing in the intrapersonal domain.

Psychosocial Maturity

Psychosocial maturity can be conceptualized as a subset of overall personal maturity, referring to the flourishing quality of the person's relationship with others:

1. Sociability operationalizes the desire (willingness) to relate to others and implies increasing ability to relate to others over time.
2. Social awareness (awareness of self-in-relationship to others), social self-control (monitoring and controlling self in relationships with others), and social self-acceptance (acknowledging the social characteristics of self) operationalize the ability to relate to others.
3. Social integration (experienced as sense of connectedness to others) is the immediate interpersonal result of relating to others in mature (socially aware, regulated and accepting) ways.
4. Social integration provides a stable basis for ongoing psychosocial maturation.

5. Ongoing psychosocial maturation operationalizes human flourishing in the interpersonal domain.

Psychospiritual Maturity

Psychospiritual maturity can be conceptualized as a subset of overall personal maturity, referring to the flourishing quality of the person's relationship with God:

1. Spirituality operationalizes the desire (willingness) to relate to God, and implies increasing ability to relate to God over time.
2. Spiritual awareness (awareness of self-in-relationship to God), spiritual self-control (monitoring and controlling self in relationship with God) and spiritual self-acceptance (acknowledgment of the spiritual characteristics of self) operationalize the ability to relate to God.
3. Spiritual integration (experienced as sense of connectedness to God) is the immediate transpersonal result of relating to God in mature (spiritually aware, regulated and accepting) ways.
4. Spiritual integration provides a stable basis for ongoing psychospiritual maturation.
5. Ongoing psychospiritual maturation operationalizes human flourishing in the transpersonal domain.

Psychological, psychosocial and psychospiritual maturity are functionally linked because integration in any one domain (intrapersonal, interpersonal, transpersonal) promotes flourishing in other domains (and undermines it when integration is lacking). Moreover, psychological, psychosocial and psychospiritual maturity are all necessary, but none alone is sufficient, for complete maturity and hence human flourishing.

PROCESS MODEL OF MATURITY

The model in Figure 7.1 is a *structural* model of maturity. However, the definitions provided previously and the description of each dimension of maturity (psychological, psychosocial and psychospiritual) imply casual linkages that can be represented in a *process* model. Such a model is represented in Figure 7.2.

Figure 7.2 suggests that maturity leads to flourishing, which in turn leads to maturity. This reciprocity demonstrates that maturity is both a prerequisite for, and an outcome from, human flourishing.

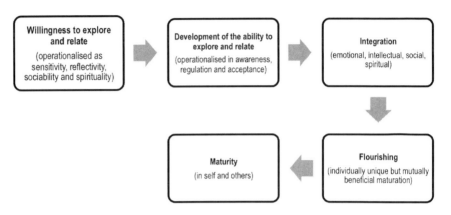

Figure 7.2 Process model of maturity.

PATTERNS OF MATURATION

In this section we propose that maturation may be synchronous or asynchronous, and that the degree of synchronicity of maturation holds significant implications for both ongoing maturation and human flourishing.

Synchronous Maturation

Synchronous maturation refers to the balanced development of the person across intra-, inter-, and transpersonal domains in such a way that development in any given domain supports development in all other domains. Synchronous maturation does not imply simultaneous maturation across domains because often development in one domain is a prerequisite for development in another domain.

Asynchronous Maturation

Asynchronous maturation occurs when awareness and/or control and/or acceptance become imbalanced within and/or across domains. The result of asynchronous maturation is personal disintegration. Personal disintegration may be experienced as tension or breakdown within the self, or between self and others.

Table 7.1 shows the *domains* of maturation as outlined in this chapter. Table 7.1 also shows the *dimensions* (psychological, psychosocial and psychospiritual), *attitudes* (sensitivity, reflectivity, sociability, spirituality), and *functions*

TABLE 7.1 Domains, Attitudes and Functions of Maturation

Domains			*Intrapersonal*		*Interpersonal*	*Transpersonal*
Dimensions			*Psychological*		*Psychosocial*	*Psychospiritual*
Attitudes			*(Emotional) Sensitivity*	*(Intellectual) Reflectivity*	*Sociability*	*Spirituality*
Functions		Awareness *(Perception)*	emotional awareness	intellectual awareness	social awareness	spiritual awareness
		Control *(Regulation)*	emotional control	intellectual control	social control	spiritual control
		Acceptance *(Integration)*	emotional acceptance	intellectual acceptance	social acceptance	spiritual acceptance

(awareness, control and acceptance) of maturation as discussed previously. The results of imbalances across these domains are outlined below.

Asynchronicity Among Functions

Imbalance within domains occurs where development with respect to any function of maturity (awareness, or control or acceptance) exceeds development with respect to other functions of maturity. Short-term imbalances may actually promote maturity—for example, if growing awareness of emotion provides the developmental impetus to regulate and/or accept emotion. However, if an imbalance persists over the longer-term, the result will be an impediment to maturity as described below.

1. If awareness in any domain exceeds control or acceptance in that domain, the person may become overwhelmed by his or her:
   - emotions,
   - thoughts,
   - perceptions of others, and themselves-in-relationship to others; or
   - perceptions of God, and self-in-relationship to God.
2. If control exceeds awareness or acceptance in any given domain, the person may experience:
   - emotional dysfunction associated with excessive monitoring and control of emotional states, such as obsessive compulsive disorder or generalized anxiety;
   - intellectual (cognitive) dysfunction associated with excessive monitoring and control of thoughts and thinking, such as rigid, or compartmentalized (black-and-white) thinking;
   - social/relational dysfunction associated with excessive monitoring and control of responses in social situations, such as social anxiety disorder; or

- spiritual dysfunction associated with excessive monitoring and control of responses to God, such as fear of God (spiritual anxiety).

3. If acceptance exceeds awareness or control in any given domain, the person may demonstrate superficial engagement with:
   - emotions—leading to a "shallow" personality;
   - thoughts—leading to a lack of critical analysis;
   - others—leading to the lack of fulfillment of deeper relational needs; or
   - God—leading, for example, to fatalism.

Asynchronicity Within Functions

As argued above, short-term imbalances among domains (e.g., imbalances in awareness across different domains) may promote maturity if the imbalance provides developmental impetus to the "lagging" domains. However, longer-term imbalances are expected to impede maturation because development in the "strongest" domain can restrict development in other domains—especially where the person becomes overly reliant or overly focused on a given element of maturity in a strong domain.

Imbalanced awareness. In the case of a between-domain imbalance in awareness, awareness in the "strongest" domain dominates awareness in other domains:

1. If emotional awareness exceeds awareness in other domains, the potential result is excessive focus on, or sensitivity to, emotions leading to inhibition in other domains, as evident in a restricted range or fluency of emotional response.

2. If intellectual awareness exceeds awareness in other domains, the potential result is excessive focus on, or sensitivity to, thoughts and thinking leading to objectification of other domains, as evident in hyper-criticism of self, others or God.

3. If social awareness exceeds awareness in other domains, the potential result is excessive focus on, or sensitivity to, others leading to loss of autonomy, as evidenced in conformity or inappropriate self-sacrificing.

4. If spiritual awareness exceeds awareness in other domains, the potential result is excessive focus on, or sensitivity to, God leading to dissociation, as evidenced in the negation of free will, or depersonalization (loss of self).

Imbalanced control. In the case of a between-domain imbalance in control, control in "strongest" domain becomes normative for control in other domains:

1. If emotional control exceeds control in other domains, the person can feel (relatively) out of control (and hence anxious) or out of place (and hence isolated) in these other domains. In such cases, the person may retreat into his or her inner emotional world in order to avoid, mask or treat insecurity arising in connection with the other domains.

1. If intellectual control exceeds control in other domains, the person may retreat into the world of thought in order avoid, mask or treat insecurity arising in connection with the other domains.
2. If social control exceeds control in other domains, the person may seek to excessively control the persona in order to avoid, mask or treat insecurity arising in connection with the other domains.
3. If spiritual control exceeds control in other domains, the person may use apparent religious/spiritual/moral scruples to avoid, mask or treat insecurity arising in connection with the other domains.

Imbalanced acceptance. In the case of a between-domain imbalance in acceptance, acceptance in the "strongest" domain becomes normative for acceptance in other domains:

1. If emotional acceptance exceeds acceptance in other domains, the person may seek to define him or herself primarily in emotional terms (i.e., the "feeling" person). This self-definition may cause the person to excuse attitudes and/or behaviors on the basis of the more-or-less unquestioned validity of emotions.
2. If intellectual acceptance exceeds acceptance in other domains, the person may seek to define him or herself primarily in intellectual/ cognitive terms (i.e., the "thinking" person). This self-definition may cause the person to excuse attitudes and/or behaviors on the basis of the more-or-less unquestioned validity of thoughts.
3. If social acceptance exceeds acceptance in other domains, the person may seek to define him or herself primarily in social terms (i.e., the "relating" person). This self-definition may cause the person to excuse attitudes and/or behaviors on the basis of the more-or-less unquestioned validity of his or her relationships.
4. If spiritual acceptance exceeds acceptance in other domains, the person may seek to define him or herself primarily in spiritual terms (i.e., the "holy" person). This self-definition may cause the person

to excuse attitudes and/or behaviors on the basis of the more-or-less unquestioned validity of his or her faith/religion/spirituality.

The analysis above suggests that imbalances in maturity may not only restrict maturation, but may also lead to a variety of deleterious psychological, psychosocial and psychospiritual consequences. Psychologists, counselors, pastors/ministers, educators, and so on would do well to investigate the possibility that these consequences are developmental as much as pathological in nature. In other words, it may be possible to treat any given "presenting condition" as a deficit in maturation—which may imply different treatment than if the same condition was attributed to non-developmental causes.

PRACTICAL APPLICATIONS

In this section we sketch some practical applications that arise from the theory outlined above. This outline assumes that professionals and organizations desire to promote maturity and maturation (and, hence, human flourishing), but may not always do so because their activities and structures unintentionally (or otherwise) in fact promote asynchronous maturation and, hence, restrictions to maturity and flourishing.

In Table 7.2 we very briefly outline positive practices of psychological, educational, social and spiritual "services" that may promote synchronous maturation. These services have primary emphases on, respectively, emotion, cognition, relationships, and spirituality. We assume that each service will adequately promote maturity in its primary "service" domain (paralleling the applicable dimension of maturity), and so focus on the other service domains in Table 7.2.

The suggestions in Table 7.2 are predicated on the assumption that maturity in any domain potentially affects maturity in every domain. As such, it is not feasible for services simply to focus on building maturity in their primary service domain. A focus on any one domain runs the risk of promoting or preserving asynchronous maturation.

CONCLUSION

Maturity is an important quality leading to positive personal and interpersonal outcomes. This chapter provides some building blocks towards a theory of maturity. In doing so, the chapter provides both a structural and a process model of personal maturity. Together these models define personal maturity as a multidimensional, hierarchically arranged and developmental construct. The chapter also defines key attitudes and functions of maturity,

TABLE 7.2 Promoting Synchronous Maturation

Service	Service Domain	Example Activity/Focus
Psychological Services	Intellectual	Actively engaging the client in therapeutic strategizing and decision making.
	Social	Exploring the history and trajectory of social relationships with the client, and the impact of social relationships on the client.
	Spiritual	Exploring the client's understanding of God and self-in-relationship to God.
Educational Services	Emotional	Teaching emotional self-awareness, self-control and self-acceptance as keys to effectiveness in learning.
	Social	Recognizing the impact of mature or immature conceptualizations of self-in-relationship-to-others as a key stimulus or impediment to learning.
	Spiritual	Recognizing mature or immature images of God and self-in-relationship-to-God as a potentially influential factor in learning—perhaps especially in "religious" learning settings.
Social Services	Emotional	Building emotional maturity as a key contributor to enduring relationships, and as a key buffer against social rejection and other relational difficulties.
	Intellectual	Teaching the impact of patterns of mature or immature thinking on the establishment and maintenance of a mature social orientation.
	Spiritual	Supporting maturity in a person's relationship with God as key contributor of maturity in interpersonal relationships.
Spiritual Services	Emotional	Recognizing that emotional maturity or immaturity may impact on the quality of a person's spirituality and mature functioning with respect to God.
	Intellectual	Identifying the effect of thoughts about God on mature functioning in relation to God e.g., how certain beliefs about of God impact the shape of a relationship with God.
	Social	Demonstrating how maturity or immaturity in relationships with others may impact the development of a mature relationship with God.

showing how asynchronous development with respect to the functions of maturity can lead to a variety of deleterious psychological, psychosocial and psychospiritual consequences. Finally, the chapter outlines ways in which psychological, educational, social and spiritual services can promote synchronous maturation and, hence, human flourishing. We hope that the chapter will provide fertile ground for further theoretical, empirical and practical investigations.

REFERENCES

Adorno, T. W., & Becker, H. (1999). Education for maturity and responsibility. *History of the Human Sciences, 12*(3), 21–34.

Allport, G. W. (1961). *Pattern and growth in personality.* New York: Holt, Rinehart, & Winston.

Allport, G. W. (1960). *Personality and social encounter.* Boston: Beacon Press.

Allport, G. W. (1950). *The individual and his religion,* New York: Macmillan.

Arnett, J. J. (2000). Emerging adulthood: A theory of development from the late teens through the twenties. *American Psychologist, 55,* 469–480.

Asendorpf, J. B., & Wilpers, S. (1998). Personality effects on social relationships. *Journal of Personality and Social Psychology, 74,* 1531–1544.

Barber, B. K., Stolz, H. E., Olsen, J. A., & Maughan, S. L. (2005). Parental support, psychological control, and behavioral control: Assessing relevance across time, method, and culture. *Monographs of the Society for Research in Child Development, 70*(4).

Batson, C. D., Schoenrade, P., & Ventis, W. L. (1993). *Religion and the individual.* New York: Oxford University Press.

Beck, A. T., Rush, A. J., Shaw, B. F., & Emery, G. (1979). *Cognitive therapy of depression.* New York: The Guilford Press.

Bornstein, M. H., & Lamb, M. E. (2005). *Developmental science: An advanced textbook.* Mahwah, NJ: Erlbaum.

Bowlby, J. (1969). *Attachment and loss: Vol. 1. Attachment.* New York: Basic Books.

Brandtstadter, J. (1999). The self in action and development: Cultural, biosocial, and ontogenetic bases of intentional self-development. In J. Brandtstadter & R. M. Lerner (Eds.), *Action and self-development: Theory and research through the life span* (pp. 37–66). Thousand Oaks, CA: Sage.

Brandtstadter, J., & Lerner, R. M. (Eds.). (1999). *Action and self-development: Theory and research through the life span.* Thousand Oaks, CA: Sage.

Brook, D. W., & Spitz, H. I. (Eds.). (2002). *The group therapy of substance abuse.* New York: Haworth Medical Press.

Carver, C. S., & Scheier, M. F. (1999). Themes and issues in the self-control of behavior. In R. S. Wyer, Jr. (Ed.), *Advances in social cognition: Vol. 12: Perspectives on behavioral self-control* (pp. 1–105). Mahwah, NJ: Erlbaum.

Cooper, A. M. (1984). Narcissism in normal development. In M. Zales (Ed.), *Character Pathology* (pp. 39–56). New York: Brunner/Mazel.

Damon, W., & Hart, D. (1988). *Self-understanding in childhood and adolescence.* Cambridge: Cambridge University Press

Deci, E., & Ryan, R. (2008). Facilitating optimal motivation and psychological well-being across life's domains. *Canadian Psychology, 49,* 14–23.

Dodge, K. (2006). Emotion and social information processing. In J. Garber & K. Dodge, *The development of emotion control and dyscontrol* (pp. 159–181). New York: Cambridge University Press.

Duval, T. S. (2001). *Self-awareness and casual attribution.* New York: Springer.

Eisenberg, N., Carlo, G., Murphy, B., & van Court, P. (1995). Prosocial development in late adolescence: A longitudinal study. *Child Development, 66*(4), 1179–1197.

Ellis, A. (1994). *Reason and emotion in psychotherapy, revised and updated.* Secaucus, NJ: Carol Publishing Group.

Elliot, A. J., & Thrash, T. M. (2004). The intergenerational transmission of fear of failure. *Personality and Social Psychology Bulletin, 30,* 957–971.

Emmons, R. A. (1999). *The psychology of ultimate concerns: Motivation and spirituality in personality.* New York: Guilford Press.

Erikson, E. (1968). *Identity, youth and crisis.* New York: Norton.

Erikson, E. H. (1994). *Childhood and society.* New York: Norton. (Original work published 1950)

Eysenck, M. W. (1998). Personality and the psychology of religion. *Mental Health, Religion and Culture, 1,* 11–19.

Fagan, J. (2005). Adolescents, maturity, and the law: Why science and development matter in juvenile justice. Retrieved November 9, 2009 from http://www.prospect.org/cs/articles? article=adolescents_maturity_and_the_law

Fowler, J. W. (1981). *Stages of faith: The psychology of human development and the quest for meaning.* San Francisco, CA: Harper and Row.

Freud, S. (1953). *The standard edition of the complete psychological works of Sigmund Freud.* J. Strachey (Trans.). London: Hogarth Press.

Freud, S. (1928). *The future of an illusion.* W. D. Robson-Scott (Trans.). New York: Liveright.

Goldberg, A. E. (2003). Constructions: A new theoretical approach to language. *Trends in Cognitive Sciences, 7*(5), 219–224.

Golomb, E. (1992). *Trapped in the mirror.* New York: Morrow.

Greenberg, J. R., & Mitchell, S. A. (1983). *Object relations in psychoanalytic theory.* Cambridge, MA: Harvard University Press.

Harris, J. R. (1995). Where is the child's environment? A group socialization theory of development. *Psychological Review, 102,* 458–489.

Helson, R., & Roberts, B. W. (1994). Ego development and personality change in adulthood. *Journal of Personality and Social Psychology, 66,* 911–920.

Helson, R., & Wink, P. (1987). Two conceptions of maturity examined in the findings of a longitudinal study. *Journal of Personality and Social Psychology, 53,* 531–541.

Hitchens, C. (2007). *God is not great: How religion poisons everything.* New York: Twelve/Hachette Book Group.

Hogan, R., & Roberts, B. W. (2000). A socioanalytic perspective on person/environment interaction. In W. B. Walsh, K. H. Craik, & R. H. Price (Eds.), *New directions in person-environment psychology* (pp. 1–24). Hillsdale, NJ: Lawrence Erlbaum.

Jahnukainen, M. (2007) High-risk youth transitions to adulthood: A longitudinal view of youth leaving the residential education in Finland. *Children and Youth Services Review, 29,* 637–654.

James, W. (1902). *The varieties of religious experience.* New York: Longman.

John, O. P., Pals, J. L., & Westenberg, P. M. (1998). Personality prototypes and ego development: Conceptual similarities and relations in adult women. *Journal of Personality and Social Psychology, 74,* 1093–1108.

King, L. A. (2002). Personal growth and personality development: A forward to the special section. *Journal of Personality, 70,* 1–3.

Kohlberg, L. (1969). State and sequence: The cognitive-developmental approach to socialization. In D. A. Goslin (Ed.), *Handbook of socialization theory and research* (pp. 347–480). Skokie, IL: Rand McNally.

Lerner, R. M. (2002). *Concepts and theories of human development.* Mahwah, NJ: Erlbaum.

Lerner, R. M., & Walls, T. (1999). Revisiting individuals as producers of their development: From dynamic interactionism to developmental systems. In J. Brandtstadter & R. M. Lerner (Eds.), *Action and self development: Theory and research through the life span* (pp. 3–26). Thousand Oaks, CA: Sage.

Maslow, A. H. (1968). *Toward a psychology of being.* New York: Van Nostrand Reinhold.

McAdams, D. P., Reynolds, J., Lewis, M., Patten, A. H., & Bowman, P. J. (2001). When bad things turn good and good things turn bad: Sequences of redemption and contamination in life narrative and their relation to psychosocial adaptation in midlife adults and in students. *Personality and Social Psychology Bulletin, 27,* 474–485.

Newman, B. M., & Newman, P. R. (2006). *Development through life: A psychosocial approach.* Belmont, CA: Wadsworth.

Ozarak, E. W. (1989). Social and cognitive influences on the development of religious beliefs and commitment in adolescence. *Journal for the Scientific Study of Religion, 28,* 448–463.

Peidmont, R. L. (1997). Does spirituality represent the sixth factor of personality? Spiritual transcendence and the five factor model. *Journal of Personality, 67,* 985–1013.

Piaget, J. (1970). Piaget's theory. In P. Mussen (Ed.), *Carmichael's manual of child psychology* (pp. 703–732). New York: Wiley.

Rask, K., Åstedt-Kurki, P, Tarkka, M., & Laippala, P. (2002). Relationships among adolescent subjective well-being, health behavior, and school satisfaction. *School Health, 72*(6), 243–249.

Roberts, B. W., Caspi, A., & Moffitt, T. (2001). The kids are alright: Growth and stability in personality development from adolescence to adulthood. *Journal of Personality and Social Psychology, 81,* 670–683.

Roberts, B. W., & Chapman, C. (2000). Change in dispositional well-being and its relation to role quality: A 30-year longitudinal study. *Journal of Research in Personality, 34,* 26–41.

Rogers, C. R. (1961). *On becoming a person.* Boston: Houghton Mifflin.

Roman, R. E., & Lester, D. (1999). Religiosity and mental health. *Psychological Reports, 85,* 1088.

Rossi, A. S. (2001). *Caring and doing for others: Social responsibility in the domains of family, work, and community.* Chicago, IL: University of Chicago Press.

Ryan, R., & Deci, E. (2000). Self–determination theory and the facilitation of intrinsic motivation, social development, and well-being. *American Psychologist, 55*(1), 68–78.

Ryan, R. M., Deci, E. L., & Grolnick, W. S. (1995). Autonomy, relatedness and the self: Their relation to development and psychopathology. In D. Cicchetti & D. J. Cohen (Eds.), *Manual of developmental psychopathology* (pp. 618–655). New York, NY: Wiley.

Ryff, C. D., & Keyes, C. L. M. (1995). The structure of psychological well-being revisited. *Journal of Personality and Social Psychology, 69,* 719–727.

Sanders, J. O. (2005). *Spiritual maturity: Principles of spiritual growth for every believer.* Chicago, IL: Moody Publishers.

Sheldon, K. M., & Kasser, T. (2001). Getting older, getting better? Personal strivings and psychosocial maturity across the life-span. *Developmental Psychology, 34,* 491–501.

Smith, D. W. (2005). Consciousness with reflexive content. In D. W. Smith & A. L. Thomasson (Eds.), *Phenomenology and philosophy of mind* (pp. 93–114). Oxford: Oxford University Press.

Thompson, B. L., & Waltz, J. A. (2008). Mindfulness, self-esteem, and unconditional self-acceptance. *Journal of Rational-Emotive & Cognitive-Behavior Therapy, 26*(2), 119–126.

Vygotsky, L. S. (1978). *Mind in society: The development of higher psychological processes.* Cambridge, MA: Harvard University Press.

Westenberg, P. M., & Block, J. (1993). Ego development and individual differences in personality. *Journal of Personality and Social Psychology, 65,* 792–800.

Youniss, J. (1980). *Parents and peers in social development: A Sullivan–Piaget perspective.* Chicago: University of Chicago Press.

CHAPTER 8

SAVORING LIFE

The Leader's Journey to Health, Resilience and Effectiveness

Stephen Smith
University of Sydney

ABSTRACT

This chapter shares some of the findings of a participatory action research study undertaken by the Churches of Christ movement in NSW, Australia. In forming a framework for sustainable leadership health, five streams of current literature (burnout, stress, coping, mindfulness, and flow) were found to add insight to the shift from the *pathogenic* to the *salutogenic*. A dynamic state of "optimal functioning" was seen to enhance leadership health, resilience, and effectiveness—this was referred to in the study findings as "savoring life." The study identified a needed shift in organizational practice from reactive to proactive attending to leaders' needs, with an emphasis on *holistic wellness* rather than merely the *absence of disease*. The result is a transformative approach to sustainability that calls ministry leaders to an inner spiritual journey, going deeper, discovering self, and seeking discernment *to result in greater energy, resilience and purpose*. Two leadership mapping and development tools are shared that are designed to help leaders explore their own

Beyond Well-Being: Spirituality and Human Flourishing, pages 151–177
Copyright © 2012 by Information Age Publishing
151

journeys—moving from *struggling* to *savoring*. These elements were foundational in an organization-wide change initiative *to change your corner of the
world by changing yourself.*

In 1580 the Archbishop of Canterbury stood before Queen Elizabeth I and
defended his inability to provide quality leaders in thirteen thousand An-
glican parishes across Great Britain. "Jesus!" broke in the Queen, "Thirteen thousand! We can't possibly find that many." Then she added, "but
if they cannot be properly educated they can at least be honest, sober and
wise" (Neale, 1934, p. 302). Almost five hundred years later this dilemma
of attracting, developing and retaining high quality leaders remains a challenging issue for organizations across every sector of industry, government,
and not-for-profit (Bradach, Tierney, & Stone, 2008). This is certainly true
in the Churches of Christ movement in NSW, a network of one hundred
church communities plus numerous aged care facilities, community projects, and refuge centers. Research conducted within this organization
(Smith, 2009) found that the current ministry leadership is aging with approximately seven-out-of-ten over forty years old. In the research, *one third*
indicate that they are seriously wounded in some way and this is impairing
their life and ministry. *One third* are operating at their peak—connecting to
God and feeling they are being used powerfully. *One third* are somewhere in
the middle—struggling at times, functional but not necessarily excelling—
wounded healers.

SEARCHING FOR FRESH HOPE

In the search for ways to develop sustainable, healthy leaders, there is growing support for the idea that spirituality is *integral* to health, and not merely
an *influence* on health (Larson, 1996). In 1999 the Executive Board of the
World Health Organization adopted changes to their definition of health
to become, "a dynamic state of complete physical, mental, spiritual and
social well-being and not merely the absence of disease or infirmity" (Bok,
2004, p. 13). Agencies with strong links to the World Health Organization,
such as the US Department of Health's Center for Disease Control and
Prevention, are now developing ways to "champion a focus on wellness that
acknowledges the roles of mental health, spirituality, and complementary
and alternative medicine across the lifespan" (Navarro, Voetsch, Liburd,
Bezold, Rhea, 2006, p. 2). While Chuengsatiansup sees the inclusion of
spirituality in the definition of health as merely a shift from a structured
reductionist approach to health that is limited to those elements that can
be measured easily using the scientific approach, he advocates a more ontological approach where "spirituality is an emergent property of a complex

living system and exists only when such a system is examined in a holistic manner" (Chuengsatiansup, 2003, p. 4).

The Churches of Christ are such a system—a diverse, complex, decentralized movement of autonomous yet interdependent *communities of fresh hope*. The health of the movement and the leaders in it are woven together with ever-shifting complexity—each affecting, and being affected, by the other. Ian Hughes (2008), in the context of action research in healthcare writes:

> Complex adaptive systems include a large number of autonomous agents (who adapt to change) and a larger number of relationships among the agents. Patterns emerge in the interaction of many autonomous agents. Inherent unpredictability and sensitive dependence on initial conditions result in patterns which repeat in time and space, but we cannot be sure whether, or for how long, they will continue, or whether the same patterns may occur at a different place or time. The underlying sources of these patterns are not available to observation, and observation of the system may itself disrupt the patterns. (pp. 389–399)

Examples of complex adaptive systems are the financial market, the human immune system, a colony of termites, or any collection of humans (Plsek & Greenhalgh, 2001, p. 625). The lessons from Complexity Science suggest that "illness and health result from complex, dynamic, unique interactions between different components of the overall system" (Wilson & Holt, 2001, p. 688), and these unpredictable agents are 1) within each human body, 2) within the choices made by each individual, 3) affected by (and affecting) the web of relationships between individuals, and 4) influencing the wider social, political and cultural systems. As such there is no simple cause-and-effect modeling that adequately predicts and solves health-related issues when relying on a system to be "constant, predictable and independent" (Plsek & Greenhalgh, 2001, p. 625).

Spirituality is now recognized in the field of management theory as making a profound contribution to both personal and organizational transformation (Conger, 1994; Renesch & DeFoore, 1996; Neal, 1997; King & Nicol, 1999; Mitroff & Denton, 1999). This is also true in education, nursing, and social welfare (Hart & Bond, 1995) perhaps because "spiritual people have a sense of inner calm which helps them stay focused and hopeful in troubled times" (Blonna, 2000, p. 11). Action research is an appropriate methodology to explore matters of health and spirituality because "contemplating our spiritual purpose and human flourishing are seen as characteristics of action research" (Reason & Bradbury, 2001).

For both leaders and community this holistic view of health is intertwined. The Churches of Christ in NSW have adopted the vision: "to develop healthy, mission-shaped communities of fresh hope." The word "church" was removed, and the ideas of "health" and "community" were added. The vision-statement was the end-product of a self review that focused on re-framing what it means to be Christians in community. This reshaped view of church is focused on health: for individuals and the group as a whole. Notice the comment by the Hebrew prophet Samuel around 3,000 years ago: "God puts poor people on their feet again; he rekindles burned-out lives with *fresh hope*. Restoring dignity and respect to their lives— a place in the sun!" (1 Samuel 2:6, The Message). This verse is now the art feature in the reception area of the Sydney office of the Churches of Christ. This shift in thinking offers a challenge to those who claim to be God's people to fo-cus on bringing life, centered on being a restorative, life-giving community. Christian community is not merely an institution, but a place of belonging; not only a gathering, but a place for genuine close-knit relationships; not limited to membership, but united in shared purpose and values. In short, it is a healthy community that brings fresh hope to burned-out lives: their own and others.

This reshaping from a focus on "church institution" to being a "healthy community" reflects a significant shift in ecclesiology. It recognizes that health is a central quality desirable for the organization as a whole and reflected by the leaders who convene the dialogues of change and future building. In his book, *Community: The Structure of Belonging*, Peter Block (2008) defines the core elements of a healthy community:

> Community... is the experience of *belonging*. We are in community each time we find a place to belong. The word belong has two meanings. First, it means to be related to and a part of something. It is membership, the experience of being at home in the broadest sense of the phrase... To belong is to know, even in the middle of the night, that I am among friends. The second mean-ing has to do with being an owner: something belongs to me. To belong to a community is to act as a creator and co-owner of that community. What I con-sider mine I will build and nurture. The work, then, is to seek in our commu-nities a wider and deeper sense of emotional ownership; it means fostering among all of a community's citizens a sense of ownership and accountability. Belonging can also be thought of as a longing to be. Being is our capacity to find our deeper purpose in all that we do. It is the capacity to be present, and to discover our authenticity and whole selves. Community is the container within which our longing is fulfilled. Without the connectedness of a commu-nity, we will continue to choose not to be. I have always been touched by the term "beloved community." This is often expressed in a spiritual context, but it is also possible in the secular aspects of our everyday life. (p. xii)

The need for belonging and community is universal. We are social beings: the need to belong is a sign of health. Community is important for every-one, in religious or secular contexts. The religious context is not dissimilar to the secular when dealing with matters of health—whether emotional, so-cial, physical or spiritual. However, all communities are complex. M. Scott

Peck (1991), author of *The Different Drum: Community-Making and Peace*, describes complex community in these terms:

> *Community* can be one of those words—like God, or love, or death, or consciousness—that's too large to submit to any single, brief definition...we consider community to be a group of people that have made a commitment to learn how to communicate with each other at an ever more deep and authentic level. One of the characteristics of true community is that the group secrets, whatever they are, become known—they come out to where they can be dealt with...a group that deals with its own issues—its own *shadow*—and the shadow can contain any kind of issue. Within an organization, community represents a forum where the tension can be surfaced out in the open and made known. You can't develop a *tensionless* organization. To the contrary, one of the conclusions at the conference was that you wouldn't *want* to develop a tensionless organization. Creating community in the context of an organization permits those tensions to be surfaced and dealt with as best they can, rather than being latent or under the table. (p. 26)

The process of redesigning the concept of community in the context of our research reported below was not without tension. However, stakeholders' redefining the terms of reference from "churches" to "healthy, fresh hope communities" enabled the organization to recognize the legitimacy of groups and settings such as refuges, aged care facilities, welfare groups, and chaplaincy settings as stakeholders in our organization. This was an intentional move towards organization-wide health:

> Our communities must support our individual freedom as a means to community health and resiliency. And, as individuals, we must acknowledge our neighbors and make choices based on a desire to be in relationship with them as a means to our own health and resiliency. (Wheatley & Kellner-Rogers, 1998, p. 14)

It became evident in our research that the Churches of Christ is not sustainable unless significant changes are made to its structure. The organization does not exist to serve itself—rather it exists to serve a purpose. However, without a depth of healthy, mission-focused leadership that is able to build healthy, purpose-driven community, it will become irrelevant over time.

The issue of sustainability is important for leadership. At a risk-assessment workshop run by Price-Waterhouse-Coopers with senior staff from the Churches of Christ in NSW in 2008, the participants agreed that the second-highest area of risk for Churches of Christ is the attraction, recruitment and retention of high-quality staff (PWC, 2008). With an aging leadership, in roles that can be highly stressful, it is essential that the physical, mental, spiritual and social well-being of leaders is dealt with proactively and as a high priority. Without a steady stream of healthy leaders making a continuous positive impact on their churches there will not be "fresh hope communities" but rather "life draining gatherings."

THE LEADER'S JOURNEY FROM "STRUGGLING" TO "SAVORING"

Our research within the Churches of Christ in NSW took the form of a participatory action research project under the supervision of the Faculty of Health Science at the University of Sydney. The project was designed to improve professional practice in the area of leadership health and intended to "generate transformational theories" (McNiff, 2000, p. 56) as leaders produced "their own theories of practice" to bring about personal and organizational change. Jean McNiff writes:

> I continue to make the case for generative transformational processes of real life. Organization practices are always changing. Organization theory needs to develop a form that embodies change. Knowers and their knowledge are changing phenomena in a changing world; people change their practice as they try to develop their lives. This means studying their own changing work, and telling the stories of their own learning processes as they tried to make a difference for good. (McNiff, 2000, pp. 56–57)

Harvesting the experiences of leaders through the collection of their comments, insights and stories was a powerful form of data collection. Lave and Wenger (1991) describe stories as "packages of situated knowledge" (p. 108). They cite examples of stories' power in Alcoholics Anonymous saying that "talk is a central medium of transformation"(1991, p. 85). The role of stories in sense-making has been given considerable attention by researchers (Weick, 1995). "Telling stories about remarkable experiences is one of the ways that in which people try to make the unexpected expectable, hence manageable" (Robinson, 1981, p. 60). Whitehead (2009) stresses that recording stories in any creative forms:

> Communicates the values that give meaning and purpose to their lives and that are expressed in their professional practice. I think of such values as ontological in that they are at the heart of the individual's sense of themselves and their ways of being. Their values are expressed with a life-affirming energy in what they are doing. The ontological significance of the explanatory principles of living theories is that these are the values used by individuals to give meaning and purpose to their lives. These values can be clarified and developed in the course of the action research. The expression of the meanings of the embodied values can be formed, in the process of clarification, into the communicable standards of judgment that can be used to evaluate

the validity of the contributions to knowledge in the production of the living theories. (pp. 93–94)

These "living theories" took the form of "cogenerative inquiry" (Greenwood & Levin, 2005) built on "professional researcher-stakeholder collaboration that aims to solve real life problems in context" (p. 54) as questions were raised, problems identified, data analyzed, and resolutions found to bring about effective social change. Theory was iterative and evolving through multiple forms of stakeholder engagement. Forums for participant storytelling, knowledge-sharing, brainstorming, and reframing created a shared analysis for the challenges to leadership health. In constant dialogue participants made posters of their thoughts, feelings, and reflections to help understand the present and co-create a preferred future.

In other areas of health research these non-linear forms of learning have been found to increase the capability of doctors and nurses to meet their role requirements (Fraser & Grenhalgh, 2001, p. 799). Whitehead and McNiff found that:

> As we practise we observe what we do and reflect on it. We make sense of what we are doing through researching it. We gather data and generate evidence to support our claims that we know what we are doing and why we are doing it (our theories of practise), and we test these knowledge claims for their validity through the critical feedback of others. The theories are our living theories. (Whitehead & McNiff, 2006, p. 32)

The resulting models were tested and refined in multiple cycles of cogenerative dialogue. A broad range of research literature was shared with participants to help inform these research conversations and develop "real world models" that would improve professional practice. Gareth Morgan (1983) highlights the power of this kind of research for individual and organizational transformation, noting that:

> In conversation, as in research, we meet ourselves. Both are forms of social interaction in which our choice of words and action return to confront us ... When we engage in action research, thought and interpretation, we are not simply involved in instrumental processes of acquiring knowledge, but in processes through which we actually make and remake ourselves as human beings. (p. 373)

As this research aimed to improve professional practice in the area of health, the question "How do we improve our practice?" was central. Creating a toolkit for individual and organizational transformation was important, as this provided a way for ideas to be tested repeatedly by practitioners. It was also a way to seep transformational knowledge into the wider system by holding up a mirror for participants to see themselves and where they are in relation to their own health and well-being. Stories were gathered as collections of deep pain, common struggles, interesting challenges, personal triumphs and great joys. They were then shared and realigned into common themes. Through multiple cycles of interaction the wisdom of participants was engaged and developed:

> The value of collective and interactive research cycling is that the individual's own learning can be fully drawn out and acknowledged; shared and put side-by-side, with the 'knowing' of others, so that individual meaning is enriched, enhanced and extended by interaction with others; and evaluated and constructively challenged by others. This concept is fundamental to the process of action learning... (Cherry, 1999, p. 85)

The central interpretive apparatus for the research was adapted from the work of Herr and Anderson (2005), providing a benchmark for the research against other established processes, and providing the following tests of valid action research:

- generating new knowledge *(knowledge quality)*;
- achieving action-oriented outcomes *(outcome quality)*;
- transforming researcher, participants and organization *(change quality)*;
- testing of research value and applicability by participants in organization *(practice quality)*;
- co-creating and sharing knowledge owned by stakeholders *(democratic quality)*; and
- confirming rigorous and appropriate research method *(process quality)*.

The approach worked in cooperation with participant stakeholders to harvest their knowledge and make it available for sharing with others. As improving practice was the chief goal, it was the *usefulness* of these tools that dictated the *validity* of the themes and models. These models had been further shaped by the literature in the field, but their usefulness was determined by the stakeholders. As Greenwood and Levin (2005) write:

> Validity, credibility, and reliability in action research are measured by the willingness of local stakeholders to act on the results of the action research, thereby risking their welfare on the 'validity' of their ideas and the degree to which the outcomes meet their expectations. This cogenerated contextual knowledge is deemed valid if it generates warrants for action. The core validity claim centers on the workability of the actual social change activity engaged in, and the test is whether or not the actual solution to a problem arrived at solves the problem. (p. 54)

IMAGES OF WOUNDED LEADERS

Images of leadership health in Churches of Christ in NSW were collected through dialogues conducted around the state and confirmed by a survey of one hundred and eight ministry leaders (Smith, 2009). The results combined quantitative and qualitative data from eighty-four paid ministering persons (church pastor, chaplain, or in another form of ministry) and twenty-four unpaid leaders (retired, board members, or volunteers). The participants were predominantly male (73% male), 32% were regionally located, and two thirds were over forty years old. Their responses yielded the following descriptions of leaders as wounded but with some strengths.

One half (50%) believe that their ministry life is not sustainable if things stay as they are. Our leadership is aging with approximately seven-out-of-ten being over the age of forty. Most of our ministers (58%) are working part-time. Forty percent believe they are overworked and 44% feel they lack leaders in their church they can rely on. Almost three-out-of-five (58%) feel they do not have enough financial support to live on and 44% lack the financial resources to do their ministry.

One third (32%) say they are really struggling. Over half (53%) describe themselves as "wounded." Of these 47% say they are "wounded but are able to heal others," and 23% feel "wounded and unable to see themselves being healed." One third (35%) are doing or thinking things that are usually out of character for them, while almost half (48%) feel their healthy boundaries are starting to blur.

One third currently feel stuck and don't know what to do. Meanwhile 37% are looking for work outside of ministry now; 32% are looking for other ministry options now; and 33% will leave ministry altogether when they have another reasonable option. Approximately one third feel they are burnt-out (31%) or depressed (31%). One third (32%) believe their spouse is depressed. One third (31%) feel limited by their own physical health, and almost half (46%) are struggling with their own inner personal stresses.

One half (49%) say their marriage relationship continues to grow deeper. One half (48%) believe their ministry is very effective. About one third (34%) believe God is using them powerfully, feel very connected to God (33%), God-empowered (29%), very healthy emotionally and spiritually (29%), feel they are doing quite well (35%), and their faith is stronger than ever (34%). Further, two-in-five (40%) have no plans to leave their ministry position and most (55%) feel supported and encouraged by their church leadership team. Almost one half (47%) wish to find God's agenda for their life, while 57% would focus on their own spiritual formation, 43% on coping with stress, 39% on becoming a spiritual leader, 31% on dealing effectively with conflict, or 61% on managing boundaries.

This research project garnered the ideas and feelings of ministry leaders in multiple dialogues across the state. Common threads were identified and with participant dialogue, testing, validating and reshaping, various models were developed. Two of these models are shared here: 1) *Adapt or Derail: the Leader's Journey from Struggling to Savoring;* and 2) *Savoring Life: The Leadership Journey to Health, Resilience and Effectiveness.* The power of these tools was that they were *co-generated* by the participants in the system, but they were also created for *personal mapping.* Mapping opens up "knowledge spaces" (Clarke, 2005, p. 30) that provide a visual way to see *where we are* and *where we want to go* (or, more importantly, who *we want to be*). This is a simple and powerful form of situational analysis that provokes a fresh way of looking at our own situation within an organizational context. The process can be transformative, as "maps are excellent devices to materialize questions" (Clarke, 2005, p. 30).

Leaders were asked to identify four key mapping actions for their lives in their ministry contexts: 1) map on this diagram where you are now; 2) map on this diagram where you want to be in six months; 3) describe what that map position is like—feelings, thoughts, actions; and 4) what positive steps are needed to move you there? The mapping process helped leaders see themselves in the stories of others. Participants regularly said, "I've been there," or "I know what that feels like," when these tools were used to discuss their health, resilience and effectiveness.

Leaders were asked to share their images of their own experiences of "struggling." Their stories often spanned a lifetime of different situations and contexts. The information was organized by participants into the following themes:

1. *Drained:* decreased energy and increasing difficulty in staying focused and "keeping up to speed" with all that's going on;
2. *Demoralized:* feelings of failure in vocation and questioning the call to ministry;
3. *Devalued:* reduced sense of reward (feeling unappreciated) in return for giving so much to the ministry;
4. *Defeated:* a sense of helplessness and inability to see a way out of current problems;
5. *Denial:* failing to accept the nature or depth of a crisis, or own role in contributing to current situations;
6. *Dogmatic:* demonstrating black and white thinking, holding on to positions in an unreasonable manner that demeans others for thinking or feeling differently;
7. *Demanding:* feelings of being "entitled" to special treatment because of position, divine will, or recognition of sacrificial service;

8. *Disconnected:* detachment from important relationships and an inability to develop closeness;
9. *Disillusioned:* cynicism and negativism about self, others, work, and the world in general;
10. *Derailing:* rationalized choices that break previous boundaries and are self-destructive, adventure seeking, addictive or otherwise out of character;
11. *Duty:* ministry service is driven by obligation and responsibility—rather than joy, meaning, faith and love;
12. *Dryness:* spiritual wilderness, feelings of emptiness, going through the motions, no sense of God's "presence";
13. *Driven:* an obsession with seeking their own personal agenda (for significance and/or security) rather than humbly pursuing God's agenda; and
14. *Depression:* feelings of overwhelming sadness, disturbed sleep, low energy, loss of ability to experience pleasure, and poor concentration.

These themes are consistent with issues arising out of the current literature on leadership impairment (Millon, Grossman, Millon, Meagher, & Ramnath, 2000; Sperry, 2002; Hoge & Wenger, 2005; Smith & Vaartjes, 2008; Berglas & Baumeister, 1993). It should be noted that these images are messy and fuzzy, crossing over in multiple ways, and may be colored by other issues such as burnout, acute stress, stage of life issues, Secondary Post-Traumatic Stress Disorder (compassion fatigue) (Rothschild, 2006; Joinson, 1992), or neurotic dysfunction (Baumeister & Scher, 1988; Kets de Vries, 2001; White, 1997).

The journey of leadership through times of personal woundedness is depicted in the mapping tool *"Adapt or Derail."* The map is described as follows: when you are born you may have predispositions towards different ways of thinking and feeling *(inherited);* your environment helps to shape you and enables you to discover your own ways to thrive and survive *(experience);* you recognize your preferences and develop complementary skills to help you achieve your goals *(consolidate);* your strengths become entrenched into patterns of behavior as you continuously "do what works for you" *(entrench);* at some point the behavioral styles that "worked for you" in the past ceased to be effective *(struggle);* increasing demands place pressure on your ability to meet expectations, so you have to make a choice *(respond).* At this point you either:

1. just keep doing the same things, but try harder—a lack of self awareness leads to extreme behavior *(derail);* this eventually manifests in unhealthy behavioral styles that entrench destructive patterns until "everything is someone else's fault" *(crash).* Or,

2. you examine your approach to life and work, making any difficult, deep changes necessary to achieve your goals *(adapt);* you continuously reassess, learn and adjust to changing demands, transforming and thriving to achieve healthy life goals *(savor)*.

Figure 8.1 is consistent with the literature on life transitions (Sheehy, 1974; Gould, 1978; Fowler, 1981; Rohr, 1990; Campbell, 1949; Hagberg & Guelich, 1995; Levinson, 1978, 1996) where, particularly in midlife, a leader hits a "crisis of limitation" (Rohr, 1990, p. 166) and realizes that the story of his or her life where he or she featured as "the hero" (Campbell, 1949, p. 245) has not come to fruition. This is the point where "doing what has worked for you" is no longer effective, and the leader is at a crossroads—to *adapt* (find a new role in the story or redefining what a hero really is and changing accordingly) or *derail* (remaining stuck, like a rabbit in the headlights, afraid to act, and afraid to do nothing until his or her soul is eroded and destructive behaviors manifest). In our research participants felt that "struggling" will likely continue until a leader can reconcile his or her "heroic dream" with his or her "current reality"—this requires a journey of deep personal transformation.

SHIFTING FROM PATHOGENIC TO SALUTOGENIC

Responding to the holistic health needs of leaders within the Churches of Christ has required a significant shift from being *reactive* to *proactive*. The shift reflects a changing emphasis across industries and disciplines to health and wellbeing. In the emerging field of Positive Psychology, Seligman and Csikszentmihalyi (2000) challenge the traditional therapeutic approach by saying that "psychologists have scant knowledge of what makes life worth living" (p. 5), and that "psychology…has become largely a science about healing. It concentrates on repairing damage within a disease model of human functioning" (p. 5). They urge a shift from the traditional emphasis on weaknesses and malfunctioning towards a focus on human strength and optimal functioning.

The need for a switch in focus from the negative to the positive is evident in recent searches of psychological journals, where Myers (2000) reported that negative emotions outnumber positive emotions by 14 to one. Diener, Suh, Lucas, and Smith (1999) conducted a similar study and found that the number of articles examining negative states outweighed those focusing on positive states by 17 to one, while Schaufeli and Bakker (2004) found a similar ratio (15 to one) in literature in the field of occupational health psychology. The imbalance is underscored by George Vaillant (2008, p. 42):

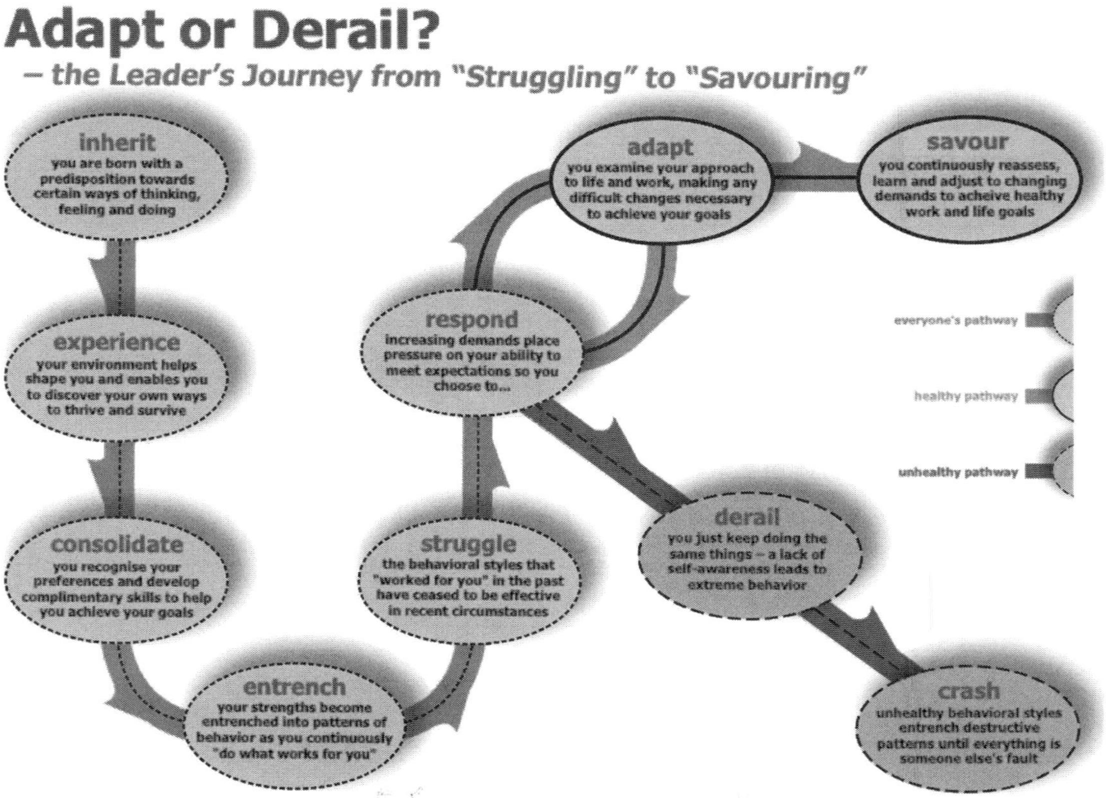

Adapt or Derail?
– the Leader's Journey from "Struggling" to "Savouring"

savour
you continuously reassess, learn and adjust to changing demands to achieve healthy work and life goals

everyone's pathway

healthy pathway

unhealthy pathway

crash
unhealthy behavioral styles entrench destructive patterns until everything is someone else's fault

adapt
you examine your approach to life and work, making any difficult changes necessary to achieve your goals

derail
you just keep doing the same things – a lack of self-awareness leads to extreme behavior

respond
increasing demands place pressure on your ability to meet expectations so you choose to...

struggle
the behavioral styles that "worked for you" in the past have ceased to be effective in recent circumstances

entrench
your strengths become entrenched into patterns of behavior as you continuously "do what works for you"

inherit
you are born with a predisposition towards certain ways of thinking, feeling and doing

experience
your environment helps shape you and enables you to discover your own ways to thrive and survive

consolidate
you recognise your preferences and develop complimentary skills to help you achieve your goals

Figure 8.1 The leader's journey from struggling to savoring.

Consider that in 2004 the leading American text *The Comprehensive Textbook of Psychiatry,* half a million lines in length, devotes 100 to 600 lines each to shame, guilt, terrorism, anger, hate, and sin, thousands of lines to depression and anxiety, but only five lines to hope, one line to joy, and not a single line to faith, compassion, forgiveness, or love.

The promise of the shift from *negative diagnosis* to *positive reinforcement* is not limited to issues of mental health but all aspects of human health (Seligman, 2008). Examples are found in therapeutic approaches to people helping such as Solution-Focused Brief Therapy (SFBT) in which "problem talk" is laid aside for "solution talk" (DeShazer, 1994, p. 80). The solution-focused approach is viewed as more likely to produce positive outcomes in a shorter period of time (Lipchick, 2002) and forms a growing basis for much of the literature on performance coaching—executive, sport and life (Berg & Szabo, 2005). This is similar to approaches to organizational change such as Appreciative Inquiry (AI) (Cooperrider & Srivastva, 1987; Watkins & Mohr, 2001). Both SFBT and AI denounce a problem-solving approach to change and rely on developing a dialogue that identifies what has worked well (the positive) and encourages participants to do more of that. This is a shift from *pathogenic* (focus on disease or disorder) to *salutogenic* (focus on health and well-being) (Antonovsky, 1987, 1996; Charlton & White, 1995).

In literature depicting this shift from pathogenic to salutogenic, there are five streams of thought of particular relevance to the holistic health of ministry leaders. The five streams are: *burnout* (Maslach & Leiter, 1997; Hakanen, Bakker, & Schaufeli, 2006; Schaufeli, Martinez, Marques Pinto, Salanova, & Bakker, 2002), *stress* (Nelson & Simmons, 2004; Quick, Quick, Nelson, & Hurrell, 1997; Seyle, 1976), *coping* (Bryant & Veroff, 1984), *mindlessness* (Brown & Ryan, 2003; Weick & Sutcliffe, 2001; Hanh, 1976; Kabat-Zinn, 1994), and *apathy* (Csikszentmihalyi, 1990, 1998). In each of these streams, for each state of negative health there is a positive counterpart, a state of "optimal functioning." *Engagement* is the positive counterpart of burnout (Maslach, Schaufeli, & Leiter, 2001; Hakanen et al., 2006; Schaufeli et al., 2002), *eustress* is the positive counterpart of distress (Nelson & Simmons, 2004; Quick et al., 1997; Seyle, 1976), *thriving* is the positive counterpart of coping (Bryant & Veroff, 1984), *mindfulness* is the positive counterpart of mindlessness (Brown & Ryan, 2003; Weick & Sutcliffe, 2001; Hanh, 1976; Kabat-Zinn, 1994), and *flow* is the positive counterpart of apathy (Csikszentmihalyi, 1990, 1998). Research supports linkages among the five positive concepts and between each concept and positive outcomes such as holistic health, resilience and effectiveness (all of relevance to the sustainable wellbeing of leaders):

1. They all recognize a positive state of being "fully present" (Kahn, 1992; Brown & Ryan, 2003; Senge, Scharmer, Jaworski, & Flowers, 2004) that has the effect of "optimal functioning";
2. There are positive correlations between these states of "optimal functioning" and positive health and well-being (physical, psychological, social, spiritual);
3. The state of "optimal functioning" has positive spillover to the emotional well-being of the family;
4. Significant positive correlations exist between being "optimal functioning" and positive business outcomes in the following areas: employee productivity, shareholder return, customer retention, employee retention, client satisfaction, personal well-being, and workplace health and safety;
5. They all recognize that the "spiritual" aspects of personal wholeness contribute positively to the state of "optimal functioning"; and
6. There is a positive correlation between the state of "optimal functioning" and leadership health, resilience and effectiveness.

The state of "optimal functioning" is referred to in our research as "savoring life." Leaders who feel swamped, stressed or bored will find that they easily slip into automatic pilot, a kind of sleepwalking, where daydreaming, "zoning out" or "black and white thinking" all seem to make life a little easier. This is not a new phenomenon, as 100 years ago William James (1911) wrote that, "Compared to what we ought to be, we are only half awake" (p. 237).

The state of "being stuck" can drain the life of passion related to work. It may manifest itself as depression or, as Kets de Vries (2001) suggests, a *quasi-anhedonia* (a mild form of mood disorder) where an individual can no longer find pleasure in a previously pleasurable activity. This emotional numbness is also characterized by the loss of ability to concentrate and enjoy living. He writes, "While hedonism reveres pleasure, its obverse, anhedonia, negates it. Anhedonia is characterized by a sense of apathy and loss of interest in and withdrawal from pleasurable activity" (Kets de Vries, 2001, p. 106). These potential challenges increase during midlife.

In contrast, "savoring life" is about being "fully present" in the moment (Hanh, 1976), single-minded, focused, and highly engaged (Langer, 1990). This dynamic state is "not so much about doing as about being" (Kabat-Zinn, 1994, p. 112). The whole person—*head* (cognitive, thinking), *heart* (emotional, feeling), and *hands* (physical, doing)—is fully absorbed in what you are doing. The state of savoring has a positive effect on physical health, psychological well-being, work-place safety, personal resilience, cognitive functioning, and life satisfaction (Weick & Sutcliffe, 2001; Segal, Williams, & Teasdale, 2002; Langer, 1990; Hopkins, 2002; Brown & Ryan, 2003), as the capacity for savoring life supports the many attitudes and actions that contribute to overall human flourishing.

The five literature streams discussed above provide insight into the state of health, resilience and effectiveness of leaders within the Churches of Christ in NSW. Bodies of research related to the five streams were introduced into the dialogues, workshops and resources shared with ministry leaders, allowing them to help co-create a mapping tool: *"Savoring Life: the Leader's Ongoing Journey to Health, Resilience & Effectiveness"* (see Figure 8.2).

The two dimensions of this model are *challenges* and *capability*. Challenges represent the range of issues that potentially drain inner resources (this is not necessarily positive or negative). They may be external (situational) or internal (psychological/spiritual). Capability is essentially the inner resources people use to learn and adapt to the challenges they face. Capability is more than competence. Leaders within the Churches of Christ in NSW (a complex adaptive system) have largely been equipped through traditional education and training focused on enhancing competence (skills, knowledge and attitudes). In a world where complexity is now nor-

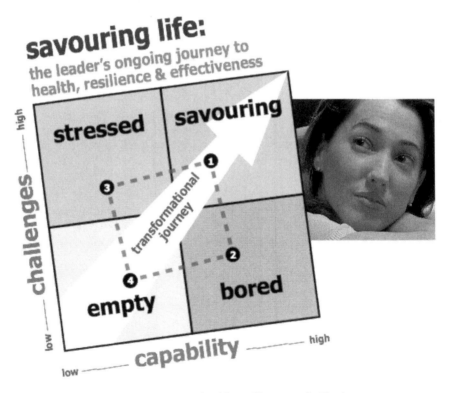

Figure 8.2   The leader's journey to health, resilience and effectiveness.

mative, equipping leaders for *competency* does not appear to be enough. Fraser and Greenhalgh (2001), in the classic British Medical Journal series on complexity, emphasize the need for educating for capability: "In today's complex world we must educate not merely for competence, but for capability—the ability to adapt to change, generate new knowledge, and continuously improve performance . . . Reflective learners transform as the world around them changes: poor learners simply complain about it" (p. 800).

The need to continuously adapt, *savoring life*, rather than merely *enduring work*, is exhibited in the following story. Participants experienced many similar feelings on their own journeys, and these experiences are shared here in one story. The mapping tool, Savoring Life, was developed to reflect the common themes of these stories—a co-created tool designed to aid personal transformation. When shared with people in other industries, the essential elements of leadership health, resilience and effectiveness remained the same. Participants were encouraged to "find their own stories within the story" and map their current positions, owning their own roles and making a *learning space* to explore their own situations, a challenge to *savor life*.

A LEADERSHIP JOURNEY

John takes a job in ministry. He is excited about the new adventure—it will be a fresh experience, stretching his capabilities as he faces new and unknown challenges. He has the ability to try creative ideas, apply things he has learned from different contexts, and build relationships with a congregation who, by and large, are looking to him to be a significant leader who can help them move ahead. Expectations are high. John is absorbed in this new role—it is fun and energizing. He knows he is making a real difference in the lives of people he encounters. He is focused and fully engaged, healthy, resilient and effective. This is the *Savoring Quadrant (1)* (see Figure 8.2).

Being in the *Savoring Quadrant* is not merely being happy in what you are doing. Aristotle argued that there were two forms of happiness: *hedonia* "the life of pleasure" and *eudaimonia* "the life of purpose." *Hedonic well-being* is about maximizing pleasure through indulging in the pursuit of appetites and desires. *Eudaimonic well-being* is optimum functioning based on the pursuit of goals and meaning. Aristotle viewed this as the higher pursuit. Each needs the other for holistic wellness. Pleasure without purpose is empty and meaningless. Purpose without pleasure is sterile and joyless. Seligman (2002) explores this duality:

> The good life consists in deriving happiness by using your signature strengths in every day in the main realms of living. The meaningful life adds one more

component: using these same strengths to forward knowledge, power or goodness. A life that does this is pregnant with meaning, and if God comes at the end, such a life is sacred. (p. 260)

Being in this quadrant is a meaningful experience for John. It is reflected in his overall wellness and effectiveness. Over time John hits some limitations in his ability to keep going. For some reason the role is no longer energizing him, and projects don't have the same excitement. They are now just regular events, and start to have a feel of "sameness" (to him and others). To remain in the *Savoring Quadrant* there must be discovery and growth, being stretched to find inner strength and resources that were previously untapped. But if he does not continue to learn, adapt proactively, and remain connected to the God-purpose that brought him to the role, he will start to slide into the *Stressed Quadrant (3)* (he does not have enough leadership abilities to deal with the significant challenges he faces) or the *Bored Quadrant (2)* (he has high capability but low challenges to face). At this point the "honeymoon" is over.

In the *Bored Quadrant* the ministry leader simply does not have enough challenges to keep the role interesting. One minister in this situation commented, "I can do what they expect of me in about two days a week." The leader may create other ancillary roles to alleviate this state, focusing on those things that provides him or her with some form of energy—perhaps writing, social activities, creative expression, research study, or service projects. Many para-church organizations have been effectively established by ministry leaders who were bored in their local ministry setting and redirected their energies into a new challenge. However, remaining in this state for an extended period will likely shift the leader into the *Empty Quadrant (4)*.

In the *Stressed Quadrant* the ministry leader does not have the capability to meet the challenges he faces. He may never have been up to the challenge, or he may have been effective in leading the church to its current state but now feels somewhat lost, not knowing what to do next. Situational context is important—there may be a range of issues that now limit the capability or capacity of the leader (such as lack of work resources, shift in health status, change in family situation, lack of personal finances). As this realization mounts in the leader and in those around him, the stress is significant and if unchecked will push the leader into the *Empty Quadrant*.

In the *Empty Quadrant* the ministry leader has mentally and emotionally "checked out." Unresolved, chronic boredom and/or stress have a natural entropy toward living on "automatic pilot." Often depressed and burned out, he is now barely hanging in there. Preoccupied with coping, he is unfocused, apathetic and disconnected from those around him. His resilience is low, and he is no longer professionally effective at all. To ease the pain he may "adventure seek" in ways that would normally be out of character for him—seeking small reprieves to an inner woundedness. These activities may be self-destructive as he moves to a point beyond caring. Derailing activities may involve addiction or pleasure seeking. With a lowered ability to experience pleasure, a person is robbed of joy and feels an emptiness within. While it is obvious to many it is time to stop, have a break, and move on to something else, issues of financial security become significant, and ministers sometimes hang on beyond the point of healthy closure. An inability to think clearly or process emotionally and limited options can result in feelings of being trapped.

Every leader moves through these quadrants, sometimes quickly, sometimes slowly, and not necessarily in a particular sequence. One participant said, "I can go through all of these in a day!" However, it is the *chronic states* of these areas that can prove troublesome, with *stressed* or *bored* sliding over time into *emptiness*. This was confirmed by multiple participants as something they had experienced in their leadership journey.

THE LEADER'S JOURNEY OF DEEP TRANSFORMATION

This research into the health of leaders indicates that the leadership depth within Churches of Christ in NSW is "winding down." It is growing older, getting tired, and not attracting, developing and retaining healthy, high-caliber spiritual leaders. Without leaders who are *safe people, skilled people, spiritual people,* there is a significant risk to the effectiveness and sustainability of this movement.

Many of the issues raised are systemic. They are entrenched and interconnected. While "quick fixes" are tempting, real change lies in deeper transformation. It is important for leaders to acknowledge their roles and responsibilities in moving forward. Edwin Friedman (1985) responds to this idea:

> A comment needs to be made in this systems context about martyrdom. There are a number of clergy of all faiths who, rather than burning out, almost seem to relish abuse, either emotionally or in their physical surroundings. If they are Christian, they might see themselves as emulating Jesus on the cross. If they are Jewish, they might justify their suffering by recalling the martyrs of Jewish history. In both cases this is sheer theological camouflage for an ineffective immune system. In any family, taking the suffering for others, or being willing to suffer because of the suffering of others, is absolutely irresponsible if it enables others to avoid facing their own suffering! . . . As one minister's spouse put it, 'I used to believe a martyr was someone who went around taking everyone else's pain without complaint and refusing praise for his actions. I now realize that is not a martyr; that's a saint. A martyr is someone who's willing to live with a saint. (p. 218)

Recognizing that ministry leaders can be their own worst enemies when it comes to self-care is vital to this discussion. It encourages leaders to seek a form of change that helps them learn to set their own boundaries, build their own support networks, and strengthen their personal resilience (spiritual, emotional and physical). This work of change cannot be done *to* them or *for* them if sustainable solutions are to be developed.

In the context of this research, the health of leaders is viewed holistically because the whole person shapes his or her health and effectiveness as a leader within the church community being served. Leaders' effectiveness is impacted by the way they: 1) cope with stress, 2) have processed their family of origin issues, 3) manage relationships around them, 4) manage their physical health, and 5) possess a sense of spiritual peace. In short, there are links between the health of the leader and the health of the organization in which they are immersed (Tetrick, 2002).

The research process—using qualitative and quantitative methods with a participative approach—helped to identify the need for a shift in organizational practice from reactive to proactive. This means an emphasis on *holistic wellness* rather than merely the *absence of disease* and an emphasis on *savoring life* as the dynamic state of *optimal functioning*. The result is a transformative approach that calls ministry leaders to an inner spiritual journey, going deeper, discovering self, and seeking discernment in order to result in greater health, resilience and effectiveness. There is an emphasis on spiritual transformation and wellness rather than merely the absence of illness.

Spiritual transformation is about going deeper. Spiritual formation and spiritual mentoring are ways to help in this journey. The pursuit of personal transformation through formation, meditation, and discipline will increase physical, emotional, and spiritual resilience. Inspiring healthy life-shaping patterns (of thinking, feeling, doing, and being) is another pathway to spiritual transformation.

Wellness is about being able to live a healthy, joyous life. Ministers can savor life, enjoy their calling, and learn how to minister safely and effectively. This should be a strength of spiritual leaders—if they cannot model this, then their influence on others will be limited. Wellness is about balancing the whole of life (spiritual, emotional, relational, and physical)—transforming lives surrendered to God and aligned with His agenda.

These elements are key in helping leaders move from "struggling" to "savoring." The idea of *savoring the moment* to the extent of being totally absorbed in God (Mulholland, 1993) is not new and involves "being fully conscious and aware in the present moment" (Senge et al., 2004, p. 13). The eighteenth-century French Jesuit priest Jean-Pierre Caussade encouraged people in *The Sacrament of the Present Moment* (1861/1982) to recognize God in every moment:

Savoring God in the small things of everyday life, not fighting it but surrendering:

> To discover God in the smallest and most ordinary things, as well as in the greatest, is to possess a rare and sublime faith. To find contentment in the present moment is to relish and adore the divine will in the succession of all things to be done and suffered which make up the duty to the present moment. (p. xx)

The pathway to *savoring life* requires an emphasis on deep transformation. This journey of formation requires:

- Going deeper through *awakening:* opening a doorway between God and self—a space of comfort (feeling the closeness of God) and threat (confronted by our lack of alignment with God).
- Going deeper through *cleansing:* bringing our motives and behaviors into harmony with the character of God. No longer avoiding discipline—the spiritual disciplines are pursued to engender constant integration of God-values into everyday life as we learn to genuinely trust in God.
- Going deeper through *illuminating:* shifting from God as "out there" to a deep sense of God within our being. Renouncing our false self, we are responsive to God's touch as the heart of our life, constantly reshaping our approach to the world around us.
- Going deeper through *savoring:* experiencing absorption with God's presence in the soul. A transforming union with God, the wholeness of a spiritual marriage with Him as God's agenda is pursued with passion and humility. Self is defined by God, not the impressions of others.

Going deeper through *awakening, cleansing, illuminating,* and *savoring* describes elements of spiritual formation reflected in various forms within Christian literature including: Jean Pierre de Caussade (1675–1751); St. John of the Cross (1542–1591); Pseudo-Dionysius (6th century); Teresa of Avila (1515–1582); Francois Fenelon (1651–1715); and more modern writers as well (Avila, 2008; Barton, 2006; Foster, 1978; Groeschel, 1984; Kabat-Zinn, 1994; Merton, 1962; Mulholland, 1993; Nouwen, 1981; Peers, 1991; Rolheiser, 1999; and Willard, 1991).

It is important to recognize the emerging patterns in a complex adaptive system (Stacey, 2003). In leadership within Churches of Christ in NSW, patterns of behavior impact the health, resilience and effectiveness of leaders—and the health and effectiveness of the "fresh hope communities" they lead. The two development tools described in this chapter capture indicators of these patterns, enabling leaders to identify their situations through visual mapping, self-reflection and peer feedback.

Leaders who *savor life* are sustainable. They are not "running on empty" and are recharged by the *who* they are, *how* they live, *what* they do and *why* they do it. There is a whole-of-life balance of spiritual, psychological, social, intellectual, and physical health that constitutes a genuine flourishing of human life. This approach has helped to shape the understanding of healthy leaders and healthy ministries within the organization. Through this process of mutual sense-making, participants identified the patterns of daily life that they believed characterized and assisted optimal functioning in leaders. Healthy, sustainable leaders:

- seek personal integrity through transparency, accountability and reflection *(this is about growing in self-awareness);*
- set personal boundaries that encourage self-discipline, renew energy and build resilience *(this is about setting appropriate limits);*
- build the capability and capacity of other leaders and delegate to them efficiently *(this is about building effective teams);*
- adapt to improve personal fulfillment and professional effectiveness *(this is about pursuing deep change);*
- live the values they espouse *(this is about knowing who you truly are);*
- nourish close relationships that challenge personal attitudes and actions *(this is about belonging in community);* and
- seek depth—balancing spiritual, intellectual, social, emotional and physical priorities *(this is about growing in wisdom).*

CONCLUSION

This chapter shares some of the findings of a participatory action research study within a complex adaptive system—the Churches of Christ in NSW. Action research is the formulation of living theory (Whitehead & McNiff, 2006), a transformational process. It provides the opportunity to journey from deep tacit knowledge through transformative practice to explicit awareness (McNiff & Whitehead, 2000). More broadly, theories were developed that contribute to human flourishing and help leaders to contemplate their spiritual purpose, helping to inform and reshape their daily practices (Reason & Bradbury, 2001). A dynamic state of optimal functioning enhanced leadership health, resilience and effectiveness—this was referred to as *savoring life*. This helped to identify a needed shift in organizational practice from reactive to proactive—an emphasis on *holistic wellness* rather than merely the *absence of disease*. The result is a transformative approach that calls ministry leaders to an inner spiritual journey, going deeper, discovering self, and seeking discernment —to result in greater health, resilience and effectiveness. Two mapping tools were shared that are designed to help leaders explore their own journeys—moving from *struggling* to *savoring*. These elements were foundational in an organization-wide change initiative—*to change your corner of the world by changing yourself.*

REFERENCES

Antonovsky, A. (1987). *Unravelling the mystery of health: How people manage stress and stay well.* San Francisco: Jossey-Bass.

Antonovsky, A. (1996). *The salutogenic model as a theory to guide health promotion.* San Francisco: Jossey-Bass.

Avila, T. (2008). *The interior castle: Teresa of Avila (1515–1582).* London: Christian Classics.

Barton, R. (2006). *Sacred rhythms.* New York: IVP.

Baumeister, R., & Scher, S. (1988). Self-defeating behavior patterns among normal individuals: Review and analysis of common self-destructive tendencies. *Psychological Bulletin, 104*(1), 3–22.

Berg, I., & Szabo, P. (2005). *Brief coaching for lasting solutions.* New York: Norton.

Berglas, S., & Baumeister, R. (1993). *Your own worst enemy: Understanding the paradox of self-defeating behavior.* New York: HarperCollins.

Block, P. (2008). *Community: The structure of belonging.* San Francisco: Berrett-Koehler.

Blonna, R. (2005). *Coping with stress in a changing world.* New York: McGraw-Hill.

Bok, S. (2004). Rethinking the WHO definition of health. *Harvard Centre for Population and Development Studies Working Paper Series, 14*(7).

Bradach, J., Tierney, T., & Stone, N. (2008). Delivering on the promise of nonprofits. *Harvard Business Review, December,* 1–10.

Brown, K., & Ryan, R. (2003). The benefit of being present: Mindfulness and its role in psychological well-being. *Journal of Personality and Social Psychology, 84*(4), 822–848.

Bryant, F., & Veroff, J. (1984). Dimensions of subjective mental health in American men and women. *Journal of Health and Social Behavior, 25,* 116–135.

Campbell, J. (1949). *The hero with a thousand faces.* Princeton, NJ: Princeton University Press.

de Caussade, J-P. (1861/1982). *The sacrament of the present moment.* K. Muggeridge (Trans.). San Francisco: Harper Collins.

Charlton, B., & White, M. (1995). Living on the margin: A salutogenic model for socio-economic differentials in health. *Public Health, 109*(4), 235–243.

Cherry, N. (1999). *Action research: A pathway to action, knowledge and learning.* Melbourne: RMIT University Press.

Chuengsatiansup, K. (2003). Spirituality and health: An initial proposal to incorporate spiritual health in health impact assessment. *Environmental Impact Assessment Review, 23,* 3–15.

Clarke, A. (2005). *Situational analysis: Grounded theory after the post-modern turn.* London: Sage.

Conger, J. (1994). *Spirit at work: Discovering the spirituality in leadership.* San Francisco: Jossey-Bass,

Cooperrider, D., & Srivastva, S. (1987). Appreciative inquiry into organizational life. In W. Pasmore & R. Woodman (Eds.), *Research in organizational change and development, Vol. 1* (pp. 129–169). Greenwich: JAI Press.

Csikszentmihalyi, M. (1990). *Flow: The psychology of optimal experience.* New York: Harper Perennial.

Csikszentmihalyi, M. (1998). *Finding flow: The psychology of engagement with life.* New York: Basic Books.

DeShazer, S. (1994). *Words were originally magic.* New York: Norton.

Diener, E., Suh, E., Lucas, R., & Smith, H. (1999). Subjective well-being: Three decades of progress. *Psychological Bulletin, 125,* 267–302.

Dionysius, P. (1984). *Pseudo-Dionysius: The complete works.* C. Luibheid (Trans.). New York: Paulist Press.

Fenelon, F. (2008). *The seeking heart.* Edmondson, R. (Trans.). New York: Paraclete Press. (Original work published 1675–1715)

Foster, R. (1978). *Celebration of discipline.* New York: Harper and Row.

Fowler, J. (1981). *Stages of faith: The psychology of human development and the quest for meaning.* New York: Harper Collins.

Fraser, S., & Greenhalgh, T. (2001). Coping with complexity: Educating for capability. *British Medical Journal, 323,* 799–803.

Friedman, E. (1985). *Generation to generation.* New York: Guildford Press.

Greenwood, D., & Levin, M. (2005). Reform of the social sciences and the universities through action research. In N. Denzin, & Y. Lincoln (Eds.), *The Sage Handbook of Qualitative Research* (3rd ed.) (pp. 43–64). London: Sage.

Groeschel, B. (1984). *Spiritual passages.* New York: Crossroad.

Gould, R. (1978). *Transformations: Growth and change in adult life.* New York: Simon and Schuster.

Hagberg, J., & Guelich, R. (1995). *The critical journey: Stages in the life of faith.* Salem, NY: Sheffield Publishing.

Hanh, T. (1976). *The miracle of mindfulness.* Boston: Beacon Books.

Hakanen, J., Bakker, A., & Schaufeli, W. (2006). Burnout and work engagement among teachers. *Journal of School Psychology, 43,* 495–513.

Hart, E., & Bond, M. (1995). *Action research for health and social care: A guide to practice.* Buckingham: Open University Press.

Herr, K., & Anderson, G. (2005). *The action research dissertation: A guide for students and faculty.* London: Sage.

Hoge, D., & Wenger, J. (2005). *Pastors in transition: Why clergy leave local church ministry.* Grand Rapids, MI: Eerdmans.

Hopkins, A. (2002). *Safety culture, mindfulness and safe behavior: Converging ideas?* Working Paper 7, National Research Centre for OHS, Canberra, Australian National University.

Hughes, I. (2008). *Action research in healthcare.* In P. Reason & H. Bradbury (Eds.), *Handbook for Action Research: Participative Inquiry and Practice* (pp. 381–393). London: Sage.

James, W. (1911). *Memories and studies.* New York: Longmans, Green and Co.

Joinson, C. (1992). Coping with compassion fatigue. *Nursing, 92*(4),116–121.

Kabat-Zinn, J. (1994). *Wherever you go, there you are: Mindfulness meditation and everyday life.* New York: Hyperion.

Kahn, W. (1992). To be fully there: Psychological presence at work. *Human Relations, 45,* 321–349.

Kets de Vries, M. (1989). *Prisoners of leadership.* New York: Wiley.

Kets de Vries, M. (2001). *Struggling with the demon: Perspectives on individual and organizational irrationality.* Madison, WI: Psychosocial Press.

King, S., & Nicol, D. (1999). Organizational enhancement through recognition of individual spirituality: Reflections of Jaques and Jung. *Journal of Organizational Change Management, 12*(3), 17–24.

Langer, E. (1990). *Mindfulness.* New York: Perseus Books.

Larson, J. (1996). The World Health Organization's definition of health: Social versus spiritual health. *Social Indicators Research, 38,* 181–192.

Lave, J., & Wenger, E. (1991). *Situated learning: Legitimate peripheral participation.* Cambridge: Cambridge University Press.

Levinson, D. (1978). *The seasons of a man's life.* New York: Knopf.

Levinson, D. (1996). *The seasons of a woman's life.* New York: Ballantine.

Lipchick E. (2002). *Beyond technique in solution-focused therapy.* New York: Guildford Press.

Nouwen, H. (1981). *The way of the heart: Desert spirituality and contemporary ministry.* New York: Harper.

Maslach C., & Leiter M. (1997). *The truth about burnout.* San Francisco: Jossey-Bass.

Maslach, C., Schaufeli, W., & Leiter, M. (2001). Job burnout. *Annual Review of Psychology, 52,* 397–422.

McNiff, J., & Whitehead, J. (2000). *Action research in organisations.* London: Routledge.

Merton, T. (1962). *New seeds of contemplation.* New York: Doubleday.

Millon, T., Grossman, S., Millon, C., Meagher, S., & Ramnath, R. (2000). *Personality disorders in modern life.* New Jersey: Wiley.

Mitroff, I., & Denton, E. (1999). A study of spirituality in the workplace. *Sloan Management Review, 40*(4), 83–92.

Morgan, G. (Ed.). (1983). *Beyond Method: Strategies for Social Research.* London: Sage.

Mulholland, M. (1993). *Invitation to a journey.* Downers Grove, IL: IVP.

Myers, D. (2000). The funds, friends, and faith of happy people. *American Psychologist, 55,* 56–67.

Navarro, A., Voetsch, K., Liburd, L., Bezold, C., & Rhea, M. (2006). *Recommendations for future efforts in community health promotion: Report of the National Expert Panel on Community Health Promotion.* Washington, DC: United States Department of Health—Center for Disease Control and Prevention.

Neal, J. (1997). Spirituality in management education: A guide to resources. *Journal of Management Education, 21*(1),121–139.

Neale, J. (1934). *Queen Elizabeth.* London: Jonathan Cape.

Nelson, D., & Simmons, B. (2004). Eustress: An elusive construct, an engaging pursuit: Emotional and physiological processes and positive intervention strategies. *Research in Occupational Stress and Well Being, 3,* 265–322.

Peck, M. (1991). *The different drum: Community making and peace.* New York: Simon & Schuster.

Peers, E. (1991). *Dark night of the soul: A masterpiece of the literature of mysticism by St. John of the Cross.* New York: Doubleday.

Plsek, P., & Greenhalgh, T. (2001). The challenge of complexity in health care. *British Medical Journal, 323,*625–628.

Price Waterhouse Coopers. (2008). *Risk assessment Report—Churches of Christ in NSW.* Sydney: Author.

Quick, J. C., Quick, J. D., Nelson, D., & Hurrell, J. (1997). *Preventive stress management in organizations.* Washington, DC: American Psychological Association.

Reason, P., & Bradbury, H. (2001). *Handbook of action research* (Concise Paperback Edition). London: Sage.

Renesch, J., & DeFoore, B. (Eds.). (1996). *The new bottom line: Bringing heart and soul to business.* San Francisco: New Leaders Press.

Robinson, J. (1981). Personal narratives reconsidered. *Journal of American Folklore, 94,* 58–85.

Rohr, R. (1990). *From wild man to wise man.* Cincinnati, OH: St. Anthony Messenger Press.

Rolheiser, R. (1999). *The holy longing.* New York: Doubleday.

Rothschild, B. (2006). *Help for the helper: The physiology of compassion fatigue and vicarious trauma.* New York: Norton.

Schaufeli, W., & Bakker, A. B. (2004). Job demands, job resources and their relationship with burnout and engagement: A multi-sample study. *Journal of Organizational Behavior, 25,* 293–315.

Schaufeli, W., Martinez, I., Marques Pinto, A., Salanova, M., & Bakker, A. (2002). Burnout and engagement in university students: A cross-national study. *Journal of Cross-Cultural Psychology, 33,* 464–481.

Segal, Z., Williams, J., & Teasdale, J. (2002). *Mindfulness-based cognitive therapy: A new approach to preventing relapse.* New York: Guildford Press.

Seligman, M. (2002). *Authentic happiness.* New York: The Free Press.

Seligman, M. (2008). Positive health. *Applied Psychology, 57,* 3–18.

Seligman, M., & Csikszentmihalyi, M. (2000). Positive psychology. *American Psychologist, 55*(1) 5–14.

Senge, P., Scharmer, C., Jaworski, J., & Flowers, B. (2004). *Presence: An exploration of profound change in people, organizations, and society.* New York: Doubleday.

Seyle, H. (1976). *The stress of life.* New York: McGraw-Hill.

Sheehy, G. (1974). *Passages: Predictable crises of adult life.* New York: Ballantine.

Smith, S. (2009). *Leadership health and sustainability of ministering persons employed by churches or ministries within Churches of Christ in NSW.* Sydney: Churches of Christ in NSW.

Smith, S., & Vaartjes, V. (2008). Advice for new practitioners: Engage your internal stakeholders. *Participation Quarterly, 11*(3) 6–7.

Stacey, R. (2003). *Strategic management and organizational dynamics: The challenge of complexity.* London: Pearson.

Sperry, L. (2002). *Effective leadership.* New York: Brunner-Routledge.

Tetrick, L. (2002). Individual and organizational health. *Current Perspectives on Stress and Health, 2,* 117–135.

Vaillant, G. (2008). *Spiritual evolution: A scientific defense of faith.* New York: Broadway Books.

Watkins, J., & Mohr, B. (2001). *Appreciative inquiry.* San Francisco: Jossey-Bass.

Weick, K. (1995). *Sensemaking in organizations.* London: Sage.

Weick, K., & Sutcliffe, K. (2001). *Managing the unexpected.* San Francisco: Jossey-Bass.

Wheatley, M., & Kellner-Rogers, M. (1998). *The paradox and promise of community.* In F. Hesselbein, M. Goldsmith, R. Beckhard, & R. Schubert (Eds.), *The community of the future* (pp. 9–18). San Francisco: Jossey-Bass.

White, W. (1997). *The incestuous workplace: Stress and distress in the organizational family.* Center City, MN: Hazelden.

Whitehead, J. (2009). Generating living theory and understanding in action research studies. *Action Research, 7*(1), 85–99.

Whitehead, J., & McNiff, J. (2006). *Action research living theory.* London: Sage.

Willard, D. (1991). *The spirit of the disciplines.* San Francisco: Harper.

Wilson, T., & Holt, T. (2001). Complexity and clinical care. *British Medical Journal, 323,* 685–688.

SECTION III

PRACTICING HUMAN FLOURISHING

Preface

Section III provides a range of case examples where spirituality was used or encouraged in order to promote the flourishing of individuals and communities. This section draws upon, but also moves beyond, theory and research in order to frame practical applications of spiritual resources in various contexts. The contexts include community development, life coaching, and psychological therapy. Practitioners involved with individual and community change will find that the case studies both illustrate theoretical issues and suggest concrete ways of promoting flourishing through spirituality.

SPIRITUALITY AND COMMUNITY DEVELOPMENT

Spirituality is often viewed as a private, individual endeavor. As such, it may not be easy to see how spirituality might be important for community flourishing. Sue Kaldor and Maureen Miner, however, argue that intentional Christian communities (formed to be communities) constitute places where individual spirituality can be nurtured and then, through increased individual spirituality, the community can flourish. In Chapter 9, they provide case studies of communities fostered within urban neighborhoods, on desert journeys, and in small gatherings. Analyses of the cases indicate that "thick" (multiply reciprocal) relationships promoted by and within communities facilitate individual actualization, enhance community

Beyond Well-Being: Spirituality and Human Flourishing, pages 179–182
Copyright © 2012 by Information Age Publishing
All rights of reproduction in any form reserved.

relationships, and thus result in community flourishing. The analyses draw upon theories of community development, Christian theology (Trinitarian theology), and theories of individual development (attachment theory). In particular, Asset Based Community Development (ABCD) theory is used to argue that networks of reciprocal relationships are essential for individual and community enhancement. Consistent with a spiritual formulation of ABCD theory by David Andrews, the nature of community relationships as reflecting the relational being of God is discussed. Hence, the chapter considers ways in which flourishing communities live out Trinitarian themes such as the Father's embrace, the Son's self-emptying, and the creative Three-Person God at play. Finally, theories of individual cognitive-affective development as depicted by attachment theory are considered, with an emphasis on attachment processes and their effects on community flourishing—specifically the giving and receiving of care within communities. Kaldor and Miner conclude that consciously nurtured spirituality is intrinsic to community flourishing because it is intrinsic to the thick connectedness of thriving communities, motivates community formation, and provides a spiritual model for asset based community development.

LIFE COACHING AND MENTORING

Although community bonds are critically important for human flourishing, individuals also need to be supported in other ways during their journeys towards flourishing. This support can be provided through programs of life coaching and mentoring. In Chapter 10 Diann Feldman and Alison Feldman consider how conscious development of client spirituality can become an intrinsic part of mentoring and life coaching. Often personal coaching and mentoring are based on the client's stated goals of work achievement and self-fulfillment. However, the authors argue that spiritual themes underpin these external goals. These themes include the search for the sacred (seeking meaning and purpose), integration (seeking holistic well-being), deep connection (seeking relationship and belonging), and congruency (seeking consistency with life values). When coaches and mentors deal only with external goals, the clients may fail to achieve an integrated sense of personal significance and fulfillment. In such circumstances, clients may continue to be governed by contemporary myths—for example, that busyness is fulfilling and that there is an ideal, unchanging work-life balance. On the other hand, spiritually founded life coaching and mentoring address underlying spiritual needs, help clients discover their core purpose, and encourage spiritual transformation. Importantly, spiritual transformation and the accompanying sense of significance can foster styles of leadership oriented to serving others rather than being focused on the self.

Feldman and Feldman illustrate their spiritual approach with comments from participants following their life coaching program. People engaged in mentoring and life coaching will find this chapter to be a cogent account of theory and techniques that bring spirituality into prominent focus as mentors sojourn with clients in their journey towards flourishing.

Rick Brouwer and Maureen Miner continue Feldman and Feldman's exploration by outlining a method of life coaching in which spirituality is integral. In Chapter 11 they present a holistic approach to life coaching that emphasizes an integrated biological, psychological, and spiritual means of maintaining well-being. In doing so, they note that contemporary society accepts biological, psychological and social explanations of health and pathways to well-being but typically ignores spirituality. For this reason, the coaching model explored in this chapter begins with tropes of sickness, dysfunction and healing but moves to tropes of sin, suffering and salvation as work with the client proceeds. The biblical figure of the shepherd is used to illustrate the consistent holistic counselor who draws healing from suffering. The authors also briefly discuss core Christian teachings concerning pathways from suffering to wholeness and flourishing.

In order to ground the underpinning concepts, Brouwer and Miner describe a case where spiritual issues were a key focus of wellbeing coaching, in the context of physical, psychological, social and financial concerns. Although the presenting problem was a medical condition, psoriasis, the holistic life coaching approach identified psychological and spiritual factors that exacerbated the condition. Through the coaching process, it also became apparent that flourishing had been compromised by a narrow medical approach. As a result of holistic coaching, the client reported significant improvement in the medical condition, and also flourishing in his personal and spiritual life. The authors analyze the case in terms of psychological diagnostic issues and treatment practices, as well as in terms of stated principles of the coaching process.

Together, Chapters 10 and 11 demonstrate how spiritually-informed mentoring can promote human flourishing among people who do not need, or do not seek, psychological therapy.

PSYCHOTHERAPY AND FLOURISHING

Many people who seek referrals to mental health practitioners are encountering life difficulties that make it very difficult for them to flourish. In Chapter 12, Loyola McLean and Marie-Therese Proctor suggest how psychological therapy, and particularly spiritually-oriented approaches to psychological therapy, can promote flourishing among people with deep psychological wounds. They liken the process of psychotherapy to a pilgrimage—a journey involving both patient and therapist in deep relationship. In the context of this relationship, psychological healing and spiritual flourishing coalesce to provide meaning and personal integration. Nevertheless, the inclusion of spiritual themes within the theory and practice of therapy is challenging for many practitioners. To direct practitioners towards the inclusion of spiritual themes, McLean and Proctor identify five secular and spiritual themes based on attachment theory and arising in many patient presentations. The themes include: identifying attachment states of mind, changing dysfunctional attachments through the therapeutic relationship, allowing secure spiritual attachment to act as a "holding space" while change occurs, growing through psycho-spiritual challenges, and searching for new purpose and meaning in life. By addressing these themes, practitioners can help patients heal and flourish.

McLean and Proctor present case vignettes that illustrate therapeutic processes in which attachment themes are addressed. In particular, they emphasize the convergence of psychological and spiritual journeys in the process of healing. The cases include presentations of depression and hypochondriasis, melancholic depression and eating disorders subsequent to sexual abuse, borderline personality disorder, and adjustment issues in a family following the death of a child. In each case, the relationship with the therapist and treatment of the patient's human and spiritual relationships are critical for healing. Further, the outcome is a movement towards flourishing for both patient and therapist: the patient finds new meaning and motivation for life change just as the therapist participates in a joyous healing connection without depletion of the self.

In summary, these four chapters illustrate and analyze cases where physical, psycho-social and spiritual issues are addressed in practices designed to effect individual and/or community change. Documented results include flourishing for individual clients/patients, communities, and change agents (therapists, community developers, life coaches and mentors). The cases demonstrate how appropriate spiritual interventions can and often do facilitate ongoing flourishing.

CHAPTER 9

SPIRITUALITY AND COMMUNITY FLOURISHING

A Case of Circular Causality

Sue Kaldor
Living Well Blue Mountains

Maureen Miner
University of Western Sydney and Wesley Institute

ABSTRACT

Within the literature on spirituality, there is much discussion of individual spirituality from a psychological perspective (e.g., Paloutzian & Park, 2005) and work from theological perspectives on the church as a spiritual community (e.g., Volf 1996, 1998). However, there is relatively little psychological examination of the nature and functions of spirituality at the level of small intentional faith communities. This omission is important because the decline in formal church affiliation means that many people may feel isolated in their individual spirituality and less able to grow spiritually. One solution is to develop small alternative communities where individuals can be nurtured in their spiritual lives. We argue that a flourishing community is an ideal place for individual spirituality to develop. Further, core aspects of spirituality are

Beyond Well-Being: Spirituality and Human Flourishing, pages 183–198
Copyright © 2012 by Information Age Publishing
All rights of reproduction in any form reserved.

connectedness and inclusiveness, and these aspects are essential for community flourishing. Finally, there is a circular causality where flourishing at the community-level impacts flourishing at the individual-level. Such flourishing is inclusive of all elements in the human experience, including the spiritual.

Urban living in the early 21st century seems far removed from the ideal of a flourishing community. Residents use their dwellings as week-day dormitories where they sleep, eat and groom before the often long and slow commute to work. It is hard to meet neighbors, even when people reside in the same place for more than a couple of years. The busyness and transience of life, as well as the contemporary emphasis upon individuality and autonomy, prevent people from experiencing a sense of real belonging with others living nearby. People may look back with nostalgia to depictions of village or town life in centuries past (as found in novels by Jane Austen or Thomas Hardy, for example) but see little ongoing community involvement in their suburb. Even in churches and among other spiritual groups there is often little sense of community and flourishing. This chapter considers how spirituality might be used to strengthen and develop communities, and in turn how flourishing communities might increase levels of spirituality within the group. Given the abstract nature of the concepts "community" and "spirituality" and their remoteness from the everyday lives of many people, the chapter begins with key definitions and assumptions.

DEFINITIONS AND ASSUMPTIONS

Community

A community can be defined in functional and structural terms. Functional definitions refer to the *purposes* of community. A general functional definition of a community is: a human community is a group of people who are voluntarily or involuntarily committed to a common purpose. For example, a family is an involuntary community where the common purpose is the support of kin; a church is a voluntary community where the common purpose is broadly understood as worship.

However, it is necessary to consider the typical *structures* of a community for a complete definition. The focal structures of interest are the networks of relationships within the community. From a systems theory perspective, a human community is a network of relationships with structure, boundaries, and energy (Minuchin, 1974). The structure is its organization; boundaries delineate what is included within the community; and communication is its "energy." Further, the community system operates within a dynamic context of other systems at varying levels of complexity (regional, state, national; political, economic, social, etc.). Hence, a well-functioning human community will demonstrate both change and movement towards states of equilibrium. Such a combination of change and periods of stability is defined as dynamic equilibrium.

A flourishing community is one in which the common purpose of the community is met, and structures allow for dynamic equilibrium. This definition allows for changes in human relationships, or levels of connectedness, within the community. However, wide and deep connections within a community are best suited to adaptation and transformation (Andrews, 2006). Structures of authority may be vertical (a hierarchy of power), horizontal (democratic decision-making) or mixed, depending upon the composition, goals, and strategies of the community members, and may likewise change to suit particular purposes. A key requirement for flourishing is that structures are flexible. A further indicator of community flexibility, and hence flourishing, is that its structures serve a range of tasks: there is celebration, creativity, and play as well as work within a flourishing community. The boundaries of a flourishing community must be sufficiently firm to provide a sense of community identity, but permeable to allow input from outside the system. The flourishing community, then, would have a sense of its own identity but also openness to engagement with others. Since communication provides energy for the human system, a flourishing community will have smooth, accurate, inclusive, and complex communication at cognitive, affective, and behavioral levels. In short, a flourishing community is able to fulfill its purpose and grow and be transformed. When community growth and transformation are planned, the processes of change may involve community development.

Community Development

Community development differs from strategic community planning. The strategic community planning approach emphasizes external direction, the assessment and planning process, targeted change consistent with the community's assessed goals, and outcome evaluation (Watson-Thompson, Fawcett & Schultz, 2008). There is involvement of community members at different phases, but the process is controlled by the external agents, or coalitions for community change. In contrast, community development emphasizes community participation as a central goal: processes support maximum decision making by grass-roots community members even when such processes are not the most efficient means of reaching ostensible goals. Hence a person facilitating community development will "work with the people on any task that the community sees as important. Hence, a person facilitating community development will not impose tasks:

rather, ways of working together and community-based tasks are given priority (Kelly & Sewell, 1988).

Contemporary community development theory is asset-based. In practice, asset-based community development assumes that all people have strengths that can be developed and used to foster positive community functioning. The focus shifts from problems and deficits requiring external remediation to solutions available within the resources of the community—and most notably, human resources. It is assumed that human resources of a community are under-utilized, that people are able to develop responsibility by being given responsibility in community, and that people within the community are best able to pinpoint problems and solutions (Andrews, 2006).

A key summary of asset based community development (ABCD) that includes the problems of the strategic planning approach is as follows:

> ABCD focuses on the strengths and capacities of local communities. It rests on the conviction that sustainable development emerges from within a community, not from outside, by mobilizing and building upon local resources. In contrast, most conventional development work can be characterized as needs-based, i.e., interventions typically focus on problems and deficiencies. This has the unfortunate effect of encouraging communities to denigrate themselves as victims and to put their worst face forward in an effort to attract external assistance. It also leads concerned outsiders into becoming charitable 'fixers.' These are not the most effective relationships for enabling long lasting change. (Bergdall 2003, p. 1)

Therefore, much of contemporary community development work that emphasizes the flourishing of people within communities is based on ABCD theory. The next section considers the nature of spirituality within a community perspective.

Spirituality

Historically spirituality has been associated with mystical experiences, relating to the ultimate, human connectedness, the human quest for existential meaning, and the personal and experiential aspects of religion (Zinnbauer & Pargament, 2005). In light of such a definitional context, Zinnbauer proposed, "spirituality is defined as a personal or group search for the sacred" (Zinnbauer & Pargament, 2005, p. 35). However, Pargament suggested that "religiousness refers to a search for significance in ways related to the sacred" (Zinnbauer & Pargament, 2005, p. 36). Within the latter definition, Pargament noted that goals of emotional well-being, human connectedness and self-development are representative of a search for significance that is broader in focus than "the sacred." Both definitions involve an understanding of the sacred as denoting God, Ultimate Reality, and the Transcendent. Yet not all spirituality is focused on an ultimate being (Spilka, 1993); there can be spiritualities focused on nature, self and others (all in the sense of transcending material existence). Hence, the search for human connectedness or connectedness with nature could arguably indicate spirituality rather than religious goals. The ideas of searching, the Transcendent, and connectedness as core aspects of spirituality require further analysis for a full definition of spirituality. The search for the sacred involves a longing for meanings and purposes that extend beyond the natural world. Such a search for meaning includes a yearning for identity—the longing to secure one's sense of self in a bigger story, which gives purpose and significance to life's routines and experiences. A core aspect of the "bigger picture" is the Transcendent; from a sense of one's insignificance in the universe across time there is a search to know something of the Ultimate. A keen sense of the Transcendent gives rise to surrender to something "more." Spiritualities that focus on God would supplement the goal of knowing God with being known by God (see Rosner and McLean, this volume). Christianity adds the particular focus of a personal relationship with God, who empowers people for their actions in the world. The final aspect of connectedness is related to a search for meaning and identity with respect to the Ultimate and other humans. It is through personal connectedness that people find their full sense of individual self as argued by proponents of attachment theory (Bowlby, 1969; Cassidy, 1999; Schore, 2003). Through connectedness, people also work out personal meaning systems and find strength to fulfill their individual tasks in life (Paloutzian & Park, 2005).

The above analysis gives a conceptual definition of spirituality but neglects human questions as people begin their spiritual search. More concretely, then, issues of searching for *meaning* are expressed in questions such as: Who am I? Where do I belong? How do I deal with suffering? Issues of *transcendence* are expressed by: Who or what can I serve? How can I know God? What is the source of my strength? Finally, issues of *connectedness* are expressed by: What is my relationship with other people? What is my relationship with creation?

These definitions of spirituality point to both individual and community aspects within Christian spirituality. The search for the sacred is a search by an individual who is likely to be located within a spiritual community of vertical and horizontal relationships. The vertical relationships comprise individual and corporate ways of connecting with God, whereas the horizontal relationships include connectedness based on a shared identity as spiritual seekers, and as pursuing a shared purpose broadly conceived as worship of God. Although worship is directed towards God, it can be expressed through actions towards creation (nature, people)—actions that indicate surrender to God. Thus, loving one's neighbor (connecting with other humans in ways that fulfill needs and potentiate the others' development) is both a means of connecting with God and with others.

In short, spirituality is a search for meaning and connectedness with the natural world, other people, and with the Ultimate. Such a search is ideally supported by a caring spiritual community. Yet the community itself, as a network of relationships linked by a common purpose, must at least demonstrate connectedness and inclusion if the community is to flourish. A flourishing community is able to nurture individual growth and to receive contributions from those who are developing through their spiritual quest.

HOW SPIRITUALITY CONTRIBUTES TO A
FLOURISHING COMMUNITY

Three case studies are presented to illustrate the contribution of spirituality to flourishing community. In each are discerned the key spiritual principles or practices which enabled or hindered flourishing. Following the case studies, the common themes are discussed in light of community development theory, attachment theory and Trinitarian theology.

Case 1: An intentional Christian Group Within a Neighborhood Community

In the late 1970s a group of young people involved in community work on an inner city housing estate decided to move into accommodation on the estate so they could move from a part time charitable involvement to becoming residents alongside those they were working with. Their thinking was influenced by many new social movements reflected in the broader society and Christian movements, such as development of Christian communes, incarnational theology, radical discipleship and liberation theology. The community members all came to join this community with an active Christian faith developed in churches of different denominations. However they were all looking for more than their middle class institutional churches were offering. They were looking to express their faith in a way that would make a difference to the world around them and where their faith was real beyond a worship service on a Sunday.

Initially three people in their twenties moved in to a run-down terrace, and over time there were four or five houses with up to 15 participants. The venture began with a strong sense of purpose to support the community work and to support each other so that they would persevere. Participants shared finances and domestic duties, lived simply, and spent a lot of time carrying out the various kids clubs, pastoral visiting, fruit co-ops, drop-in centers, and other programs on the estate. Their lives together were also structured around meals together on a daily basis and meetings to grapple with issues in communal life, to reflect on their practices, and to focus on new learning and spiritual nourishment such as prayer, worship and celebration.

This Christian community was the support-base for the community work on the local housing estate and helped to resource other ventures such as the establishment of a church dedicated to the estate residents, a neighborhood center, and various lobbying groups. It was also the hub of many individual nurturing relationships with local residents, who were often struggling with low incomes and a variety of social problems. All of these relationships and activities were demanding, as the social pressures on these inner-city residents were great. Residents felt powerless in the face of poverty, drug taking, wild teenage behavior, and inadequate housing. As individuals, the community members would have found it difficult to stand with these residents in their despair, but as a group with a spiritual center, they had a sense of purpose that enabled them to stay and thrive for many years.

Members of the faith community struggled with low incomes and demanding living conditions, housing was cramped, and local teenagers often put a lot of pressure on these community members with their anti-social behaviors. The sense of taking a path of "costly discipleship" due to one's faith and a need to draw strength from a greater power were foundational to the ability of members to stay committed.

As the community work and relationships formed touched the lives of local residents and teenagers, many of them wanted to explore faith, meaning, God, and what it means to become a Christian. These residents had no relationship with local institutional churches but discovered ways of building on their own spirituality when they encountered the members, and group life, of the Christian community. People became volunteers, looking more closely at what the Christians were doing and exploring their own spirituality. They engaged with the "bigger picture" issues and became part of an inclusive spiritual community.

Over time the members of this Christian community expanded their involvements, and many moved on, although most would still see this experience as having contributed greatly to their own personal growth and identity, their spiritual direction, and their commitments to justice and community involvement long term.

This first case demonstrates five ways in which spirituality affected community flourishing:

1. The spiritual formation of the intentional group members provided the human qualities and motivation to work with the community for change. The human qualities, or virtues, included the foundational

commitment to whole of life spirituality and core values such as justice. Motivation for long-term, costly community engagement was derived from a more radical theology than had been encountered in their suburban churches. The spiritual foundations had been given to these young people as part of churches that taught concern for others and reliance on God rather than one's own strength. These spiritual foundations gave them spiritual power, strength, and vision to engage in such a committed way with the inner city community. In short, spirituality was the catalyst for initiating and maintaining the project of community development. In other literature, some of the qualities of effective catalysts have been suggested, such as honesty, consistency, transparency and accountability (Bergdall, 2003). However, the spiritual qualities and resources of effective catalyst (such as deep compassion for others and reliance on God) have been neglected and should be recognized.

2. The gathered spiritual community allowed for group support, celebration, shared stories and "thicker" connections within the broader community. The community nurtured the lives of members as they grew in maturity while dealing with the challenges of ministering to people struggling with poverty. The process of reflection in the community also helped members to learn from the spiritual journeys of those whom they sought to serve. Thicker connections are bonds that allow for sensitivity, subjectivity, and objectivity (Andrews, 2006). Such thick connections constitute reciprocal relationships of mutual caring. Indeed, John McKnight (2003) depicts caring as the connection of citizens:

> It is one of the quiet tragedies of the 20th century that we have accepted the idea that institutions, rather than families, neighbors, and associations, are the primary sites of care. This mistaken understanding is the cause, rather than the solution, of many of our social problems. Who among us looks forward to old age under the "care" of a nursing home, now called a "care" facility? And what young person surrounded by professional "servicers"—educational, recreational, psychological, correctional—is aware that these professionals are creating a counterfeit community that can never replace the concern, insight, experience, support, and love of a genuine community of care? (p. 10)

and

> Community building is basically about understanding our neighborhood assets and creating new connections among them. (p. 13)

Since deep connectedness is a mark of spirituality, processes of connecting and shared reflection facilitated further spiritual development among members of the spiritual community.

3. The intentional group members had a spiritual focus and thus catalyzed discussion of transcendent issues (meaning, connection to God, etc.). Hence, members of the broader inner city community were challenged to consider and develop their own spirituality.

4. There was an emphasis on recognizing the strengths of individuals within the community. Such recognition allows individuals to "discover their own mental health and innate capacity for wisdom, well-being and resiliency" (Mills & Naim, 2007, p. 49). Further, drawing upon individual strengths directly impacts positive community change (including spiritual flourishing—Andrews, 2006):

> Feelings of respect and appreciation for what each group or person brings to the table have unleashed creativity, insight, and new ideas that get to the core issues and root causes. Perhaps most poignantly, we have witnessed thousands of people who felt they were no good and who had lived for years in fear, guilt, shame, and insecurity, begin to embrace the birthright of their simple beingness: the capacity for intelligence, strength, and loving feelings that are part and parcel of it. This dimension of *human wisdom,* accessible to all—our natural capacity for fresh, insightful thinking—seems to us the missing link to sustainable, positive change. (Mills & Naim, 2007, p. 54)

5. The underlying theory of the community intervention was a spiritual model. Although the asset-based theory of community development had not been articulated at the time of the inner city project, in retrospect the implicit model was of ABCD (Andrews, 2006). There was a focus on individual strengths, empowering people, and walking alongside people. The processes of change were consistent with the roles and processes of ABCD catalysts (Bergdall, 2003), namely realistic reflection, connection, active partnership in the problem and solution, building trust via shared life in the community, encouraging change from and by the community, and communicating a clear ABCD agenda. The ABCD model is also a spiritual model because it draws explicitly from Trinitarian theology (Andrews, 2006). Relationships within God as Trinity are an ideal form of relationships within a flourishing community. The exact nature of Trinitarian relations and their implications for community are discussed more below, but it is sufficient at this point to note that spirituality was implicated in the flourishing of the inner city community because the underlying theory of community development as used implicitly by the intentional group was profoundly spiritual.

Case 2: An Intentional Short Term Spiritual Community to Promote Individual Flourishing

Desert Journeys are trips into desert country in Central Australia for seven to nine days, involving about 16 people of all ages who choose to have an adventure together in wilderness and allow the experience to open them up to a journey in their spiritual landscape. Participants are informally spiritual companions for each other on the journey. Everyone sets out in 4WD vehicles that can take the group away from all signs of civilization, into the vastness, beauty and harshness of the Australian deserts. Participants do not all know each other beforehand and come from all walks of life. Yet they choose immersion in this wilderness with an openness to exploring their sense of spirit, their purpose in life, their relationship to others and to creation itself. Such immersion and openness weaves their stories together, and a strong sense of community is born. Each day travelers help each other with simple tasks of lighting campfires, cooking, setting up beds, exploring the wonders around them, and they begin to step out of their everyday persona and become more present to themselves and each other in work and play.

Over time the conversations around the campfire become filled with what people have noticed from the day and reflections on the vastness of the creation and the creator. People marvel at signs of life in such harsh conditions, they wonder at the variety of landscape and beauty in a supposedly barren place, and they begin to laugh and play with or interact with their surroundings in a way that reminds them of who they are deep down and what they value. They begin to reflect on their own lives and spiritual experiences. The community develops its own shared stories and daily rhythms and adds meanings to the way members relate to each other. All members are included and find their place and their way of contributing so that by the end of the journey, they have a sense of belonging to each other despite relational annoyances or distance caused by age, role, religion, and so on.

This second case addresses the topic of how spirituality of the desert and community in the desert impacts human flourishing:

1. a focus on the spirituality of creation—creation demonstrating the activity of God—brings out wonder and awe that is part of being fully human. In the desert one has a chance to recognize the smallness of one's place in the universe and the intricacy of the creation, the complexity of the ecosystems of life, and the diversity of spaces that at first glance may seem to be characterized by nothingness. In the busyness of life we often lose track of ultimate questions, of our place in the universe. We lose touch with the big picture, of being part of the broader creation and of fitting into the grand scheme of

things. The desert experiences prompted a sense of meaning and connectedness with God and nature. That sense of wonder and awe is a spiritual experience (Otto, 1917/1950), consistent with a sense of spiritual well-being. In addition to being a spiritual activity in itself, meaning-making is also a form of spiritual coping conducive to psycho-social health and flourishing (Paloutzian & Park, 2005).

2. The structure of the program allows people to simplify life and experience the spirituality of connectedness to others. Simplicity of living forces one to take time to look around, both at the desert and one's own life. The fact of being part of a team in a remote place forces individuals to depend on each other and on each other's strengths. In such a community people discover each other, are forced to interrelate and depend on each other and grow a space that is greater than the sum of each part. In such connectedness there is a stripping of pretence, roles, or persona so a real relationship can develop. The false self hinders the capacity for stillness and feeling touched by God. Simplicity and self-emptying of all that is false or superficial are spiritual principles. In Christian terms they mirror the kenosis (self-emptying) of God, as depicted in Philippians 2. Self-emptying is a pre-requisite for spiritual formation, as Rolnick (2007) states:

> Following the example of Christ, being drawn out of the self has a kenotic quality, an emptying and humbling of the self (Phil. 2:5–8). As we 'let the same mind be in [us] that was in Christ Jesus,' humility is a prerequisite, an invitational openness to being formed by Christ, the source, exemplar, and measure of all that is true, good, and beautiful. In being formed by Christ, we become active partakers of the strange narrative in which the first become last, he last become first, the master becomes servant of all, and sinners are turned and sanctified. (p. 256)

As a consequence of self-emptying and simplicity, there is space for human and spiritual embrace. The metaphor of embrace is used by Volf (1996) to indicate welcoming one another as Christ welcomed us (Romans 15:7). Kenosis and embrace are central Christian themes found in Trinitarian theology (as Father, Son and Holy Spirit give themselves in love to each other), Christology (as in the outstretched arms of Christ on the cross towards the godless), and the doctrine of salvation (the open arms of the father receiving the prodigal son). As individuals experience and respond to God's embrace, they are able to connect to (embrace) others. Hence, the desert journeys' emphasis on emptying invites spiritual flourishing via divine and human embrace.

3. In such a desert context there is space and encouragement to reflect and play. Both children and adults benefit from play—not just as a break from work demands, but as valuable self-expression, learning

and interaction. In everyday life responsibilities can reduce one's focus to role-demands, over time even affecting one's psychological well-being and blocking sensations of the real world. Some forms of therapy emphasize playful expression as a way of fostering healthy development of the self (Meares, 2005). Simplicity can open people to sensations that have previously been dulled. Time and space can enable playfulness to be rediscovered and, in the process, people become attuned to God at play in the world. This attunement can open space in one's spirit to allow God's touch, thus allowing for individual spirituality to emerge and flourish. The image of the securely attached child at play with the fully-attuned parent (Benjamin, 1995) can be applied, by analogy, to one's relationship with God. A believer's relationship with God has been depicted as an attachment relationship (Kirkpatrick, 1999; Miner, 2007), although qualities of playfulness have not been fully addressed in theoretical models. Since creativity and play are linked, there is often a sense of "God at play" as humans ponder the created universe. Further, just as the child enjoys the responsiveness of the parent to her play, so the believer enjoys a sense of God's responding in play, or to play, in the world. Thus, Biblical images of children playing signify the presence and blessing of God in the world (Zechariah 8:5). Further, the child seeks parental touch in play and in stillness. Similarly, believers enjoy the sense of God's touch in their play and in stillness and awe.

Case 3. From Individual Flourishing to Community Flourishing

The Gathering is an informally organized faith community in the Blue Mountains where 20 to 30 people of all ages seek to express their Christian faith or their searching for faith in a communal context. For the past eight years they have met together weekly to share a simple meal and share their lives, their spirituality, their struggles and joys. When they meet they may pray, discuss scripture, learn about social justice issues they are involved in, or explore creative worship together. Their concern for each other is expressed beyond the meetings in working bees at their homes, support when members are sick, and sharing the parenting challenges of the group. This commitment beyond the meeting times arises out of an understanding of discovering God as present in the whole of their lives. There is also a strong commitment to social justice issues beyond the group, and this is expressed in activities such as the community meal. Once a week lonely or isolated members of the broader community are invited into a family home: everyone contributes what food they have with much laughter, argument, friendly discussion, eating and drinking. A simple night of hospitality helps people who are often known mainly as clients find a place to belong. Perhaps the best way to express the benefit of a safe place of hospitality is in the following words of a participant when asked at his birthday to make a speech about what really matters to him and he replied, "What I value in life is spirit expressed through community, and I find it here in this group."

This faith community has been a safe place to bring up children and allow them as adolescents to explore and challenge beliefs and spiritual directions. The teenagers in the community have seen adults grapple with their spiritual journeys with some openness, and the young people are constantly drawn in to discussion and directions for the group. This is a place for teenagers to speak to and be heard by all age groups, which gives them an alternative to the pressures of identification with peers alone. As all of us sit around a candle to hear what our spirits are grappling with, these teenagers can stay a part of a community that offers them belonging at the same time as they move to explore their own worlds in the process of individuation. These young people flourish and make a mature contribution to the broader community, as they have deep spiritual roots developed by many and diverse caring mentoring relationships and experiences. This intergenerational inclusiveness also benefits the vitality of the faith community, which cannot stay with practices that serve only one generation.

This third case study explores how individual flourishing within a community works to promote further community flourishing.

1. Individuals have the chance to find their full potential in the context of others, and this is most easily done where people have some commitment to each other. Those who realize their potential in community are most able to contribute to others.
2. Communities are important for nourishing and developing the spirituality of young people through mentoring, modeling, teaching, and allowing space to explore and challenge. Young people are able to experience relationships and explore the world beyond the family without simply being abandoned to the peer group and mass culture. Again, those young people who are spiritually more mature within a community are more likely to seek avenues for caring for others within and without the community.
3. Christian hospitality provides a space for people to be nourished in a home environment. Where the provision of food is a shared task, community members both give and receive hospitality according to their means. Reciprocal nurturing is enjoined within Christianity (e.g., Galatians 6:1–10; Ephesians 5:33) as a way of contributing to individual and group flourishing. Thus, Christian spirituality puts high value on mutual care, where people are encouraged to give in

love and not just take from each other. People who are nourished then contribute to the community. The purpose of such community is not purely for the sake of those involved in it, but for the mutual empowerment of each other to make a positive difference in the world—in communities, in homes, among friends, and in wider society. The reciprocal and inter-generational development of people through care-seeking and care-giving is recognized by attachment theory (George & Solomon, 1999). At an individual level, those who are securely attached (and emotionally well-nourished by their attachment relationships) are best able to promote secure attachment in others. Since communities are webs of human relationships, including relationships based on attachment functions, it is not surprising that a similar causation has been observed for community care-seeking and care-giving.

CONCLUSION

The case analyses revealed themes relevant to understanding spirituality and community flourishing from perspectives of community development theory, Trinitarian theology, and attachment theory.

From an Asset Based theory of Community Development (ABCD theory), key issues were connectedness and a focus on strengths. The theory of ABCD holds that paternalistic, hierarchical, problem-focused interventions to change communities are very limited and may alienate people, or even worsen community functioning. Instead the primary goal of community development is seen as fostering relationships for their own sake (Andrews, 2006). Associated with the emphasis on multiple, reciprocal relationships is a positive nurturing of individual strengths (Mills, 2007). Together, the positive and relational approaches to community development mirror the nature and activities of the Christian Trinitarian God who is the source of all relationality and human strengths, and expresses relationality and reciprocal caring within the Godhead (Gunton, 1993, 1997, 2002). Hence, community development based on spiritual principles that mirror the nature and activities of God are most likely to promote individual and group flourishing.

Christian theology further highlights important themes of kenosis, embrace, and play as qualities of the Trinitarian God of relevance to intentional spiritual communities (Gunton, 1993, 2002; Rolnick, 2007; Volf, 1996). It is not immediately obvious that self-emptying, intentional embrace and play would be critical qualities for flourishing communities. However, in the present Western culture, dominated by assumptions of autonomy, control and self-interest, it is important to consider the counter-cultural ideal of self-emptying with all of its implications for vulnerability. There is a longing for connectedness, yet Christian theology points to the sacrifice of embrace. Work dominates people's lives, to the extent that work can seem the major source of meaning and purpose (Pines, 2000). However, play is crucial to the growth of the self (Meares, 2005). It is salutary to be reminded that play is also encouraged in Christian theology and contributes to the openness and vulnerability that are necessary for individual and group flourishing.

Finally, attachment theory clarifies the reciprocal relationship between individual and community flourishing by its analysis of care-seeking and care-giving behavior systems. Within attachment theory is the often-overlooked point that the purpose of secure attachment relationships is not just proximity and security for the individual, but such security is also the basis for optimum expression of the care-giving system. The reciprocity found in attachment theory is also consistent with Christian theology's emphasis on mutual caring. People who are nurtured in a spiritual community are likely to develop secure attachment relationships, develop expectations around mutual caring, experience spiritual empowerment to care for others, and hence promote secure attachment relationships with others by their sensitive care-giving.

In conclusion, reflection upon case studies of intentional community development has revealed themes of connectedness, inclusiveness (embrace), kenosis, and play as important for community flourishing. Within flourishing communities, individuals can explore identity, meaning, and relationships with God and others. Not only do flourishing communities foster individual flourishing, but those flourishing individuals, in turn, contribute to flourishing communities. Spirituality is inherent in the thick connectedness of community life; spirituality motivates individual attitudes and actions conducive to community formation; and Christian spirituality provides a model for asset based community development. In these ways spirituality is intrinsic to community flourishing.

REFERENCES

Andrews, D. (2006). *Compassionate Community Work.* Carlisle, UK: Piquant Editions.

Benjamin, J. (1995). *Like subjects, love objects: Essays on recognition and sexual difference.* New Haven: Yale University Press.

Bergdall, T. (2003). Reflections on the Catalytic Role of an Outsider in 'Asset Based Community Development' (ABCD). Internal report retrieved on December 9, 2010 from: http://www.abcdinstitute.org/publications/downloadable/

Bowlby, J. (1969). *Attachment. Vol.1 of Attachment and Loss.* New York: Basic Books.

Cassidy, J. (1999). The nature of the child's ties. In J. Cassidy & P. R. Shaver (Eds.), *Handbook of attachment: Theory, research, and clinical applications* (pp. 3–20). New York: Guilford.

George, C., & Solomon, J. (1999). Attachment and caregiving: The caregiving behavioral system. In J. Cassidy & P. R. Shaver (Eds.), *Handbook of attachment: Theory, research, and clinical applications* (pp. 649–670). New York: Guilford.

Gunton, C. (1993). *The one, the three and the many: God, creation and the culture of modernity.* Cambridge: Cambridge University Press.

Gunton, C. (1997). *The promise of trinitarian theology.* London: T&T Clark.

Gunton, C. E. (2002). *Act and being: Towards a theology of the divine attributes.* London: SCM Press.

Kelly, A., & Sewell, S. (1988). *With head, heart and hand.* Brisbane: Bollarong.

Kirkpatrick, L. A. (1999). Attachment and religious representations and behavior. In J. Cassidy & P. R. Shaver (Eds.), *Handbook of attachment: Theory, research, and clinical applications* (pp. 803–822). New York: Guilford.

McKnight, J. L. (2003). *Regenerating community: The Recovery of a space for citizens.* The IPR Distinguished Public Policy Lecture Series, May 29, 2003, Northwestern University, Evanston, IL.

Meares, R. (2005). *The metaphor of play: Origin and breakdown of personal being* (3rd ed.). New York: Routledge.

Mills, R. C., & Naim, A. C. (2007). Towards a peaceable paradigm: Seeking innate wellness in communities and impacts on urban violence and crime. [Electronic version]. *National Civic Review, 45–55.* DOI: 10.1002/ncr.194

Miner, M. (2007). Back to the basics in attachment to God: Revisiting theory in light of theology. *Journal of Psychology and Theology, 35*(2), 112–122.

Minuchin, S. (1974). *Families and family therapy.* Cambridge, MA: Harvard University Press.

Otto, R. (1950). *The idea of the holy: An inquiry into the non-relational factor in the idea of the divine and its relation to the rational.* London: Oxford University Press. (Original work published 1917)

Paloutzian, R., & Park, C. L. (2005). *Handbook of the psychology of religion and spirituality.* New York: Guilford.

Pines, A. M. (2000). Treating career burnout: A psychodynamic existential perspective. *Journal of Clinical Psychology/In Session, 56*(5), 633–642.

Rolnick, P. (2007). *Person, grace, and God.* Grand Rapids, MI: Eerdmans.

Schore, A. N. (2003). *Affect regulation and the repair of the self.* New York: Norton.

Spilka, B. (1993, August). *Spirituality: Problems and directions in operationalizing a fuzzy concept.* Paper presented at the Annual Conference of the American Psychological Association, Toronto, Canada.

Volf, M. (1996). *Exclusion and embrace: A theological exploration of identity, otherness and reconciliation.* Nashville, TN: Abingdon.

Volf, M. (1998). *After our likeness: The church as the image of the trinity.* Grand Rapids, MI: Eerdmans.

Watson-Thompson, J., Fawcett, S. B., & Schultz, J. A. (2008). Differential effects of strategic planning on community change in two urban neighborhood coalitions. *American Journal of Community Psychology, 42,* 25–38.

Zinnbauer, B. J., & Pargament, K. (2005). Religiousness and spirituality. In R. Paloutzian & C. L. Park (Eds.), *Handbook of the psychology of religion and spirituality* (pp. 21–42). New York: Guilford.

CHAPTER 10

GUIDANCE AND HUMAN FLOURISHING

The Contribution of Spirituality Explored Through Mentoring and Life Coaching

Diann L. Feldman
Feldman and Associates

Alison D. Feldman
University of Southern Queensland

ABSTRACT

Mentoring and life coaching are relationship-based helping and guiding processes. When these processes foster a spiritual journey in response to someone's searching, clients uncover a higher order of living that enables them to flourish. This spiritual journey is a more sustainable journey in the long term; this journey is not defined by, or reliant upon, destination or attainment only. In this paper we explore how a life-direction or noble purpose, drawn from a spiritual framework and integrated into all areas of one's life, orients human existence to one of meaning and significance beyond oneself.

Beyond Well-Being: Spirituality and Human Flourishing, pages 199–214
Copyright © 2012 by Information Age Publishing

We live in an era that promotes success mainly through the pursuit of high performance and perfection. Success is often perceived as high attainment in five areas: prosperity, prestige, position, power, or pleasure (Jensen, 2002). High attainment in any or all of these five areas is not inherently negative, but it nevertheless has considerable impact on whether people flourish. To flourish is to thrive through growing vigorously and reaching a heightened level of development or influence. Yet one can be accomplished in any or all of the five areas and not feel or experience the wellness, hope or even satisfaction with everyday life and living that is associated with flourishing. Attainment and accomplishment without development or influence often leave people searching for more. Hence attainment in itself does not confer flourishing, but may initiate the search towards flourishing. One vehicle that people use to enhance attainment and flourishing is life coaching.

Today, life coaching is one of the fastest growing "helping professions," evident in the significant number of new coaching businesses established each year (30,000 in the last ten years, according to Burkes, 2008) and the number of qualified counselors re-establishing themselves as life coaches. At the same time, mentoring is experiencing a strong resurgence both in community and organizational settings. More and more, people are being thrown onto their own resources in order to thrive amidst today's increasingly complex life-pressures. Institutions have proven to be less concerned with an individual's struggle or circumstances (Bowsher, 2007), or in providing a nurturing environment where spiritual growth and thriving may occur. People have become disenchanted and lost confidence in institutions (Klein, 2000). Spiritual direction, however, is inherently personal and very individual. Human thriving, therefore, may best be addressed through processes that remove the pressure of an institution, its agenda and/or its inherent power structures.

The pursuit of success in terms of "how much I do" is unsustainable in the long term. It is unsustainable because achievement in something usually leads people to recognize how much more remains to be attained. The authors propose that spirituality, including spiritual intelligence, is an essential element in human flourishing.

> Spiritual intelligence is the intelligence with which we accept our deepest meanings, values, purposes and highest motivations. It is the intelligence with which we exercise goodness, truth, beauty, and compassion in our lives. It is, if you like, the soul's intelligence. If you think of *soul* as that channelling capacity in human beings that brings things up from the deeper and richer dimensions of imagination and spirit into our daily lives, families, organisations, and institutions. (Zohar & Marshall, 2004, p. 3, emphasis in original)

A life that embraces spirituality at its core moves beyond a focus of attainment in the five areas (although these may be a by-product of the journey).

Instead people flourish because of the progressive realization and internalization (Jensen, 2002) of who they are and how their "being" is part of something greater beyond themselves. This spiritual journey is a more long-term sustainable journey, not defined by, or reliant upon, destination or attainment only.

In this chapter, the authors propose that a sustainable journey is most profound when individuals are conscious of the dimension of spirituality. The thesis is that guiding individuals through the helping processes of mentoring and life coaching (Schein, 1999) can shape someone's life direction and leadership and accelerate their discovery of spirit and human flourishing. First, the importance of the practitioner's perspective is discussed, followed by an analysis of the meaning and importance of spirituality for one's life journey. Next, processes of mentoring and life coaching are described. How spirituality can be incorporated into guidance processes is then addressed. The chapter concludes with some comments on the transformative power of mentoring and life coaching.

A PRACTITIONER'S PERSPECTIVE

This chapter is written from our perspective of working in the field as practitioners in learning, personal and leadership development, mentoring, and coaching. This experience incorporates the development of a project that has reached over 10,000 women from across the globe, including the United States of America, England, Australia, and New Zealand; the life coaching resource book has also been translated for use in the Philippines, France, Spain, Africa, Middle East, Central America, South America, Greece, Netherlands, and South Asia. During 25 years in organizational development, human development, mentoring, coaching, counseling, community engagement, adult education, learning and development, the authors have walked alongside people of all ages, cultures, and experiences both in Australia and from across the globe, in their journeys of discovery and growth. What has become evident is that most people acknowledge a desire to flourish or achieve beyond where they are, and seek a pathway that reaches a maximized state of development and fulfillment. A fellow sojourner is critical in supporting the individual's discovery and possibilities on this journey. In contemporary language, such a fellow sojourner can be a mentor or life coach. Mentoring and life coaching are two particular helping processes (Schein, 1999) that generate in others a greater realization of the unique way in which they, as humans, can flourish. Both help people to seek and experience wellness, significance, and fulfillment. Both work best when drawn from a "positive" psychology (Seligman & Csikszentmihalyi,

2000). Positive psychology suggests that spirituality, one of the six core virtues, is a means to attain wellbeing and flourishing.

SPIRITUALITY

What is spirituality? There is no single, absolute answer to this question. Whereas most definitions "include a descriptor of transcendence, ultimacy, or divinity, other components of the definitions vary greatly" (Giacalone & Jurkiewicz, 2003, p. 6). Some treat spirituality as a behavior (the personal expression), others as an objective reality (that which involves ultimate and personal truths), or a subjective experience. In some definitions it is described as a search (emerging from moments in which the individual questions the meaning of personal existence), while in others it is "an animating force" or "capacity" (Giacalone & Jurkiewicz, 2003, p. 6).

We also live in a global society where spirituality is expressed in many forms, embedded in many cultural and religious heritages, and conceptualized in many ways. Despite this, however, we have identified in our work some common threads or intents verified by other researchers.

Firstly, spirituality is living out a noble purpose or life direction that transcends one's self, situation, barriers, or seasons of life. Stephen Covey defines purpose as the voice of the human spirit—full of hope and intelligence, resilient by nature, boundless in its potential to serve the common good—your voice, your calling, your soul's code (Covey, 2004). Spirituality as purpose and direction acts like the magnetic force of a true north position on a compass in someone's life. "For those of us who spend our lives in organizations, this means listening to the voice of the soul and the deep yearning for the sense of purpose, meaning, belonging that echoes in the cubicles and corridors of our workplaces" (Klein, 2000, p. 64).

Secondly, it is an inner energy, resource, or state (Nash, 2003) that is expressed in outward behaviors and actions that are aligned with a person's spirit, noble purpose, or life direction. Thirdly, it is a framework of principles and values (natural laws) that are able to stand the test of time and result in predictable acceleration of human expression and experience. "Spirit comes from the Latin word *spiritus*, meaning 'breath' and is often viewed as a vital principle or animating force traditionally believed to be within living beings, one's essential nature" (Anderson, 2000, p. 16).

Lastly, spirituality, when uncovered, both inspires and animates human existence because it acts as a "tipping point" (Gladwell, 2002). This term comes from the world of epidemiology and describes a seemingly unpredictable moment when a slight incremental difference creates a disproportionate momentum for change (Nash, 2003).

Spirituality draws people to a higher order or place beyond oneself—sometimes expressed as divine or supernatural equanimity. It draws someone's focus away from the compelling challenges of the immediate circumstance, and provides them with a higher order view of who they are, their story and purpose, and from this place defines behaviors and actions that respond to the present situation or circumstances.

> Imagine you have been flying in an airplane through dark clouds and turbulence. Suddenly the plane soars above the dark clouds into a clear boundless sky. You are inspired and exhilarated by this emergence into a new dimension of freedom . . . As this new awareness begins to become vivid and almost unbroken, there occurs what [ancient Hindu writings] call a 'turning above in the seat of consciousness,' a personal, utterly non-conceptual revelation of what we are, why we are here, and how we should act. This 'amounts in the end to nothing less than a new life, a new birth, you could say a resurrection.' (Rinpoche, 1992, p. 40)

Our extensive experience has identified that no matter who the client is, their needs can usually be translated into one of four spiritual searches: the search for meaning and purpose (the sacred); the search for wellbeing (integration); the search for belonging (deep connection); and the search for congruency (consistent principles and values). Our work focuses on empowerment and amplification as critical elements in a person's search. Both elements create a stronger tipping point than a more traditional methodology of deficit or gap assessment.

Spirituality offers something beyond the tangible measures of success and points individuals towards a potential flourishing of the human spirit expressed in a higher order of living. The Greek term *sophrosyne* identifies the uniquely-tempered balance of wisdom, intelligence and care upon which one relies in order to integrate spirituality into practical everyday living (Goleman, 1995). Spirituality uniquely shapes the elements of human flourishing through increased awareness of, or attachment to, a divine presence, which acts as a transitive force. The impact of such awareness or attachment is evident in all behaviors and actions that follow in an integrated way across all areas of a person's life.

MENTORING

Mentoring is a long-term mutual partnership between two people—the mentor and the mentee/client. Mentoring originated in Greek literature (circa 800BC) in Homer's *Odyssey*. Mentor is depicted as a companion and confidante of Odysseus, the king of Ithaca. Mentor becomes the guardian and teacher of Odysseus' son Telemachus when Odysseus leaves Ithaca to fight the Trojan War (Alter, n.d.). Homer provides insight into the character of Mentor when he describes Mentor as a trusted friend whose wisdom in the ways of the world was tempered with gentleness (Bell, 2002). Mentoring is a process of ongoing dialogue that focuses on discovery, exploration and support, addressing needs (known and yet to be identified) as expressed by the mentee. A mentor helps the mentee to release his or her inner wisdom; such wisdom comprises knowing and sensing grounded-in values and beliefs, and underscores the individual's part in a larger purpose. This inner wisdom enables a mentee, with the support and counsel of a mentor, to find his or her unique purpose, equip him or herself for the journey, tackle issues, and address blockages in a more intentional way. A mentor engages the mentee in open dialogues, which develop capacity and experience through his or her spiritual framework. Each individual (whether mentor or mentee) brings his or her own uniqueness to the process. Just as a thumbprint identifies each of us uniquely, mentoring works to enhance one's individual uniqueness. Mentoring helps to uncover one's spiritual core, shapes his or her uniqueness and inner wisdom, and empowers him or her to move to higher intentions aligned with noble purpose.

Mentoring that explores spiritual needs involves four searches—meaning and purpose, wellbeing, belonging, and congruency. Spiritually-oriented mentoring addresses something that cannot be met by traditional training or learning methods, which tend to focus on knowledge or skills and rules or norms, usually set by others (Vilnai-Yavetz & Rafaeli, 2003).

In contrast to general mentoring, spiritually-based mentoring is a joint, deep engagement: "Having found our own sense of values, gifts and legacy, we will naturally engage with our colleagues in a deeper conversation" (Klein, 2000, p. 64). The mentoring relationship rests on the mutual commitment and common human desire of living one's noble purpose and life-direction, of searching and exploring together.

Mentoring may be sponsored or even formally advocated by an organization. The mentor's role is to focus on the individual and his or her needs, and to absorb the pressure of the organizational agenda and power in a manner that enables the individual to flourish more freely, and over time to respond effectively to the challenges of organizational life.

LIFE COACHING

Life coaching is a short (usually less than 12 months), fixed term (Stanley, 2006); outcomes-oriented (Dilts, 2003), future focused (Coutu, 2009), and co-active (Longhurst, 2006) helping relationship between the coach and the client. In a survey of 2,298 coaches conducted by the International Coach Federation in 2003, 66% indicated a relationship between three to

12 months in length (Grant & Zackon, 2004). Life coaching focuses on behaviors and actions that move people from where they are to higher levels of outcome effectiveness. The methods and tools used in the process are activated by the coach, while outcomes are owned by the client. A life coach helps a client to reshape his or her mental infrastructure in order to build conscious competence (Dilts, 2003) in behaviors that shape life-purpose. The purpose of life coaching is to incorporate spiritual actions aligned with an individual's spiritual framework into a level of living that is consciously competent. An individual's uniqueness is always upheld in the life coaching process. Life coaching enables a person to behave consciously in ways that will allow him or her to achieve his or her unique noble purpose.

Life coaching has close affinities with the forward-looking, goal-centered emphases of brief solution-focused counseling, with added emphases on explicit psycho-education and the client's motivation and practice to bring about change (Chapman & Skerten, 2006). Organizations may sponsor life coaching for their people. The life coach is normally not a member of the organization. Such an external perspective removes the pressure of the organization's agenda and expectations so that clients, in time, develop habitual behaviors that best respond to these pressures. Coaching both demands and causes a fundamental change in the way people perceive themselves and others (Whitmore, 2002).

GUIDANCE PROCESSES

There are many opportunities and tools that move people towards a greater experience of human flourishing. We have identified mentoring and life coaching as two such distinct and unique guidance processes because of their relationship-ethos and foundation rather than any reliance upon structure, hierarchy, status, or power as drivers for transformation. See Table 10.1 for a comparison between features of mentoring and life coaching.

Both mentoring and life coaching are sojourner-relationships between two people—the guide (mentor or coach) and a client. They share common elements including: establishment of an authentic, honest, open, high-trust and confidential relationship between the guide and the client; the creation over time of chemistry between the sojourners, which shapes the open space in which these relationships evolve; and the collaborative exchange of wisdom (knowledge combined with insight, experience, and perceptiveness). A mentor or life coach will use influence in the process of discovery and exploration, yet honor fully any decisions by the client to transform, change or adapt. Such honoring of the client's autonomy is the ultimate empowerment of another because it removes from the process any real or perceived power differentials.

TABLE 10.1 Comparison of Mentoring and Life Coaching

Comparison of:	Mentoring	Life Coaching
relationship "chemistry"	exemplar chemistry	regard chemistry
Length	a long term mutual partnership between two people	a short, fixed term, helping relationship between two people
Process	ongoing dialogue of ever deepening discovery, exploration and shaping of spirituality through 4 searches and transitions	outcomes-oriented and co-active conversations responding to the presenting needs within the 4 searches at a given point in time
Focus	life transitions, intentions and choices, insights and inspirations	immediate present → future aspirations, needs, decisions and aspirations
Quality	reflective, evolving, interdependent	reflexive, proactive, catalyst
Guide's role	seasoned travel companion	local tour guide

HOW SPIRITUALITY CAN BE INTEGRATED INTO MENTORING AND LIFE COACHING

Challenging Contemporary Myths

Imperative in our work has been the rejection of contemporary myths that shape how people exist and find greater life satisfaction and contentment. The first myth is that "busyness" is good. From our experience people are caught in busyness and the "super person" status trap, believing that doing, controlling, performing, and having more will increase life satisfaction and contentment. Pride in this status trap pervades our society and its workplaces. Even those employed in a spiritual occupation, such as pastors, are caught in this busyness trap. In a recent study of 270 pastors (Chandler, 2009), it was found that spiritual dryness was a result of inordinate ministerial demands, draining their emotional, cognitive, spiritual, and physical energy reserves, and was a primary predictor of emotional exhaustion, which is the stress dimension of burnout. This finding establishes a link between the state of the spirituality of pastors and burnout (Chandler, 2009). "I rarely meet anyone who is not proud to claim that they are 'too busy.' To be 'too busy' is treated as a sign of being deeply engaged in life, yet as anyone who has ever been in love, cooked a meal, tended a garden, or raised a child knows, being in a bonded and deep relationship is not based on busyness. It is based on stillness and listening" (Klein, 2000, p. 64). Helping people to discover the empowering release of themselves through pausing, listening to an inner presence—a wisdom and voice—and reflection, frees them from the trap of busyness.

We have also focused on challenging a second myth; the notion that there exists a magical success equation that will fulfill someone's life, or that luck will provide a miraculous life experience and outcome. Instead we reshape people's mental infrastructure by helping them find their individual stories (paths or journeys). This involves a combination of embracing their uniqueness and core values, exploring their passion for making a difference for others and self, and discovering their individual spiritual core or noble purpose. These foundations of story, making a difference, and purpose, both orient their searches and shape their life-directions. This life-direction then acts like a true north magnetic force throughout the life journey. Life-direction is then integrated across all areas of life, drawing each individual toward a place of significance and contentment, a fulfilling presence today and in their future, and a more holistic and deeply satisfying path. See Figure 10.1 for the "directions" of mentoring and coaching conversations.

Another third contemporary myth relates to work/life balance and relies upon the assumptions that (a) some perfect balance can be found, and

Direction	Focus	Description
	Orient self	explore uniqueness - beliefs, values, culture, ethnicity, preferences, dynamics, life experiences, capacity, and situation (meaning)
	Discover one's compelling	discover identity and one's story – one's compelling narrative (noble purpose) beyond one's self
	Embrace life	explore habits, behaviours and actions that honour, build and shape uniqueness in alignment with noble purpose (congruency)
	Accelerate	embrace, amplify and activate transitive elements - priorities and opportunities of the pathway, and empowered capacity to live this noble purpose

Figure 10.1   The multi-direction nature of mentoring and life coaching conversations.

(b) this balance will remain constant over time. Instead, through our guidance, a person experiences freedom by integrating his or her noble purpose across all areas of life and discovering how easy it is to align with, and best reflect, his or her spirituality. This integration removes the exhausting experience of juggling many priorities, an experience that often leaves people feeling that something has been sacrificed in order for something else to be gained. Integration is a process that utilizes energy and resource, rather than spending it. For example, behaviors and actions in one area of life may in fact bring value and outcomes into another area of life, which means a person does not need to expend energy catalyzing two or more actions.

A fourth contemporary myth is that success in work is a result of meeting the pressure to perform and to advance one's career, or doing more, or progressing through layers and levels at an expedited rate. Instead, "with a clear personal vision and intention, work flows organically. We feel in tune with the task, and alive with energy and enthusiasm. Nothing stops us from our purpose. It is this inherent strength of focus that gives work meaning" (Toms & Toms, 2000, p. 24).

When work flows from a focus on others rather than individual success, it is spiritually oriented and brings personal happiness. Denis Waitley, psychologist and author, draws attention to the concept of happiness. He considers that happiness is a spiritual experience of living where individuals live every moment from a higher-order place of love, grace and gratitude (Waitley, 1984). Happiness is not a destination, the assets we own, the prosperity we achieve, how we look or dress, nor is it something we buy and consume. This is similarly acknowledged by Tenzin Gyatso, the 14th Dalai Lama, who notes that "the more we care for the happiness of others, the greater our own sense of well-being becomes...However capable and skillful an individual may be, left alone, he or she will not survive. Interdependence, of course, is a fundamental law of nature" (Gyatso, n.d., n.p.). Grasping the essence of happiness as being directed towards others leads people towards embracing leadership in their settings.

Fostering Spiritual Leadership

A spiritual concept of leadership based on the happiness of others leads to recognition that leadership is not for the elite, but for all:

> Leadership is first and foremost a spiritual—emotional, inner-focused, feeling, affective, thinking—activity. The core theme of the conception of leadership is this: *leading is inner-based and outer-focused, not outer-based and inner-focused*...Everyone has both the opportunity and the responsibility to take on leadership roles. (Braskamp, 2008, p. 1, emphasis in original)

We draw upon the work of Robert K. Greenleaf, author of many seminal works on servant-leadership, in our mentoring and coaching. Servant-leadership helps shift people from a "what's in it for me" consumeristic and self-only view of the world, to a more compassionate, caring and others-oriented perspective. It is about being deeply moved to enhance the long-term welfare of others, and in so doing we free ourselves from the desire for personal gain (Kurth, 2003). Servant-leadership draws people toward the opportunity to expand one's service to others through leadership, and in achieving beyond one's own capacity.

Robert Greenleaf articulated his social vision based on servant leadership:

> This is my thesis: caring for persons, the more able and the less able serving each other, is the rock upon which a good society is built...If a better society is to be built, one that is more just and more loving, one that provides greater creative opportunity for its people, then the most open course is to *raise both the capacity to serve and the very performance as servant* of existing major institutions by new regenerative forces operating within them. (Greenleaf, 1991, p. 49, emphasis in original)

When someone explores, through coaching and mentoring, how he or she serves others unconditionally through just and loving means, he or she traverses a new landscape in life, a landscape that is diverse and beautiful and beyond oneself.

> *Love* is an undefinable term, and its manifestations are both subtle and infinite. But it begins, I believe, with one absolute condition: unlimited liability! As soon as one's liability for another is qualified *to any degree*, love is diminished by that much." (Greenleaf, 1991, p. 38, emphasis in original)

The sacred search of purpose and meaning is recognizing that one's life is not only about oneself, but how one serves others and makes a difference for others.

> Spiritually inspired service is *selfless action, inspired and actuated by love and the intent to contribute to the highest good of all, with no immediate concern for personal gain.* (Kurth, 2003, p. 448, emphasis in original)

Our work focuses on life direction (or personal mission), as an expression of the spirituality inherent in noble purpose, as creating a difference for others, and through serving others, finding meaning in a higher place, beyond one's own desires (see Figure 10.2 for role of spirituality in coaching and mentoring). Servant-leadership is about everyone, together, making a difference through serving where they are—no matter what their circumstances. The servant leader is servant first; leadership begins with

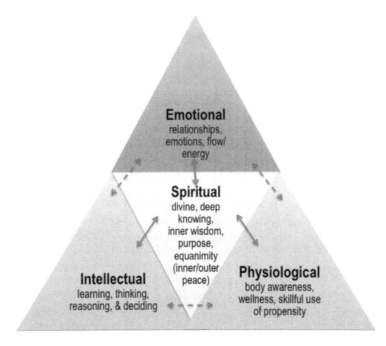

Figure 10.2 The connectivity of four human intelligences in mentoring and life coaching.

a natural feeling that one wants to serve first, and then conscious choice brings one to aspire to lead (Greenleaf, 1991).

Leadership, then, involves embracing an opportunity to serve with others on a larger scale, and inherently exists in relationships between people. When people experience serving others in real and authentic ways, although it may not be the focus of serving, one sees the enormous power of the human spirit. When one glimpses the depth and breadth of the human spirit, even in the most difficult of situations, one cannot leave without being moved more deeply within oneself. When one is living out his or her purpose through acts of service (love and compassion without limits), he or she meets and experiences spirituality in human expression. It is in experiencing this expression that a renewed sense of awe and wonder emerges. This draws people to a deeper and more real place, a place of knowing, awareness and consciousness that to flourish in our human form is to recognize that our lives have meaning and purpose beyond just the living of them.

LIFE COACHING AND MENTORING AS TRANSFORMATION

There is transformative power in spiritually-based life coaching, as demonstrated by the following communication from O'Neal and Stockdale concerning a life coaching program developed by the authors of this chapter. The program, "The Significant Women," has currently reached over 10,000 women from across the globe including the United States of America, England, Australia, and New Zealand. The resource has been translated for use in the Philippines, France, Spain, Africa, Middle East, Central America, South America, Greece, Netherlands, and South Asia. The principles of spiritually-informed coaching are embedded in this life coaching program.

> I just recently finished coaching two groups of women through The Significant Women, and I don't think I've ever seen this much life change in just 10 weeks time. I have been a women's ministry director and pastor for six years and the hardest concept for women to grasp is that they are truly acceptable, lovable, worthy—exactly as they are. As women walk through this resource, they come to a place of not simply accepting who they are, but loving themselves and their story. They see that God designed their personality, gifts, and abilities and even their story for His specific purposes, and then He provides the tools to live it out in His grace. The freedom that comes from living as God designed you to live affects every relationship and every aspect of life. It has been exciting to watch women move forward in this freedom." (Participant, "The Significant Woman," USA, personal communication, March 3 2008)

> This time last fall 2007, we were very excited about offering The Significant Women. The format was different from our traditional format for Bible studies. The value of looking closely inward was difficult for some but the majority of ladies left with greater purpose, a deeper understanding of their gifts and talents and a solid mission statement for life. The testimony of a young wife and mother has been life changing. She expressed to me that she now could say 'no' and set stronger boundaries without feelings of guilt after she had worked through her mission statement. She was convinced of the truths and how they could help other ladies in their walk with Christ. The relationships that are developing with life coaches/peer coaches are powerful. The material is excellently done and we are finding that it is bringing up so many issues that women are facing today in their spiritual journey and I feel that it is a call back to the basics of where we need to go to find our significance. I see women using this tool for a lifetime of searching and getting back to the essentials of their purpose of Kingdom building using the time, gifts and talents in an honoring way to bring glory to God. (Participant, "The Significant Woman," USA, personal communication, March 3, 2008)

As these perspectives show, individuals seeking the fulfillment experience of human flourishing can be aided and assisted by the care of a fellow sojourner—a mentor or life coach. This fellow sojourner helps someone navigate his or her integrated life journey of noble purpose with a tempered balance of wisdom, intelligence and care.

CONCLUSION

The growing business of life coaching, guidance and mentoring must consider the process of living, and not just external goals. People often seek coaching, guidance and mentoring to foster a sense of wellness, significance, and fulfillment. These goals are intrinsically spiritual since they relate to four spiritual searches commonly underpinning clients' stated aims: the search for meaning and purpose (the sacred), the search for wellbeing (integration), the search for belonging (deep connection), and the search for congruency (consistent principles and values). Hence, life coaches and mentors must consider spiritual searches and processes if they are to meet clients' needs and goals.

In practice, coaches and mentors can help clients in their spiritual searches by debunking common myths (such as that busyness is good, and that there is a magical formula for success) and fostering an orientation towards others rather than a focus on self-fulfillment. Further, coaches and mentors foster spiritual leadership where the person is living from a sense of "noble purpose." Spiritual interventions appear to be successful because they orient clients to their core purposes and allow them to experience a valid sense of significance. Spiritual leadership approaches are transformative, as illustrated in the evaluations of life coaches who have implemented spiritually informed programs. Since spiritually informed coaching and mentoring programs meet clients' deep goals for transformation, significance, and purpose, they are an important means of fostering human flourishing.

REFERENCES

Alter, J. (n.d.). *Mentoring works*. Retrieved September 8, 2009, from http://www.mentoring.org/downloads/mentoring_969.pdf

Anderson, P. (2000). This place hurts my spirit! *The Journal for Quality and Participation, 23*(4), 16–17.

Bell, C. (2002). *Managers as mentors: Building partnerships for learning* (2nd ed.). San Francisco: Berrett-Koehler.

Bowsher, A. (2007). Spiritual direction, life coaching and culture. *Journal of Alternative Spiritualities and New Age Studies, 3*, 142–153.

Braskamp, L. A. (2008). Leading as a spiritual endeavor: living, leading, and developing community with vocation. *Spirituality in Higher Education Newsletter, 4*(3), 1–9.

Burkes, P. (2008). *Business coaches aim for big league: growing industry helps companies improve*. Retrieved September 8, 2009, from http://www.newsok.com/business-coaches-aim-for-big-league/article/3315500

Chandler, D. (2009). Pastoral burnout and the impact of personal spiritual renewal, rest-taking and support system practices. *Pastoral Psychology, 58*(33), 273–287.

Chapman, L., & Skerten, B. (2006). Life coaching and counselling making connections. *New Zealand Journal of Counselling, 26*(3), 26–40.

Coutu, D., Kauffman, C., Charan, R., Peterson, D. B., Maccoby, M., Scoular, P. A., et al. (2009). What can coaches do for you. *Harvard Business Review, 87*(1), 91–97.

Covey, S. (2004). *The 8th habit: From effectiveness to greatness.* London: Simon & Schuster.

Dilts, R. (2003). *From coach to awakener.* Retrieved September 8, 2009, from http://www.nlpu.com/Coach2Awakener.htm

Giacalone, R. A., & Jurkiewicz, C. L. (2003). Toward a science of workplace spirituality. In R. A. Giacalone & C. L. Jurkiewicz (Eds.), *Handbook of workplace spirituality and organizational performance* (pp. 3–28). Armonk, NY/London, England: M. E. Sharpe.

Gladwell, M. (2002). *Tipping point: How little things can make a big difference.* Boston, MA: First Back Bay.

Goleman, D. (1995). *Emotional intelligence: Why it can matter more than IQ.* London: Bloomsbury.

Grant, A., & Zackon, R. (2004). Executive, workplace and life coaching: Findings from a large-scale survey of international coach federation members. *International Journal of Evidence Based Coaching and Mentoring, 2*(2), 2–15.

Greenleaf, R. (1991). *Servant leadership: A journey into the nature of legitimate power and greatness.* Mahwah, NJ: Paulist Press.

Gyatso, T. (n.d.) *Compassion and the individual.* Retrieved September 8, 2009, from http://www.dalailama.com/page.166.htm

Jensen, R. (2002). *Personal life coach—developing authentic leaders.* Temecula, CA: Future Achievement International.

Klein, E. (2000). Partnership and the soul. *The Journal for Quality and Participation, 23*(3), 64.

Kurth, K. (2003). Spiritually renewing ourselves at work: Finding meaning through serving. In R. A. Giacalone & C. L. Jurkiewicz (Eds.), *Handbook of workplace spirituality and organizational performance* (pp. 447–460). Armonk, N.Y./London, England: M. E. Sharpe.

Longhurst, L. (2006). The 'aha' moment in co-active coaching and its effects on belief and behavioural changes. *International Journal of Evidence Based Coaching and Mentoring, 4*(2), 61–73.

Nash, L. (2003). A spiritual audit of business: from tipping point to tripping point. In O. F. Williams (Ed.), *Business, religion and spirituality: A new synthesis* (pp. 53–78). Notre Dame, IN: University of Notre Dame Press.

Rinpoche, S. (1992). *The Tibetan book of living and dying.* London: Rider.

Schein, E. (1999). *Process consultation revisited: Building the helping relationship.* Harlow, UK: Addison-Wesley Publishing.

Seligman, M., & Csikszentmihalyi, M. (2000). Positive psychology: An introduction. *The American psychologist, 55*(1), 5–14.

Stanley, B. (2006). *Life coaching and well-being.* Retrieved September 08, 2009, from http://www.biblesociety.org.uk/exploratory/articles/stanleywint06.pdf

Toms, J., & Toms, M. (2000). Working in the zone. *The Journal for Quality and Participation, 23*(1), 24–25.

Vilnai-Yavetz, I., & Rafaeli, A. (2003). Organizational interactions: A basic skeleton with spiritual tissue. In R. A. Giacalone & C. L. Jurkiewicz (Eds.), *Handbook of workplace spirituality and organizational performance* (pp. 76–92). Armonk, NY: M. E. Sharpe.

Waitley, D. (1984). *The psychology of winning.* New York: Berkley.

Whitmore, J. (2002). *Coaching for performance: Growing people, performance and purpose* (3rd ed.). Boston, MA: Nicholas Brealey.

Zohar, D., & Marshall, I. (2004). *Spiritual capital: Wealth we can live by.* San Francisco: Berrett-Koehler Publishers, Inc.

CHAPTER 11

WHOLISTIC COACHING

A Case Study and Analysis

Rick Brouwer
Total Wellbeing Ministries

Maureen Miner
University of Western Sydney and Wesley Institute

ABSTRACT

The purpose of this chapter is to introduce wholistic coaching, developed and practised at a total wellbeing center by a total wellbeing coach, as an example of spiritually-informed life coaching. It seeks to create alternative ways of addressing human suffering and need in settings that may not normally embrace a spiritual framework. After defining what is meant by wholistic coaching, the principles of wholistic coaching are described and justified. A case account of one person's experience of wholistic coaching is offered, followed by a critical analysis based on psychological theory and practice. The case illustrates the successful use of spirituality within a life change process leading to greater flourishing.

Beyond Well-Being: Spirituality and Human Flourishing, pages 215–230
Copyright © 2012 by Information Age Publishing
All rights of reproduction in any form reserved.

As health professionals become more specialized in their fields of practice, the more integrated needs of the human person can often be neglected. In the same way wholistic approaches to human health in therapeutic settings are often put aside. In practice, the delivery of medical care is most commonly separated into two discreet specializations for physical and mental health with the "gatekeeper" a general (medical) practitioner (GP) acting as the go-between. A GP is trained within a medical model that provides an atomistic, symptom-based perspective. Similarly, psychiatrists are trained to recognize and treat mental illness; their use of drugs as a primary mode of treatment indicates their physiological focus and medical model. Where treatment is provided by community-based teams, other specialists may be used to provide psychological and support services. Their coordination depends upon the case manager, the quality of shared communication, and the capacity of the patient to consult every specialist team member as required. There is little emphasis within health care systems on the provision of wholistic care without the biases of a medical model.

Wholistic coaching, or total wellbeing coaching, which is a variation of life coaching, is one attempt to remedy this lack of wholistic care. A helpful definition of life coaching is given by Feldman and Feldman in Chapter 10 of this volume:

> Life coaching is a short (usually less than 12 months), fixed term (Stanley, 2006); outcomes-oriented (Dilts, 2003), future focused (Coutu, 2009), and co-active (Longhurst, 2006) helping relationship between the coach and the client. (p. 204)

Life coaching is broader than health and wellbeing in its scope, but its goal is to achieve a state of harmony in the whole person. Thus wholistic coaching is justified in co-opting life coaching into its framework to produce high-level outcomes for positive human living.

Wellbeing is often associated with physical and mental health, but it refers more specifically to wholeness. Commonly, the notion of health is equated with the absence of disease, or problematic symptoms. However, the word *health* comes from an old English word *hal*, which means *whole*, and thus to be healthy means to be whole. The World Health Organization (1946) defines health as a state of "complete physical, mental and social well-being" and not merely the absence of disease or infirmity (Official Records of the World Health Organization, no. 2, p. 100). Because we have lost this aspect of wholeness in the meaning of the word health, we now need to add words like *wholistic* to the word health to remind us of its actual meaning.

A further description of health is given by the Christian Medical Commission of the World Council of Churches (1990):

Health is a dynamic state of well-being of the individual and society, of physical, mental, spiritual, economic, political and social wellbeing; of being in harmony with each other, with the material environment and with God." (p. 6)

Similarly wholistic concepts of health and wellbeing are found within Christian texts. The Old Testament blessing, *Shalom*, carries with it the meaning of peace, soundness, completeness, maturity, life, salvation, wellbeing, therapy and cure. Likewise, the New Testament concept of salvation (Greek: *sozo*) carries with it the idea of saving one's soul and healing one's body (see, for instance, Matthew 18:11 and Mark 6:56).

With these rich accounts of health and wellbeing in mind, we in our center have defined total wellbeing as: *the state of enjoying maximum physical, mental, emotional, relational, financial and spiritual wellbeing.* Hence, the goal of wholistic coaching is to assist people to achieve maximum health and wholeness—across all life domains. In practice these outcomes are achieved through a series of personal coaching sessions ranging from only a few sessions to as many as twenty sessions over the course of two years.

The aim of this chapter is to offer a justification of a wholistic approach to coaching and provide a critical case analysis, which demonstrates the importance of wholistic coaching for individual life coaching.

JUSTIFICATION FOR WHOLISTIC COACHING

Many factors in society in the present day warrant a renewed understanding and approach to health, wellbeing and flourishing. Two such societal factors are listed below with a brief redress offered by the wholistic coaching approach. A further justification within Christianity for the specifically spiritual focus within wholistic coaching is also given.

Escalating Cost and Corporatization of Health Care

An aging population and lifestyle-induced diseases place escalating strain on the community's health resources. Better ways of keeping people well, not just treating disease, are needed. Further, medicine as a commercial enterprise is increasingly being driven by financial considerations and feeds into the rising costs of providing medical solutions in public healthcare. Costly research and investment in medical care are funded by global pharmaceutical corporations, who value shareholder profits, not to members of the community, who value wellbeing.

Wholistic coaching offers a non-medical view of health that seeks to balance medical interventions as an aspect of a person's journey in and towards wellbeing, rather than a primary intervention. Staying well rather than treating disease is the focus. In addition, wholistic coaching proposes that people take greater responsibility for their ongoing wellbeing. It teaches clients the skills necessary to utilize personal and community resources for health outcomes that are cost-effective and to free them from reliance on government-funded health care alone.

Individualistic Spirituality

There is a rise in interest in spirituality across society on many levels, yet skepticism against formal religion and prejudice towards the church remain. Alongside an increasing interest in individualistic spirituality, there exists a misunderstanding of what the Christian faith community can offer human wellbeing. Many people turn to alternative remedies (some of which have a spiritual base), yet do not understand the relevance of biblical Christianity to their problems. One example of the perceived irrelevance of church-based Christianity is contemporary denial of the concept of sin, which is seen as outdated. Our society is, however, suffering various forms of disease, distress, anxiety, relational breakdown and dysfunction, which may be a direct result of personal or societal sin in some cases. These negative effects occur whether or not sin is acknowledged as a cause or agent. Since many people do not see sin as a problem, there is no need of a "Savior from sin," and much Christian teaching about Jesus as One who forgives sin and heals is seen as irrelevant.

On the other hand, people are very familiar with the concept of sickness and the need for healing and wellbeing. Wholistic coaching seeks to remedy this disconnect among sin, sickness, salvation and healing by emphasizing a person's journey from sickness to health, and integrating concepts of right, wrong (sin), and salvation morphs into the metaphor of the healing journey. Wholistic coaching engages a person at an individual level in the first instance and incorporates broader understandings of church and the faith community at later stages of a person's spiritual development. It also seeks to highlight the benefits of seeking spiritual, as well as physical, wellbeing.

JUSTIFICATION WITHIN CHRISTIAN TEACHING

The goal of wholistic coaching is to assist people to achieve their maximum potential for physical, mental, emotional, relational, financial and spiritual wellbeing. This goal is consistent with biblical mandates of care and concern for others' welfare. For instance, in Ezekiel 34: 2–4 the shepherds of Israel, (who may parallel a modern day wholistic wellbeing coach or pastor) were given both a warning and a job description by God: "Woe to the shepherds of Israel who only take care of themselves! . . . You have not strengthened the weak or healed the sick or bound up the injured. You have not brought back the strays or searched for the lost. You have ruled them harshly and brutally" (NIV). From this passage we may deduce that a shepherd or a modern day wholistic wellbeing coach is to assist people toward flourishing, whether their need is for strengthening or major healing. In addition, coaches are to seek ways of connecting actively with those who may be totally disconnected from wellbeing.

Likewise, in Luke 4:18–19 (and earlier, in Isaiah 61) we learn that Jesus (the Good Shepherd) defined His ministry in terms of taking people on a journey from poverty to good news; from broken heartedness to being made well; from captivity to freedom; from blindness to sight; from mourning to comfort; from grieving to providence; from ashes to beauty; from despair to praise; and from devastation to restoration. These verses well depict the journey on which the wholistic wellbeing coach engages his or her clients; working together towards healing and flourishing in all facets of life.

These verses in Luke's Gospel also indicate the starting point for the journey. That starting point is often *pain*. Wholistic coaching engages a client at his or her point of pain. Pain is a universal language. It is an unwelcome messenger, but it is also an invitation to engage in the journey of restoration. Wholistic coaching uses the concepts from Isaiah 61 and Luke 4 to depict Jesus as the ultimate physician, who guides people on a journey from pain to flourishing. Pain is thus the beginning of a journey that God can use to take a person beyond the purely physical arena into healing and wellbeing for the whole person. This journey will often touch on the spiritual side of a client's life. It is a journey whose means and destination may be a relationship with God.

In conclusion, the corporatization of medical care and the emerging interest in individual spirituality demonstrate the need for alternative routes towards human flourishing—approaches that routinely incorporate a spiritual dimension and a wholistic approach to health and wellbeing. On the basis of the foregoing discussion then, wholistic coaching is offered as a functional healthcare process, targeted towards the needs of individual people, and consistent with core teachings of the Christian faith concerning wholeness. In the next section a case study of wholistic coaching was written in March, 2010, by a client (A. H.) who had suffered for many years from the aggravating skin disease psoriasis. The case is followed by an analysis in terms of psychological principles and premises of wholistic wellbeing coaching.

CASE OF A. H.

My Personal Experience of Wholistic Coaching

My story begins in 1977 when I was diagnosed with the skin condition psoriasis at the age of eighteen. My father had been given the same diagnosis six months previously. I came from a family of five children, but none of my brothers or sisters suffered from this disease.

I had never heard of this skin condition, and there was no internet in those days to do my own research. Although I consulted several doctors, it was almost two years before anyone in the medical profession offered me any sort of treatment. There are six different types of psoriasis, and I have gone through stages where I have had one type or all six at the same time.

The symptoms of psoriasis vary significantly depending on the severity of the disease. Most people think it is just a skin condition that causes redness, itching and flaking of the skin. However in severe cases such as mine, it is much more than that. For the first eighteen years or so my symptoms were relatively mild. Areas of my body affected were the fingernails, toenails, and patches on the elbows and knees, with the most severe area being the scalp. Most of the treatments offered to me were steroids based and had very little effect on the disease.

Although I have described the symptoms in those years as relatively mild, they had a profound effect on me. My confidence and self-esteem took a downward spiral mainly due to the mess my fingernails were in. They looked ugly and appeared to be diseased. If I had to buy something from a shop, I would ask my wife to do it, as I was too embarrassed and ashamed to let anyone see my hands. My scalp was another area that caused me great concern and discomfort. The skin had thickened on my scalp so much that it felt as if I was wearing a hat twenty-four hours a day. My concern was that people would see the problem I had and make negative comments.

During this time I was employed as an electrical tradesman; but because of the condition of my fingernails, it was becoming more and more difficult to do my job. An opportunity to take up employment as a storeman for a large public utilities company came my way in 1990. I spent six years there, and in the second half of that period I took up a position as a purchasing officer. This was to prove to be a big mistake. The position came with a high degree of stress, and that stress manifested itself in my skin. The psoriasis became chronic and caused me a great deal of grief. As I couldn't be without an income and on a dermatologist's advice, I began a course of chemotherapy. This involved an injection into the thigh once a week with a drug called Methotrexate. After being on the drug for five months, my skin was about 98% clear and stayed that way for another twelve months, after which the symptoms slowly started to return.

Over the next 10 years my psoriasis continually flared up and down, causing me to take various chemotherapy and steroid drugs. This course of treatment was to last nine months and caused my general health to suffer significantly. At times, my kidneys and liver were showing signs of failing because I had been on the drugs for so long. I quit my job so I could recover. One particularly stressful job caused my skin condition to become the most severe it had ever been. I only managed to keep that job for two years through using some different steroid type drugs. I got to the stage where I was having real difficulty just walking. The pain in my legs was almost unbearable, and I would never have believed that a skin condition could cause so much discomfort.

Early in 2008, Pastor Rick Brouwer, who was a wholistic coach, visited our church. His teaching was on the "total wellbeing" approach to life and health. Previously I had come to realize that stress was a trigger that would cause the psoriasis to flare up in my body. A dermatologist had also told me that diet might play a part. But I had never considered Pastor Rick's approach of integrating body, mind, and soul. He covered so many different aspects that day it was difficult to take it all in. I felt God had placed on my heart the need to speak further about this.

So in June of 2008 I made an appointment to see a total wellbeing coach (TWC) at the Total Wellbeing Medical and Counselling Centre. I met with a coach, who made it completely clear to me that he offered no guarantees of a "cure" for my psoriasis, but at the very least I would learn how to cope better with the disease. In that first session the TWC got me to rate my wellbeing using some simple gauges to highlight the areas of finance, health, emotional state, mental state, relationships, and spiritual wellbeing. This opened up a road I had never travelled on before. My expectation was that God would simply release me from the bondage of this skin condition. So it came as a surprise that the TWC covered areas of my life that I thought were unimportant in relation to the disease.

Together with the TWC and the leading of the Holy Spirit, I was given insight and understanding as to why this disease was having such a profound effect on my *whole* life. The psoriasis had robbed me of my self-esteem, taken away my confidence, caused me problems in relationships, and made it difficult to find suitable employment.

I know people with the same skin condition as me, and some of them cope with the disease a lot better than I did. I can't give an answer as to why I struggled so much with psoriasis, but it had become clear through the TWC that I had to change my thinking. My coach made me realize that nearly every area of my life was dictated by this disease. Almost every decision I made centered on my skin condition. I would say "I can't go there because it's warm and there is no shade. I can't do that because I will have to sit for too long. I can't stay there because the cream I use stains everything.

I can't go there because too many people will see my ugly hands." I was being robbed of life itself by this disease. I was always making decisions based on how I was feeling physically at the time. It affected my relationships with other people and, more importantly, with my wife. When this was pointed out to me, I was stunned to realize just how much of life I was missing.

Then the TWC gently asked me how I thought Jesus saw me and my skin condition. I replied, "Washed clean by His holy blood." In that instant I understood that I should not call (my skin) unclean what God has called (my skin) clean. I can honestly say that this was a moment when I really was released from the grip of this skin condition.

I came away from that first session with a different outlook on my situation. I had always been embarrassed and ashamed by the look of my skin and didn't want anyone to see or stare at me. But God had made it clear he did not see me that way. So when people did not like the look of my skin, that was their problem, not mine. It took time for me to be confident again with people, as I had been trying to hide my condition for over thirty years; yet over time I developed greater confidence and self-esteem and a different outlook on life.

The thing that impressed me about the TWC was his ability to get me to look at myself in a different way. He got me to stop looking at myself as a diseased person and, as I have said before, he asked me how I thought Jesus saw me. It was uplifting to think that my Savior saw me as a whole and complete person, not diseased. However I still had it in my mind that this was not the way the world saw me. I never expressed this to the TWC, but in one session, he did something that had a profound effect on me. While we were both in prayer, he took both my hands in his and held them. This might seem like a simple act of kindness towards me, but it was in fact a great release. Here was a man who had no issue taking my diseased hands in his, the only person outside of my own family who had done this. I have experienced medical professionals who would not touch my hands unless they first put on rubber gloves, even knowing the disease is not contagious. A simple act like this may not mean much to other people, but for me it meant a great deal. Here, for the first time since I was diagnosed with psoriasis, was a man who could see past the disease and see me, the person, instead. My confidence and self-esteem were lifted greatly.

In one session, the TWC asked me to identify areas of my life that caused me stress and, as we spoke about them, it became apparent that there was a common theme to all the things that I found stressful. What was common to all of them was *anger*. I had always been a person who lived on a short fuse. The question I asked myself was, "Why am I short tempered?" As the coach helped me follow this train of thought, he asked me about my relationship with my father and what sort of person he was. I told him, "My father was a good man but he also had a short temper. What came from my mouth then, came from my heart." I really wanted to be just like my dad, short temper included. What a revelation this was to me! From an early age I said to myself, "Yeah, I'll be just like my dad, and he will be so proud." I never fully understood that I took on the negative traits of my father as well. Now that I could see where the anger in me came from, it was so much easier now to say to God, "This is not mine, it's not me, I give it all to you, Lord." This for me was a life lesson—to be who God made me to be, not someone I thought I should be. In releasing the anger I nullified the negative aspects it had on my life, and I felt better on the inside, despite my circumstances.

Each week I really looked forward to my TWC appointment. I left each of the sessions invigorated, energized, encouraged and, more importantly for me, my skin condition was improving. I was making terrific progress, and the proof was that my skin and overall wellbeing were improving.

Another area of concern to me at the time was my financial situation. I realized that the savings my wife and I had would not last forever and, in time, would become much more of a concern. I had no idea when I would be fit enough to seek full time employment. The TWC pointed out that I was in a storm and that I couldn't see my way out of it. I expressed to him that knowing this didn't really help me much, but it was then that he explained that this was a point in my life were I had to learn to trust in God to bring me through. God was in effect saying to me, "Yes I know you can't see past this storm, but I can. So trust in me." My thoughts were running along the lines of, "Yes, God, I do trust you, but I don't know if I have enough trust to believe for this." It was then that the TWC said something that has changed my life. He told me to "Rest in God, don't be concerned about the storm in your life; God is in charge. Put your feet up and enjoy this time of rest and spend time with God." I was lost when the coach said, "Rest in God." I was at a loss as to how to do this when your life has been turned upside down. Yet, the explanation was simple enough: "Give all your worries over to God, and he will give you His peace." And indeed, when I did give my worries over to God, he did give me a great sense of peace that stayed with me during my time of unemployment and allowed me to rest in peace! My anxiety over money issues was replaced with quiet trust.

Another area explored by the TWC was the effect negative thoughts had on me. If asked, I would say that in general my outlook on life was positive, but when this opened up in one session, it became clear that was not the case. I had in fact become rather cynical in my outlook. I felt justified in this cynicism, because after all, I was the one who was sick. What a mistake that was. My cynical attitude created anger in me, and my anger was causing stress, which caused my skin to flare up. Changing my thinking to a more positive outlook took away my cynicism, anger and stress and, in doing so, I made progress towards my wholistic (total) wellbeing. The key here I believe is having a greater self-control over my thoughts. Focusing on positive thoughts gave me an overall feeling of wellbeing. I never thought something so simple would be so profound and life changing. I had never thought about how much my mind and thoughts could impact on my health

I'm not saying that I'll never get angry or stressed again in my life, but now I can walk away from it, taking charge of these negative thoughts so that they have little impact on me. I needed to discover the reason for my anger and then deal with it. This has helped me gain more self-control. I've learned through this to do the same with all negative thoughts that I may have. My mental health has improved even though I didn't think at the time I had any real problems in that area. The fact is that now I am more focused and my mind is clearer. It is no longer cluttered with negative thoughts and a sense of hopelessness due to my sickness. A sound mind means a sound body.

In summary, I learned that:

- The disease had taken control of my life.
- I looked upon myself as diseased and unclean. I felt ashamed of my condition.
- Negative thoughts about myself and how I thought other people viewed me only served to feed the disease.
- Stress was having a major impact on me, which I believe was caused by anger.
- My focus had been on the problem, not the solution.
- My relationships were suffering.
- My confidence and self-esteem were low.
- I needed to be myself, not who I thought I should be.
- I needed to rest and trust in God.

With the TWC's help and guidance I have learned to recognize and deal with these issues. God has supplied me with the tools to overcome the sickness that was ruling my life, as well as teaching me how to use them. No longer am I a slave to negative thoughts. Although these thoughts still occur from time to time, I know how to deal with them now. I'm happier and at peace with myself and no longer concerned how other people see me. I still don't know exactly what caused this disease to develop in my body, but I now understand that having an unhealthy mind created the perfect environment for it to thrive. I came to realize that stress caused my skin to flare up, but to me this was an outside influence and had nothing to do with me, as I believed I had no control over it. The TWC taught me how to control stress and showed me how other things like negative thoughts manifest in my body.

So if I take a look back at the time I spent with the TWC and ask myself the question, "What was the most important lesson I learned?" my answer would be that I now understand myself better and understand how important a healthy mind, body and soul are to my overall wellbeing. After suffering with this disease for over thirty years, I now realize that I was stuck in a never-ending cycle of remission and reoccurrence. Over the last 33 years I had used everything from prescription drugs to all natural products and in the process spent thousands of dollars. Nothing that I have used had cured the disease, and with the prescription drugs (chemotherapy, steroids) more damage was caused to my body. Yet now God is changing me on the inside and in doing so, the results show on the outside.

Through these sessions with the TWC and the Holy Spirit, mountains have been moved in my life. The psoriasis is 99.9% gone, and I believe that God will heal my body completely in the future. He is healing me from the inside, not the outside. The TWC didn't deal with the symptoms of psoriasis; he searched for the root causes in me. In searching for the cause so much more was revealed to me regarding my overall wellbeing. There were many things in me that this disease fed on, and as they were identified my situation began to improve.

Now that I understand that this cycle can be broken with a sound mind, I can look forward with great confidence to the future, knowing and believing that, in the fullness of time, my body will be completely healed. A man once said to me many years ago, "You are what you are." Well no, I'm the result of my decisions and what the world has made me to be. But with God's grace, I am now becoming the person that God intended me to be.

—A. H.
March 23, 2010

Case Analysis

The following case analysis is offered as a commentary on the report by A. H. from the perspective of a practicing clinical psychologist. The analysis is limited because it is based solely upon the client's perspective; it was written independently of any discussion of the case with the TWC. The main purpose of the case analysis is to consider the degree to which the practice of the TWC follows: a) recognized psychological theory and clinical practice (even if such theory and links with practice are not articulated by the coach) and b) the stated principles and goals of wholistic coaching. Hence, the consideration of diagnostic issues and case formulation attempts to reflect upon the case in light of psychological theory, and the consideration of treatment reflects upon the case in light of psychological practice.

Diagnostic Issues and Case Formulation

According to the DSM-IV-TR (American Psychiatric Association, 2000) A. H. displayed symptoms of Generalized Anxiety Disorder (GAD) and Social Anxiety Disorder. The presence of worry and irritability (and possible unreported muscle tension, arousal and sleep disturbance) is an indicator of GAD. The longstanding fear of embarrassment in social situations, avoidance of social situations, and the effects of such avoidance on his marriage and other relationships are indicators of a Social Anxiety Disorder. However, these anxiety symptoms are associated with a diagnosed medical condition of psoriasis. Hence an inclusive diagnosis would be one of a number of diagnoses within the general category of Psychological Factors Affecting a Medical Condition. The most appropriate diagnosis would appear to be Anxiety Affecting the Cause and Severity of Psoriasis, although an alternative possibility is a Stress-Related Physiological Response Affecting the Cause and Severity of Psoriasis. Treatment would depend on the case formulation; a formulation is suggested within a cognitive-behavioral framework and with attention to attachment issues. However, other case formulations and treatment approaches are possible from other theoretical frameworks.

The case history includes information about early childhood experiences with his father, who was chronically short-tempered. Such early experiences, together with the expressed wish to win his father's approval, suggest an anxious-ambivalent attachment style of relating to his father (Bartholomew & Moretti, 2002). Consistent with the anxious-ambivalent pattern are mental representations or schemas of a) the self as "not good enough" and generally unworthy of care and nurture; and b) others as sought after in times of distress but inconsistent in their nurturing. When symptoms of psoriasis appeared, the responses of others would have been interpreted according to the negative schemas of the self, and hence perceived as rejecting and/or ridiculing. Perceived rejection is stressful and hence precipitates anxiety symptoms and further diminishes a sense of competent self. The coping strategies of over-vigilance (constantly alert to the threat of rejection in order to respond quickly) and flight (avoidance of situations in which rejection could occur) are helpful in the short term but have negative long term consequences: chronic physiological arousal; felt stress; negative emotions such as anxiety, shame and anger; and distorted relationships with others (Young, 2003). Hence, recommended psychological interventions would include psycho-education about the nature, causes and effects of the symptoms; development of a supportive therapy relationship; and cognitive-behavioral strategies to reduce arousal and anxiety and to change negative schemas of self and others.

Treatment

The components of wholistic coaching reflected aspects of psycho-education, cognitive-behavioral therapy (CBT), and brief insight oriented therapy. Psycho-education related to the underlying ABC model of CBT: how antecedent events (A) activated maladaptive behaviors (B) by triggering distorted cognitions (C). Through psycho-education A. H. realized that the eruption of psoriasis triggered avoidant behaviors through absolutist thoughts such as "I can't."

Cognitive interventions to target absolutist thinking included the use of more adaptive thoughts, such as, "Avoidant coping is robbing me of life," and intentional strategies to change cynical patterns of thinking. Another cognitive strategy involved taking an external perspective on the problem: A. H. was encouraged to consider how Jesus saw his psoriasis. It is noteworthy that this externalizing strategy also involved the use of spiritual material. The use of Jesus as a reference figure was important because of associated biblical material relating to God's perception of his skin disease as "clean" and hence God's embrace of A. H. as a wholesome person capable of inclusion among those welcomed by God. Hence, the strategy resonated with core attachment themes of rejection and self-worth (Ainsworth, 1985; Bowlby, 1969) and helped to modify maladaptive schemas.

Behavioral strategies comprised modeling of unconditional regard through the TWC holding A. H.'s hands despite their disfigurement due to psoriasis and using prayer as a coping behavior (Pargament, 1997). As reported by the client, the holding of his hands greatly affected the "therapy relationship" or bond between the coach and client. It represented acceptance of the client as a person. These behavioral strategies helped to reinforce more positive self-schemas and led to a change in self-image from "diseased" to "complete."

An intervention targeting "hot" emotion (Lazarus, 1999) was also used when the coach asked A. H. to trace the antecedents of his anger. The client had identified anger as a consistent response to stressful events, and it was found to be associated with early experiences with his father. Such a pursuit of the antecedents of primary emotions is characteristic of insight (or psychodynamic) therapies (Fisher & O'Donohue, 2006), and A. H. gained cognitive-emotional insight into his previously uncontrollable feelings of anger. As a result he was able to take a controlled response of "giving his anger to God"—a more adaptive coping response that is also a spiritual response with the potential for direct spiritual effects.

The intervention to deal with financial stressors combined acceptance therapy (Orsillo & Roemer, 2005) with a spiritual focus. When A. H. was anxious about his financial prospects, the therapist used a version of spiritual acceptance through the strategy of "resting in God," with the result that a sense of worry and anxiety became a sense of peace. Other spiritual images were used to reinforce a more positive sense of self and more adaptive coping, such as the change from being "robbed of life" to being "washed clean by the blood of Christ."

Together, these strategies covered a range of recognized psychological therapy techniques. The strategies were also consistent with the principles and processes reported as characteristic of TWC. They directly addressed psychological (cognitive and emotional), relational (the client-coach relationship), spiritual and financial domains but did not focus on the physical issue of which the client was particularly aware. The strategies allowed for healing by the overcoming of anxiety symptoms underpinning the course and severity of the physical disorder. The sessions also produced a strengthening of the client as maladaptive schemas of self and others were apparently replaced by more adaptive schemas. More adaptive schemas of self and others reflect the development of a more secure attachment style. The use of TWC also represented a path from pain to flourishing as the physical and psychological pain engendered by psoriasis was replaced by a more positive sense of self in relation to God (implied in A. H's statement that "God is changing me").

The case may raise professional issues, such as the use of psychological therapy techniques by people who are not trained psychologists. If training in counseling and therapy is inadequate, then clients may be exposed to inadequate or unnecessary intervention, and the therapist may be exposed to burnout and other forms of emotional overload (Morrissey & Reddy, 2006). In the case reported above the TWC was trained in basic counseling through his pastoral ministry studies and was supported in a wholistic center with medical and psychological specialists on hand. However, people who offer counseling and psychological therapies within a coaching framework should understand the need for training, supervision, ongoing professional development, accountability through peer scrutiny, and networks for referrals, at the very least. Ideally, all coaches should be members of professional bodies that offer training, credentialing and professional codes.

CONCLUSION

The case represents an illustrative journey from disorder to flourishing through the use of wholistic coaching. Noteworthy in the case is the use of spiritual material in addition to well-recognized psychological techniques. The use of spiritual means of change was appropriate in this case because A. H. knew that the TWC was a pastor and was engaging in the coaching in full knowledge that spiritual material would be used. Although the TWC used a somewhat eclectic mix of techniques, they were appropriate for the presenting problem and clearly contributed to the outcome. Initially the techniques could be seen as an alternative approach, but actually the TWC was using well recognized psychological interventions. Hence the case raises the need for ongoing professional scrutiny and support for life coaches. For A. H. flourishing meant a process of ongoing spiritual change in which his troubling symptoms disappeared, his ambivalent attachment relationship style was apparently modified to a more secure style, and ineffective coping strategies of worry and avoidance were replaced by more adaptive coping strategies of acceptance and problem solving. The multidimensional approach of TWC provided a powerful context for meaningful change and flourishing.

ACKNOWLEDGEMENTS

Thanks to Dr. Alan Gijsbers for his insights into the factors that necessitate change in our Australian health care system.

Thanks also to A. H., who willingly wrote his personal appraisal of the role that wholistic coaching played in his life when dealing with psoriasis.

Thanks also to the team at the Total Wellbeing Medical and Counselling Centre for their continuing efforts to bring wholeness and wellbeing to many hundreds of patients every year.

REFERENCES

Ainsworth, M. D. (1985). Patterns of infant-mother attachments: Antecedents and effects on development. *Bulletin of the New York Academy of Medicine, 61*(9), 771–791.

American Psychiatric Association. (2000). *Diagnostic & statistical manual of mental disorders* (4th ed. text revised). Washington DC: Author.

Bartholomew, K., & Moretti, M. (2002). The dynamics of measuring attachment. *Attachment and Human Development, 4,* 162–165

Bowlby, J. (1969). *Attachment and loss: Volume I, Attachment.* New York: Basic Books.

Fisher, J. E., & O'Donohue, W. T. (Eds.). (2006). *Practitioner's guide to evidence-based psychotherapy.* New York: Springer.

Lazarus, R. (1999). *Stress and emotion: A new synthesis.* New York: Springer

Morrissey, S., & Reddy, P. (Eds.). (2006). *Ethics and professional practice for psychologists.* South Melbourne: Thomson.

Orsillo, S. M., & Roemer, L. (Eds.). (2005). *Acceptance and mindfulness-based approaches to anxiety: Conceptualization and treatment.* New York: Springer.

Pargament, K. (1997). *The psychology of religion and coping.* New York: Guilford.

World Council of Churches, The Christian Medical Commission. (1990). *Healing and wholeness: The church's role in health.* Geneva: AGL FM Production.

World Health Organization. (1946). Preamble to the Constitution of the World Health Organization as adopted by the International Health Conference,

New York, June, 19–22, 1946; signed on July 22, 1946 by the representatives of 61 States (Official Records of the World Health Organization, no. 2, p. 100) and entered into force on April 7, 1948. Retrieved October 15, 2010 from http://www.who.int/suggestions/faq/en/index.html

Young, J. E. (2003). *Schema therapy: A practitioner's guide.* New York: Guilford.

CHAPTER 12

THE PILGRIM ROAD TO HUMAN FLOURISHING

When the Psychotherapeutic and the Spiritual Journeys Meet

Loyola M. McLean
University of Sydney

Marie-Thérèse Proctor
Griffith University and Wesley Institute

ABSTRACT

Human beings develop in the matrix of relationship and meaning-making. It is therefore unsurprising that, at times, the journey of healing (through psychotherapy and the acquisition of a more robust mind) shares the road with a spiritual path (a path towards flourishing that can be likened to pilgrimage) since both journeys embrace deep purpose and meaning. Certain concepts are valued and held in common by both paths: the pursuit of Truth and Integrity; Mature Love and Intimacy; Acceptance and Forgiveness; Tolerance of Paradox and Difference; and a movement towards a deep Knowing of Self and Other. These become the landmarks in the journey of integration due to

Beyond Well-Being: Spirituality and Human Flourishing, pages 231–255
Copyright © 2012 by Information Age Publishing
All rights of reproduction in any form reserved.

231

the meaningful and transformational nature of these experiences. Allowing for, and deeply respecting, the convergence of the psychological and spiritual is a challenge for some psychotherapists and clinicians. This may be especially the case if they come from theoretical and clinical models that are reductionist and/or from spiritual perspectives and traditions that differ from those of their patients. Making space for their patients' psycho-spiritual needs and issues within the healing and recovery process invites clinicians to extend their thinking and practice beyond a biomedical model of healing to engage more fully with a bio-psycho-socio-cultural perspective. Case material is presented to show how skills and goals common to many relational therapies can allow the mind and spirit to journey together with the shared goal of helping human beings heal and flourish. These cases are framed within Attachment Theory and contemporary theories of self to suggest that ultimately a real sharing of this therapeutic journey can be joyous for clinician and patient alike, no matter the road traveled, and it is in this joyous connection that healing, flourishing, and mutual transformation occur.

> *We are pilgrims on a journey,*
> *We are [family] on the road,*
> *We are here to help each other*
> *Walk the mile and share the load.*
>
> —Gillard, 1977

At the heart of psychodynamic psychotherapy lies a relationship that is founded on an agreement to pursue truth, development, and integration. It is fostered through curiosity and empathy for the patient's experience and the story he or she makes of it, led by the therapist, but encouraged by both parties. Often an implicit goal is the nurturing of a more autonomous/secure state of mind and a lively sense of self within the individual presenting for therapy. This includes the collaborative nurturing of the capacities to work, play and love in healthy balance.

This nurturing process is grounded in the desire to help the individual heal and flourish, and is especially crucial following times of illness, trauma, loss and bereavement, or the discovery of the effects of chronic dissociation or neglect. The path to recovery is often difficult, and from this context of the *shared journey undertaken with deep purpose and in the hope of transformation* we draw the analogy with *pilgrimage*. The therapist is at times implicitly expected to be the "stronger and/or wiser" one (Bowlby, 1979, p. 129) and to hold the other in mind until the capacity to do so for oneself emerges. Being held in mind can help make whole and allow one to flourish. However, the therapist also is usually challenged to change on the journey, and the therapeutic process aims for real collaboration.

Trauma, loss, bereavement, and/or illness can significantly destabilize the individual's emotional, cognitive, and in some cases spiritual, life. Relationships with others, with self and with the world can become bruised or broken. Yet the process of recovery is a universal challenge, not one limited to mental illness: we all suffer, we must all heal and if we are to flourish, we must be transformed. The situation is compounded if psychopathology (re)emerges and/or it becomes clear that the older ways of managing the self are insufficient to surmount current life challenges. Spiritual themes can emerge in both the clinical and psychotherapeutic setting that warrant attention as individuals plow through often old and painful past events. Within this context, trauma can be both the road into and out of pain. *The crisis, the crux, the crossroads, the turn in the road* are all metaphors for the chance or the call to change. The shift can be emotional, embodied, cognitive, social and/or spiritual, or some combination of all of these, with psychotherapy providing an opportunity for fostering healing and ultimately flourishing, especially if healing reinvigorates the self and relationships and promotes mindfulness.

Previous work has explored a) the utility of assessing a patient's spirituality as part of the broader clinical assessment, and b) the applicability of using an attachment perspective both when formulating a clinical profile and managing patients with a religious/spiritual worldview (McLean, 2008; Proctor & McLean, 2008, 2009; Proctor, Miner, McLean, Devenish & Ghobary, 2009; Proctor, 2009). However this chapter begins with an argument for considering spirituality and attachment theory in various clinical contexts and with reference to specific cases.

ATTACHMENT, TRAUMA, LOSS, AND SPIRITUALITY

Spirituality is clearly utilized by some as a coping mechanism during periods of crisis (Proctor & McLean, 2009). For example, palliative care and end of life decision-making can include spiritual considerations for the ill individual and his or her family. This raises the question: *How do we respond to, and work with, individuals and families who experience and process healing, caring, dying, death and bereavement within their context of their spiritual and/ or religious beliefs?* Furthermore, whether the spirituality is overt or not, we contend that the nature of the journey through trauma and loss has spiritual aspects for many. The journey may be viewed explicitly as spiritual, or its spirituality may become known more implicitly. As psychotherapists, we are asked to accompany people on their journeys—hence the notion of pilgrimage emerges. In this chapter we extend our prior work in an endeavor to demonstrate how the journey to psychological healing and the spiritual journey can intertwine as individuals (and families) seek to resolve past and present traumas and losses.

A helpful perspective for psychotherapists engaged in the spiritual-therapeutic journey is attachment theory. Attachment theory provides a bio-psycho-social model for understanding holistic human development and human responses to stress, loss and trauma (Hesse & Main, 2000; Main, Goldwyn, & Hesse, 2002; Crittenden, 2006; Maunder & Hunter, 2001). In brief, the earliest attachment relationships with care-givers initially define how people experience themselves and others and how they behave in relationships. Critical questions are: Did they experience being loved, protected, comforted and cared for, or were their needs for safety, care and comfort rejected (and they were endangered)? Were others helpful, or did they dismiss their bids for help? Did others only meet their needs inconsistently, or were they frankly harmful? Depending on people's experiences and how they organize them psycho-physiologically, they arrive at an internalized schema that they tend to carry forward in future relationships with self and others. Figure 12.1 describes the four types of internalized schemas, or "attachment states of mind."

If people experience adequate safety and comfort, they are likely to internalize a secure strategy/schema to predict a) their own lovability, and b) the usefulness of others (Autonomous/Secure: B). If care is less safe and comforting, then people tend to organize their strategy to make the most of those less hospitable environments in one of two ways: a) by privileging their own practical and cognitive competence and down-regulating emotional dependence (Avoidant/Dismissive: A); or b) by attempting to draw in an inconsistent carer with up-regulated signals of their dependency needs and thus experiencing a diminished explicit sense of personal competency (Ambivalent/Preoccupied: C). In experiences of abuse, neglect, trauma and loss, people are likely to become temporarily disorganized. Without adequate opportunity for resolution, this chronic experience of terror/terrorizing is not far from the surface. It then becomes the background template, brought to the foreground by traumatic triggers (Disorganized/Unresolved: D) and interwoven with use of the A, B, or C strategies (Hesse & Main, 2000). Acute and chronic traumas have negative consequences: both mental illness and bereavement are highly associated with disorganized or incoherent strategies and a sense of incoherence in one's narrative/story (Main, Goldwyn & Hesse, 2002; Fonagy, Gergely & Target, 2008). The four templates, although powerful, are not necessarily permanent. Throughout the lifespan there are normative periods where templates can be revisited and shifted, especially in line with normal development or an altered environment (Crittenden, 2006). Hence, each new crisis again challenges the underlying preferred strategy and is an opportunity for the template to transform.

The aim of psychotherapists committed to human flourishing is to nurture the capacity for the more flexible and cohesive strategies and ul-

A: Avoidant /Dismissive
I have to do it myself

As

Others are not helpful/reject me/intrude
I feel shameful/contemptible when I need help
I avoid/minimize much feeling
I focus on:
- being independent/strong/proud
- achievements/fun/things
- material success
I have few rich memories

B: Autonomous/Secure
I am free to ask for help

As

I am lovable/deserve help
Others are useful and reliable
I am free to:
- value relationships
- express emotion openly and directly, receive comfort
- be vulnerable
- remember clearly
- feel joy and grieve safely

C: Ambivalent/Preoccupied
I can't do it myself

But

Others are unreliable
I feel unreliable and uncertain
I feel intensely:
- anxious/angry/blaming
- lost in memories/distressed
- helpless/hopeless/useless
If I ask loudly for help, someone may come
I remember too vividly

D: Disorganized/Unresolved
(I) can't do it myself

But

Others will make it worse!
Those who should help are frightened/frightening
I am unlovable/undeserving
I feel:
- dreadful/disconnected/confused/bad/fragmented
- afraid/terrified/shocked/horrified/numb
My memories have gaps/are absent/conflict

Figure 12.1 Attachment states of mind (modified from McLean, 2004, 2005, 2009), printed with permission.

timately a more coherent mind and narrative. This change can become possible where an acceptance of the current personal, environmental and relational truths can be integrated, when past trauma or loss is resolved, and when the individual has the capacity to respond reflectively rather than reflexively. One is not locked into the traumatic past, yet neither is one naïve with respect to dangers. Similarly it appears that if one is more secure in mind and comfortable with one's own and others' limits, one is capable of, and disposed to, forgiveness (Main et al., 2002; see also Chapter 4 in this volume). Research suggests that an autonomous state of mind and reflective functioning allow the capacity for metacognition: to understand appearance-reality distinctions; to hold uncertainty and paradox; and to have a theory of mind applicable to self and other (Main et al, 2002; Fonagy, et al., 2008).

"For Mourning, the Oil of Gladness"

Bowlby and others make it clear that many do this work of recovery from trauma and loss best within relationships (Bowlby, 1980; Meares, 2005). We were not meant, from an evolutionary perspective, to grieve alone; we have evolved to seek comfort socially, if our early experiences do not counteract this expectation. In the context of grief the power of joy is beginning to be understood. Joy is a quintessentially communal emotion. In a particular kind of healing conversation, we experience the joyous intimacy of sharing a moment, no matter what the notional content of that moment is—a story of pain, of anger, of terror, of loss. If we have entered into that moment in a resonant way, there is a connection that is inherently satisfying and integrating. Something heals; something grows.

Attachment relationships and templates "organize" our cognitive, emotional and relational lives. An attachment state of mind describes the way the individual constructs himself or herself in a particular relationship—for example, with the therapist, with others, or with God. Hence there is utility in the notion of attachment to God, (for reviews and discussion see Granqvist & Kirkpatrick, 2008; Miner, 2007; Proctor & McLean, 2009). For some, God is the stronger or wiser one who always accompanies them. In this chapter, attachment, including attachment to God, and contemporary models of self are the underlying paradigms for the shared pilgrim road to transformation; we may feel alone and our sorrow/pain is our own, but when we share the journey, something is transmuted. *Our capacity to flourish is largely determined by our capacity to be recreated after loss and trauma, to journey accompanied back to wholeness.*

APPLICATIONS OF ATTACHMENT THEORY IN CASE ANALYSES

Vignettes drawn from a series of intensive psychodynamic therapies (used with the patients' permission, de-identified, and disguised) illustrate how spiritual issues: 1) have manifested within the therapeutic setting, 2) were assessed, and 3) were implicitly or explicitly addressed as part of the process of holistic healing. Similar patterns in the processes among the cases emerged. These patterns represent important themes in therapies that address human and spiritual attachment issues. The following process-descriptors mark these similarities:

P1: *Identification of the underlying attachment states of mind with their possible points for exploration/interpretation.*

This refers to the process of formulating the case from an attachment perspective (described in Proctor & McLean, 2009). Case formulation occurs with reference to the attachment states of mind crystallized in the template in Figure 12.1 and arrived at by a process of listening and experiencing. There is listening with an ear for attachment (Slade, 1999, pp. 581–591) to the full history, including both form and content. There is also experiencing what passes procedurally between the patient and therapist (transference/countertransference), analyzed as experiences of attachment templates. Attachment states of mind affect the patient's presentation and the management of the case ("the road"). Hence, attachment issues are explored and reflected on in the therapy.

P2: *Change in the templates of relationship during therapy.*

This refers to way that other attachment templates, hopefully including the secure template, will open up in therapy and lead to the person being more free to respond and not captive to the past.

P3: *Identification of attachment to God (ATG) in providing a "holding space" during illness or recovery.*

Not all attachments to God are secure, but any secure aspects can be a source of resilience and aid the person in illness or allow the therapy/recovery to proceed.

P4: *The emergence of other spiritual challenges and maturity.*

Challenges of acceptance, forgiveness, tolerance of difference and paradox, and a move to mature love and personal maturity are among the fruits of resolution of trauma/loss. These fruits can emerge during healing and offer an opportunity for post-traumatic growth.

P5: *The search for meaning, purpose and true vocation.*

As the sense of self is strengthened and the trauma system dissolves, a sense of purpose and meaning in one's life emerges, and the call to be and to become can be heard, arising from a deep sense of being valued (Meares & Graham, 2008). The narrative self that was damaged or restricted is restored, and one is able to re-story the past and open up possibility for the future.

In addition, narrative material about one family's bereavement journey following the death of a child family member is presented. The family's explicitly spiritual approach to naming and processing the grief is highlighted, with notes about the convergence and divergence among family members' experiences of loss and grief. The vignettes illustrate the proposition that experiencing the other (therapist or support person, human or spiritual) as a companion on the healing journey is central to the transforming experience. In an attempt to retain the essence of the experience of the therapies/narratives, the first person pronoun is used for the practitioner. The reader is intentionally invited into the story of the participants to mirror the "experience near" quality of the encounters.

#1: The Case of "Single-Handed": Attachment to God as Mind-Map to the Buried Self

A 55 year old man presented with treatment-resistant major depression and a history of dysthymia (i.e., "double depression"). His previous wife (described as his soul-mate) likewise had serious mental illness. The (His) story was of "running"—constant activity and rescuing others. His motto, "Work twice as hard as everyone else," was attributed to having one hand damaged early in life. He had been an active Christian since troubled teenage years when he was taken in by a pastor.

In speaking of his life "Single-Handed" described intense experiences of meditative, contemplative prayer and times of spiritual intercession and healing for himself and others. In the face of cumulative losses and depletion, he had "broken down" and presented for treatment. Symptoms included prominent depression and anxiety, with the emergence of very clingy and dependent behaviors. These were formulated as the breakdown of his usual attachment strategy. He now moved, often oscillating quickly, between his more usual dismissive attachment state of mind and an ambivalent attachment state of mind (See Figure 12.1). In brief, he moved with discomfort between a harsh rejection of his need for help and an overwhelming and exaggerated sense of his own helplessness. This process of "flipping" states of mind was due to an underlying disorganization of his attachment state of mind. Disorganization is a toxic state due to loss or trauma that we quickly try to resolve by moving into one of the three organized states (A–C) if possible, but a resolution here could not yet be sustained. The loss or trauma had probably arisen during early childhood and then been reactivated by his cumulative and triggering recent losses (P1). Past trauma, previously unresolved and triggered in the present, was affecting his current sense of self and relationships.

His developmental history was important in tracking this potential early disorganization and subsequent relational history. His mother, whom he described as "loving," had experienced depression. His father had died when he was five and was not well remembered. He had been cared for in a "bossy" way by older sisters. His first wife had been an empathic person and a brilliant theologian but had succumbed to serious mental illness as a young woman, leaving him to struggle to care for her and their two children. Their relationship ended with a reluctant, but eventual divorce, necessitated by her incorporating him into her delusions.

His case formulation emphasized the breakdown of a dismissive strategy and underlying loss. Consequently, therapy focused on the need for him to stop and grieve for his huge losses, which had been largely dismissed until the present (P1). Early in therapy the techniques focused on active listening and attuning, waiting for the self to be less "stimulus-entrapped" (Meares, 2005), and on contemplation. Contemplation—*being with, staying with, and journeying with in time, over time*—is at the heart of all intensive therapies and forms part of the intimate work of the therapeutic conversation. Truly staying with the feeling of the moment, whether pain, emptiness, rage, disgust, madness, excitement, or so on until something shifts is essential to real and abiding change (Meares, 2005). It requires the therapist to be both participant and observer (Meares, 2000). Many can experience the deep intimacy of contemplation as sacred space or as sacred journey: it resonates with the experience captured by Isaiah: *Do not be afraid, for I am with you* (Isaiah 43:5, NJB).

After some time, a shift in affect and experience did occur and for a long time therapy with "Single-Handed" entered a period of "sitting in the aloneness/togetherness" (Meares, 2005, pp. 203–204). Terrible memories of pain, distress and anger were revealed and experienced. These became deeply shared, rather than avoided, feelings. After a long period of this deeper conversation, he somewhat surprisingly revealed one day that he had stopped praying in a heartfelt way. This was explored for some time in the session but eventually, as a partner in the pursuit of truth and integrity, I had to share the disconnect I felt about this:

"You believe in a Loving God, but you don't seem to feel you can take these most important and difficult feelings to Him. I wonder, what is happening?"

Guilt, shame, fear and an Aha! moment followed.

He said that he didn't believe God could stand it; didn't believe he, Single-handed, deserved it. He said: "That's just crazy, isn't it?"

"Crazy sad . . ." I replied.

This moment in therapy then allowed us to explore the familiarity of this moment in his life journey—other times when such feelings had been experienced. The oldest and most significant was his past sense of the impossibility of overburdening his father or mother with his anxiety or grief. His fantasies involved wondering about whether he had killed his father, "just about killed" his mother, and sent his wife mad. We stayed in those moments of horror for a long time, digesting the fear, guilt and shame. This period of deep *contemplation* seemed to lead to an understanding and a forgiveness, and hence a repair of relationship with self and repair of his relationship with God (P2). This improved sense of self and other are among the hallmarks of work on repairing attachment, marking a move to a more secure state of mind (Slade, 1999; Magai, 1999; Fonagy, 2001; Holmes, 2001) and are achieved through a particular kind of therapeutic conversation (Meares, 2005).

This improvement flagged the termination phase of an initial successful long-term therapy that helped achieve control of the serious "treatment-resistant" depression experienced at that time. An important part of this was a return to accessing care in spiritual and social circles as well as in his therapeutic relationships. He admitted he needed others and became less anxious about this—a move towards a secure state of mind (P2) (Figure 12.1). He joked that I was "the doctor who told [him] to pray more." I never had directly instructed him to do so, but had confronted him about his withdrawal from a relationship that he had said was so central to him (P1), with this attachment state serving as a deep entry point into the need for dissolution of his trauma and transformation.

Changes in the Template with Convergence of the Spiritual and Human Attachments

"Single-Handed" returned years later after his second wife developed psychosis. She left him precipitously, and he once more found himself "on the run" emotionally, understandably afraid of intimacy. His mood relapsed and we tried to mourn another significant relational loss. However, much of his feeling was now hidden behind physical symptoms. Hypochondriasis had him focused on illness; perhaps unsurprisingly, symptoms affecting heart and breath emerged as probable signs of heart-break, grief and panic. He had one intense episode where his whole body felt "toxic." This dissonant music in his body was seen ultimately as an expression of the deeply disorganizing experience of significant trauma and loss: he was being "poisoned" by what he was taking in from the world, rather than helped (see D: Disorganized, Figure 12.1). His wife, whom he had hoped would be a safe harbor, had become both frightened and frightening, and he was again disconnected from himself and others (P1). He had a brief hospital admission at this time. He began looking for the perfect cure from the perfect doctor. He was burdening his adult children who already had another seriously mentally-ill parent to manage. We needed to understand his deep need for reassurance that manifested as wanting several "second opinions" or expert consultancy about severe mood disorders. He was commenced on a monoamine oxidase inhibitor as a powerful higher-order treatment for resistant depression. It had some effect, but his fretfulness persisted.

Eventually, in a moment where I felt the huge cost of his situation, I challenged him in a way that felt like the putting down of a paternal foot, pointing out that while he had so much to accept that was heart-breaking, he also had so much in his life to actually enjoy and delight him: two children, two grandchildren, friends, and a community that loved him. The timing and tone of this intervention had to be deeply discerned. Any sense that I dismissed his great suffering would have led to unregulated shame and an entrenchment of the dismissive position he had adopted but which had proved unhelpful. After I spoke he remembered something of his father: "*I have an image of the old childhood home with my father fixing the roof with me watching and helping.*" This was a very poignant moment, as he had few memories of his father.

Soon he spoke of wanting to move the whole old house of his childhood to his farm, which already demanded too much upkeep. He began making plans and lists, and so on. I felt the "running" begin again and felt that "brakes" were again needed, suggesting:

> Maybe it's time to think about how we can more fully integrate that beautiful experience of your father working on repairing your house with you—how to hold it deep inside you rather than needing it on the outside where it costs you so much. The stories you've found don't have to be lost again, and now you can find ways to share them that don't cost you more than you can afford. Your household needs a functioning father and grandfather. They need someone to help fix the roof.

Tears streamed down his face; he initially clenched his good fist and sobbed. He then settled and eventually left the session beaming, standing taller and crushing my hand in his good hand in a very manly hand shake. He returned to a period of "working through," during which we discussed the parallel of his spiritual Father, who still helped him "repair his roof," as well as the biological and internal fathers. Not long after, we were again able to break from the intensive work. He is currently practicing "plodding" rather than running or hiding, but comes back to touch base, often needing help with applying some "brakes" or to share moments of joy and/or suffering.

Clinical Reflections

At presentation this man had openly acknowledged the importance of his attachment to God, experienced in the past as a source of immediate and healing presence and as the foundation for accessing a community of care. His faith and earlier experiences of some security in his relationship with God and others from his community probably allowed him to stand in a place where he hoped to be helped by me in therapy. However, our work came to illuminate what had been hidden: that early experiences of his parents being overwhelmed or frightened/frightening had led to a disorganized state of mind that had damaged his relationship with himself, leading to intense inappropriate guilt and shame (P1) (Main, Goldwyn & Hesse, 2002). This dismissive and disorganized state of mind had also restricted his spiritual relationship at this time of breakdown. By deeply respecting his relationship with God as foundational, we then gained access to other fundamental memories and experiences that required transformation and integration: to allow him to experience and find himself to be lovable (P2). It is possible that the second divorce of a wife with psychosis had opened up places in his bodily-centered memories, his earliest procedural memories of feeling "toxic" to his mother and she to him during his early infancy and her post-natal depression. Even understanding these circumstances was insufficient to bring about cure. In this case the healing force appears to have been a complex and reparative experience, remembered with his father but deeply felt to be applicable to his relationship with God the Father, and triggered by our "paternal" interaction. This experience was to restabilize his unstable attachment states of mind and move the current template more towards security. In this case there was a developmental challenge to a man now in his 70s, to move into the Eriksonian stage of integration (Erikson, 1959) —to mature and take on the mantle of real emotional responsibility as a patriarch and story-teller and maker of restorative meaning in his family (P4, 5).

#2: The Case of "Mouse at the Hole": The Spiritual as "Sheltering Place"/Holding Space

A single woman in her thirties was referred for a disorder of self and recurrent melancholic depression, which at times needed electro-convulsive therapy (ECT). During psychotherapy her background emerged as one of neglect due to maternal depression, followed by sexual abuse by an older family member. Eating disorders, harsh treatment of self, and terrors of all kinds were repeating themselves, as she was trapped in a cycle of care for others while receiving nothing for herself. She experienced intense self-loathing. Her previous therapist had been unable to give her more frequent sessions when she had plucked up the courage to ask for a twice-weekly frame. They ceased therapy and she felt punished and abandoned. Mostly in desperation, she took her psychiatrist's advice to try another therapy/ therapist, with a view to undertaking the more intensive work that seemed to be needed.

Mouse was a worshipping Christian but spoke very little about her faith. Her terror was such that she wanted to flee during every session. Every silence, every tiny sense of me not being attuned, every misstep was threatening. I had to be patient, steadfast and wait, often simply making "cooing" sounds until her disorganized state of mind could settle within a new and safe experience (P1). I thought and felt that *She needs faith in the process and in me, and I must also deeply believe—any doubt on my part will scare her away.* After much close and careful work together, where she startled at every real or imagined movement on my part, she began, like a mouse at the hole, to emerge tentatively, looking for cheese. She talked of her old church group, where it seemed she was in the same cycle of being neglected and used up. She moved to a new house and considered changing churches. I heard the music of change and tentatively offered the following: *Maybe you are considering things can be different from how they have always been; maybe it is safe to be hungry.*

She began to attend the new church and their "home group" where she met a fixed group of people once a week. Sometime after, she admitted that she wanted a partner—she wanted not to be alone. Again we marveled at her courage in expressing her desire; that it was safe enough for her to attempt to feel and voice her longing. One day she came in and said:

> You asked once about my favorite ice-cream flavor. Do you remember? I said, "I hardly ever eat it" and "I had no idea." You said "Huh! Well maybe there will come a day when you try what you like the look of and find out." Well, it's hazelnut!

We laughed together—someone who had spent most of the first three years of therapy scowling or frozen in horror could laugh and connect with herself and me—and it was good! Not long afterwards she met a friend at the "home group," and they began walking home together. He asked her out to a ball. She laughingly chastised me when I brought up Cinderella: "Let's not get carried away," she said. But she was: they fell in love. She felt they worked and played well together. During the period of working through that followed, I asked with intense curiosity: *How do you think you hung on all those years?* Her reply was: *I think it was 'cause I believed God loved me. I couldn't feel it, but I clung to it and now I understand what I hoped for but could never really hope for* (P3).

"To err is human, to forgive divine": The Emergence of Spiritual Challenge and Maturity

Attachment theory teaches that a secure state of mind often allows implicit or explicit forgiveness of attachment figures and rueful recognition of one's own limitations (Main, Goldwyn, & Hesse, 2002). After some time in therapy this young woman disclosed to her family the abuse she had suffered and admitted her need for help, utilizing the support of her general psychiatrist in her disclosures. She was able to proceed in her relationships with them in a more open way, aware of their limits, drawing on friends for more intimate support. She also softened towards herself, her demands on her body and her diet. She allowed for, and accepted, her need for holidays and rest. She began more thoughtfully to consider her own human limits. Currently she is waiting patiently for her partner, a child of divorced parents, to reconsider his deep terror of marriage (P2, P4, P5).

> I never thought that loving someone would mean that I would even consider accepting that I might never be married. But at the moment I can't abandon him, and he can't choose to marry me yet, as he is terrified. It has made me rethink what love means: to wait and to challenge; to wait as long as I can, but to not abandon myself.

Clinical Reflections

Mouse's attachment to God was little spoken of but deeply held and appears to have offered her a place to shelter and hope, with a hidden hope that would not have survived early open (re)cognition and expression (P3). It is possible that it was held in an emotional/cognitive space that defied her actual experiences of human others. However, it was salutary that her attachment to God was not to be analyzed away as irrational or unproved. It was actually helpful for her to be allowed to hold onto it quietly until human experience, including her treatment of herself, had finally begun to shift in her life. That slim portion of hope and faith was something we drew on until there were new experiences of love and lovability. It also appears that the therapy/spiritual path interaction was reciprocal, as it seemed it was necessary for her to heal her expectations of herself and others in therapy before she could ask for more from her community (P1, 2) and give more deeply and safely to others (P4,5). This in turn enriched our conversations with more food for thought and a productive and enlivening upward spiral of transformation began.

#3: The Case of "Martha-Dutiful Daughter": A Vocation to be More than a Martyr?

A young woman in her twenties, the daughter of divorced parents, came for therapy. At the time of the divorce, which occurred during her teens, "Martha's" father had a life-threatening illness and her mother had an intractable and severe mental illness. After many years of a more overtly dismissive attachment strategy and "hidden" somatization, "Martha" was now experiencing a breakdown of strategy and exhibiting new and unfamiliar borderline features: cutting/dissociation, affect dysregulation, idealization of her current physician, and recent difficult experiences with idealizing/de-idealizing others.

"Martha" had maintained a strong Christian faith in the past but early in therapy was disenchanted with God, describing a distant, judging experience of Him: she expected the judgment that she was "not dutiful enough." After initially deciding unilaterally that I, her therapist, was "an accursed atheist," she began to worry about the fate of my eternal soul. She doubted everything I said as "devil talk." Any affirmation to care for herself was seen as a seduction into selfishness versus submission to duty and selflessness. I challenged her on the scripture she quoted: *Love your neighbor as yourself* (Mark 12:31, NIV), wondering about the quality of love she could realistically offer others if she didn't love herself.

She was locked into experiencing me as she expected me to be, to the point of apparently not acknowledging possible cues about my spiritual heritage such as a Catholic name. I commented: *You seem to feel that you know who I am, what I think and what I feel. But is it possible you are confusing me with someone else?*

Learning at the Feet of the Master

After a year or so in therapy (on the anniversary of which she gave me a small babushka doll, which we talked about as a symbol of care and holding), she started to pray in a more intense way. She brought beautiful images from prayer of being a sparrow in God's hand, able to approach for food and comfort at need (P2). She instructed me via her described relationship with God about how to let her quietly approach and not startle or intrude (P3). The therapist was challenged to shift, respond, and change.

Ask and You Shall Receive

"Martha" began to ask for healing prayer in her church congregation and requested gifts from God, including a gift to make music. She took up the guitar and began writing spiritual songs. She began to feel that an unusual synchrony was happening. She felt that the therapy and her spiritual path were intertwining: that is, the people who were praying with her were saying similar things about her internal blocks and challenges as those we were discussing in therapy.

The Moment of Unspeakable Truth

Without any clear precipitant, "Martha" called and left a long, emotional message on my voicemail, full of rage, disgust, hopelessness and coercion. I felt violated and sensed a strong association to her mother's violent outbursts, which had only been hinted at. I did not phone back for 24 hours in order to be calmer, hoping I would be able to articulate my experience. By the time of her session I still could not articulate what I had felt. *"Knew you couldn't take it!"* was her comment when I challenged her about the tone and feeling of her message. I then tentatively offered my feeling that it wasn't what was said but the way she said it. I admitted both my association and my difficulty in articulating the reason the message felt so harmful. She then remembered and related periods of uncontained violent attacks by her mother on her father and on others that her mother knew closely. We had entered that traumatic moment: *This is how it feels when unspeakable things happen. Unspeakable things have happened to you and we have felt it now.*

She phoned me between sessions and said, *I prayed about my actions and I did know the message I left was an assault on our relationship but I left it anyway. I want you to know I know.*

Working in Concert: The Music of Joy

On her return she related with some pleasure that what I had said was what the spiritual healer who had visited her church had said to her: *unspeakable things have happened to you.* I replied: *It's a safe and comforting feeling to think that others are working in concert for your benefit a bit like a mother and father might, but not like you have often experienced it.*

She began writing songs for church and performed them: *not the triumphant worship the healer wanted but, my version of joy, where darkness and the void ends in something lighter, something less alone But the healer told my congregation: "Do not let her stop singing!"* She showed me a "picture of us": dog-owner and puppy gazing into each others' eyes: *I am only just learning to hear joy, you know.*

She has begun both physically and psychologically to find her voice, and that spiritual call that she located in prayer seems to be her first clearly articulated experience of being invited to be more than the dutiful daughter, to come to receive and to find herself.

Clinical Reflections

"Martha" begins therapy with a terrified sense that she is unloved and unlovable and that others, including God, will "make it worse" (P1). While we simply listen and stay with her experience, her relationship with God begins to heal (P2). "Martha" uses this healed spiritual relationship (P3) to help us articulate how she needs me to be with her (P2). Her moment of unspeakable truth is as much a spiritual challenge for her as it is a therapeutic one: we must face truths about her past and the way she has dealt with it (P4). She repeats something of her traumatic experience in her emotional outburst, but in the role reversal of being the "perpetrator." After this integrative experience she then begins to engage in a freer search for her true self and her true vocation. (P5). She has her own voice, hears her own call, not just that of an internalized and traumatic experience of her mother.

Summary

This triptych of intensive psychodynamic therapies demonstrates several intersections and divergences with a spiritual journey. In the first case, "Single-Handed" might have been shifting his attachment state of mind in the relationship with the therapist, but his traumatic withdrawal from his personal relationship with his God needed to be noticed and addressed. The exploration of a lack of continuity between his expressed position and his practice, a lack of integrity, allowed an integration of the disavowed experiences of his own fear, fantasized guilt and unregulated shame. Revisitation of the trauma, in a different atmosphere, allowed an opportunity for integration to be reworked and deepened when deep body memories were activated. The pilgrim must return to the site of the injury. The image of body as "temple" and home allowed transformation of the way he abided with himself and others. He can then be more fully rehabilitated.

In contrast "Mouse" had a sheltering place (Isaiah 32:2, NJB) deep in her largely unspoken faith that helped her endure psychologically until we could construct a therapeutic space safe enough for her self to re-emerge and seek nourishment. Furthermore, the social world of her church, while initially repetitive, was able to become a place of opportunity for change and then flourishing. The very sacredness of her notions of marriage was then held in tension with what she felt were the sacred demands of love. She thought deeply on the integrity of her actions as they reflected her understanding of her own and her partner's limits. In a kind of mirror she asked of me a steadfast faith in the process of our relationship. She also discovered an implicit forgiveness as a fruit of her more secure state of mind.

Healing and making whole are intrinsically connected to a holding place in the therapeutic joining of minds. In the third case and with the "tuition" she gives me "at the feet of the Master" "Martha" showed me *intuitively* how better to care for her. She could trust God with a restored idealizing transference before she could openly acknowledge it with me, but much silent restoration of her capacity to trust preceded her shift in her image of God. "Martha" ceased being a martyr to her ill mother and began to pick up the thread of her development. She experienced the honesty of our fateful interchange as meaningful, she was safe to remember more, and we shared an aspect of the unspeakable truth of her trauma. She was beginning to reflect and to acknowledge that another is with her; she wanted me to know that she knew. She trusted me with the knowledge. She became separate but connected in that moment, rather than submerged in her mother's experience, and her true self begins to emerge. Bowlby, Janet, and Meares (Bowlby, 1980; Brown, Macmillan, Meares, & Van der Hart, 1996; Meares, 2005) all describe the need for the traumatic moments to be shared in a way that dissolves them. Stern et al. remind us that these incredible moments of sharing in the "now" are healing in a way that interpretation alone does not provide (Stern et al., 1998).

A FAMILY'S JOURNEY THROUGH LOSS

A time that can be especially challenging for families is when children are seriously ill. The diagnosis of a life-limiting or life-threatening condition in a child is devastating for parents and represents an experience that quintessentially activates the attachment system. The parents' role is to strive to save and comfort the child. In the case of life-threatening/limiting illnesses, they cannot save and protect their child in the obvious sense. This inability elicits a range of responses, including for some the need to draw upon spiritual beliefs and practices in their search to make sense of an untenable situation. In many settings clinicians may find religious/spiritual themes emerge as families negotiate a potentially life-changing event. Death of a child or adolescent can further challenge families already tired and depleted. A family's grief and sense of loss is often defined and processed within their given spiritual paradigm.

Generally pediatric health care involves working directly with families towards the shared goal: the ill child's recovery. However, where children have life-limiting and/or life-threatening illnesses, long term recovery ceases to be an option (Stevens, Rytmeister, Proctor & Bolster, 2010), and the direction of care changes to that of supporting the child or adolescent and his or her family through the process of dying and mourning. In bereavement, families are challenged to move through their distress, to resolve feelings of anger and despair, hopefully coming to a place where the family as a unit and as individuals can reinvolve themselves in life. This task of mourning as integration is described by Freud in his classic paper "Mourning and Melancholia" (Freud, 1917) but reconceptualized afresh by each generation of therapists (Bowlby, 1980; Meares, 2005). Some families have available to them, and draw upon, a specific religious/spiritual paradigm within which they experience their journey. Accepting that some families experience illness, loss and bereavement from a particular spiritual worldview is challenging, even confronting, for some.

- What, if any feelings, thoughts and behaviors are overtly reported by each individual/family member that reflect some aspect of the family's spiritual paradigm?
- Does the individual/family's spiritual paradigm provide tools that help them as they search for meaning in the context of their experience of loss/trauma?
- Are individuals/family members drawing upon their spiritual/religious beliefs, experiences and practices to help them to understand and make sense of their loss/trauma?
- To what extent do family members vary in their use of and adherence to the family's spiritual beliefs and practices in the context of processing their loss/trauma?
- Does use of a spiritual paradigm appear to aid individual family members in processing their grief/trauma?
- Is the family's cohesion strengthened when family members use a commonly shared framework for exploring, negotiating, and processing their grief/trauma?

Figure 12.2 Some questions to consider when working with individuals/families of a spiritual/religious worldview in the context of loss and bereavement or trauma. *Source:* Proctor (2011), printed with permission.

As Figure 12.2 suggests, we need to consider how an individual or family's spiritual worldview functions in the context of trauma, loss and bereavement and to consider how family members can vary in their responses to these events. As a result, there will be different presentations of grief among family members as they draw upon their familial spiritual narrative to help them negotiate and integrate the loss of a loved one.

In some cases loss and spirituality come together to facilitate recovery. At other times negotiating the journey of loss within the context of a particular spiritual paradigm can be challenging, even turbulent, with some beliefs and practices abandoned along the way. As witnesses and at times participants in such journeys, clinicians may find their own spirituality is challenged, affirmed, or undermined (Proctor, & McLean, 2009). How then can the family be supported to journey together through loss, or to accept and support that one or more members may take a different road to recovery? Case 4 highlights the challenges of interweaving a spiritual narrative cohesively into a family's journey of loss.

#4: The Case of the Traditionally Religious Family—The Death of a Daughter and Sister

Mary was an 11 year old girl who died from a cancerous tumor. Her family participated in a study exploring Australian families' experiences of car-

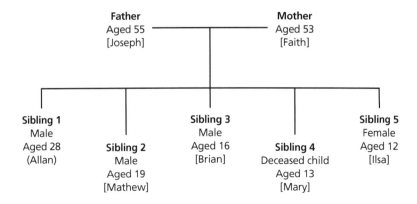

Figure 12.3   Genogram of Mary's family.

ing for children and adolescents with life-limiting or life-threatening conditions (Stevens, Lord, Proctor, Nagy & O'Riordan, 2010). The genogram in Figure 12.3 provides an overview of the family system. Each family member was invited to contribute his or her story, and each accepted. All were interviewed in private and remained unaware of the nature or content of the stories shared by other family members. Collection of the interviews spanned several months, providing time for the family to be informally observed, including during the sharing of a meal and informal social conversations. It was evident that they were a close-knit family, very active in their faith community. All attended regular services and engaged in various leadership roles in their faith community relevant for their ages and stages in life. The family conformed to a traditional patriarchal model of authority. This position of authority was further emphasized by the father's participation in the local faith community.

Since the family's world view is so firmly grounded in their religious beliefs and practices it is appropriate to speak about how they functioned *psycho-spiritually* in the face of their loss. In this family, what is spoken of spiritually is also lived and practiced, with all family members adhering to a common psycho-spiritual narrative with its origins in the teachings of their faith tradition. In time, like all stories, the family's personal collective narrative had become flavored with the family's handling of their tradition's larger faith story. However there was a strong adherence to ideas of purity and non-contamination such that family life centered around, and was grounded in, both their ethnic and faith traditions. These traditions formed the terrain upon which daily life was overlaid, continuing to provide a stabilizing focal point during Mary's illness and after her death. By the time of our meeting, Mary had been deceased for just over a year. This period represented early days of bereavement from an attachment perspective (Main, Goldwyn & Hesse, 2002).

There is a rich interplay between the grief of any individual and their family. This becomes clearer when those who have sustained a loss share elements of their worldviews: how they approach, respond to, interpret, and process the trauma associated with significant life events. In the case of Mary's family, each member in some way recounted a story of loss that defined it as a spiritual experience. Some chose to articulate this more clearly, explaining it in terms of the Christian story of death and resurrection (e.g., Joseph, the father) or in terms of Mary appearing to become wiser during her illness (Isla, the sister). The right to grieve and feel the depth of maternal loss was countered by the promise of new life for Mary at the feet of her heavenly Father (e.g., Faith, the mother). At times the story was delivered in a very matter of fact manner (e.g., Brian, the brother), while other family members struggled with balancing their deeply-felt sense of personal loss within the larger story of what it meant to live and die as a Christian (e.g., Mathew and Isla, the siblings).

Individuals within the family differed in how overtly they couched their loss within a clearly spiritual narrative. Indeed, at times it seemed that some members found it hard to make sense of the psychological pain they felt in the light of the available spiritual framework. Sharing a common spiritual heritage and an understanding of death as entry into eternal life did not ameliorate the pain linked to Mary's absence. I wondered how easy or difficult it might be for individual family members to openly express the human cost of their loss in the face of a powerfully held religious position: to admit to confusion, deep grief or the pain of separation without the risk of being seen to deviate from the "correct" explanation of how to grieve? Not surprisingly, the youngest child, who was only 10 or 11 at the time of her sister's death, was struggling to deal with the empty space in their shared bedroom and had no reference point (other than a faith based one) for the pain she felt at her sister's absence.

More generally, while admitting to speaking about Mary and things that they had done together, family members' narratives suggested limited open shared grieving. In withdrawing from my time with this family, I was left feeling that despite a commonly-held spirituality and their very obvious love of each other, some individual family members were alone in their experiences of grief and potentially at risk of unresolved loss. There was, at times, a sense that this family's spirituality was "double-edged"—holding both the potential to empower and unify and the potential to foster disconnectedness and isolation.

The family had not yet achieved that "aloneness-togetherness" or the intimacy that appears to be healing (Meares, 2005). Their loss was recent: attachment theory reminds us the disorganizing effects of bereavement may exceed 12 months (Main, Goldwyn & Hesse, 2002). It is likely that they were still disoriented and disconnected from their normative strategy as a family and might move naturally back towards a more cohesive state. Perhaps the psychospiritual challenge for this family will be to find a way to validate each story of grief and to resolve any paradoxes with the family's faith in steps analogous with those seen in the above therapies (P1-5). In some ways the challenge can be described as one of deepening the capacity of the family to contain and reflect, to hold in mind all these differences—clearly a challenge when the normal carers, the parents, are themselves bereaved. In this case it is unclear how each can journey accompanied through their grief and then authentically give and receive "the oil of gladness" (Isaiah 61:3, NJB). Will they require that accompaniment from human others, either within or outside the family, or will the sense of spiritual accompaniment by God be sufficient?

CREATING HEALING, HOLDING, WHOLE-MAKING SPACE

In resolution of conflict or crisis and in therapy, we often struggle to find "the third"—a fresh position that is not repetitive of the past but is integrative. The therapies above exemplify how the patient's spiritual relationship and journey may offer an opportunity to experience or deepen this "third" position. However, this is not universally true for the spiritual interface with therapy. At times as in the case of "Single-Handed" or the "Dutiful daughter," the relationship with the Divine can initially illustrate the old way of being, and the therapy must first provide the experience of the new. Which aspect of relationship in this drama becomes new and which is expressing the old may shift, but the relational world of healing can be richer for this opportunity to include the spiritual.

These therapies/ journeys are not narrated as proof of a God. They are presented as examples of how spiritually meaningful experiences can work with a therapy or arise within it, rather than being analyzed away as obstacles to coherence. These deeply-held beliefs can be fruitfully challenged— but within the patient's own worldview: "Single-Handed's" withdrawal, challenged by the therapist; "Mouse's" self-reflection on her ethical/moral dilemma within her relationship; the challenge to "Martha's" martyrdom; the grieving family's question of how they may grieve without leaving anyone behind and allow all to flourish. Attachment theory, especially aligned with notions of the developing self as capable of reflection (Meares, 2005; Fonagy, Gergely, & Target, 2008), provides a useful background theory for working with spiritual issues and experiences in the clinical and psychotherapeutic setting. It clearly outlines the human need for relationship and positions an autonomous/secure state of mind as the source of freedom to think, feel, act, remember and change. One can hold in mind, reflectively, that another may see the situation differently. In this theory the therapist is also free to hold the patient contemplatively in mind and not to judge any experience out of hand, but to join with the other in a collaborative journey to arrive at a new understanding. It should not be surprising that the "now moments" described so lucidly by Stern et al. (1998) have the spiritual quality of revelation; for they are moments of communion, of a light of understanding shining in the darkness, where something/someone lost is found—all refrains of old and familiar spiritual themes.

Bowlby (1980) maintained it was this synchronous and inherently joyful sharing of deep emotion that allowed grief to resolve. Schore (2001) and other researchers affirm that human beings were not meant to be or to recover alone. In this moment of communion, of aloneness/togetherness, trauma and grief dissolve (Meares, 2005; Stern et al., 1998). We have evolved to need companions on our journey, especially our pilgrimages, to grow, heal, transform and flourish. Psychotherapy provides a human way of building upon that need for companionship to help repair damaged or broken relationships, whether spiritual or human, and to help the self and other/s flourish.

> *I will weep when you are weeping,*
> *When you laugh, I'll laugh with you*
> *I will share your joy and sorrow*
> *Till we've seen this journey through.*
> —Gillard, 1977

ACKNOWLEDGEMENTS

The cases were originally presented with this theme at the RANZCP Congress 2008, Melbourne, Australia (McLean, 2008; Proctor & McLean, 2008) and at the *Spirituality, Human Development and Well-Being UWS Psychology and Spirituality Society 2008 Conference*, Sydney Australia (Proctor, Stevens, Nagy, Lord, B., & O'Riordan, 2008). We also acknowledge the support of PASS members and executive in supporting the development of this work via the 2009 Sydney Conferral and feedback.

REFERENCES

Brown, P., Macmillan, M. B., Meares, R., & Van der Hart, O. (1996). Janet and Freud: Revealing the roots of dynamic psychiatry. *Australian and New Zealand Journal of Psychiatry, 30*, 480–491.

Bowlby, J. (1979). *The making and breaking of affectional bonds*. London: Tavistock.

Bowlby, J. (1980). *Attachment and loss. Vol 3: Loss: Sadness and depression.* New York: Basic Books.

Crittenden, P. M. (2006). A dynamic-maturational model of attachment. *Australian and New Zealand Journal of Family Therapy, 27,* 105–115.

Erikson, E. H. (1959). *Identity and the life cycle.* New York: International Universities Press.

Fonagy, P. (2001). *Attachment theory and psychoanalysis.* New York: Other Press.

Fonagy, P., Gergely, G., & Target, M. (2008). Psychoanalytic constructs and attachment theory and research. In J. Cassidy & P. Shaver (Eds.), *Handbook of attachment: Theory, research and clinical applications* (2nd ed.) (pp. 783–810). New York: Guildford.

Freud, S. (1917). *Mourning and melancholia.* London: Vintage.

Gillard, R. (1977). The servant song, verses 2 and 4. In *Scripture in Song.* San Clemente, CA: Maranatha!Music.

Granqvist, P., & Kirkpatrick, L. A. (2008). Attachment and religious representations and behavior. In J. Cassidy & P. Shaver (Eds.), *Handbook of attachment: Theory, research and clinical applications* (2nd ed.) (pp. 906–933). New York: Guilford.

Hesse, E., & Main, M. (2000). Disorganized infant, child and adult attachment: Collapse in behavioural and attentional strategies. *Journal of the American Psychoanalytic Association, 48,* 1097–1127.

Holmes, J. (2001). *The search for the secure base: Attachment theory and psychotherapy* (1st ed.). Hove, East Sussex: Brunner-Routledge.

Magai, C. (1999). Affect, imagery and attachment: Working models of interpersonal affect and the socialization of emotion. In J. Cassidy & P. Shaver (Eds.), *Handbook of attachment: Theory, research and clinical applications* (1st ed.) (pp. 787–802). New York: The Guildford Press.

McLean, L. (2008). Attachment to God: Exploration of spiritual attachment relationships in clinical care and psychotherapy. *Australian and New Zealand Journal of Psychiatry, 42*(S1), A34.

Main, M., Goldwyn, R., & Hesse, E. (2002). *Adult attachment scoring and classification systems,* Unpublished manuscript, University of California at Berkeley.

Maunder, R., & Hunter, J. (2001). Attachment and psychosomatic medicine: Developmental contributions to stress and disease. *Psychosomatic Medicine, 63,* 556–567.

Meares, R. (2000). *Intimacy and alienation: Memory, trauma and personal being.* London: Routledge.

Meares, R. (2005). *The metaphor of play: Origin and breakdown of personal being* (3rd ed.). New York: Routledge.

Meares, R., & Graham, P. (2008). Recognition and the duality of self. *International Journal of Psychoanalytic Self Psychology, 3,* 432–446.

Miner, M. (2007). Back to the basics in attachment to God: Revisiting theory in light of theology. *Journal of Psychology and Theology, 35*(2), 112–122.

Proctor, M-T. (2011, March). 'A delicate balance': The intersection of the spiritual and psychological in healthcare—A place for conversation. Peer-reviewed presentation and paper presented at the Spirituality in the 21st Century: At the Interface of Theory, Praxis and Pedagogy 1st Global Conference, Prague, Czech Republic.

Proctor, M-T. (2009). In sickness and in health: Including the spiritual domain as an aspect of psychological assessment. *In Psych, 31*(4), 14–15.

Proctor, M-T., & McLean, L. (2008). Assessing attachment to God and spirituality as an aspect of psychological health and wellbeing. *Australian and New Zealand Journal of Psychiatry, 42*(S1), A34.

Proctor, M-T., & McLean L. M. (2009). Reviewing the place of the spiritual domain in the clinical and psychotherapeutic setting: Framing issues within an attachment perspective. In M. Miner, M-T. Proctor & M. Dowson (Eds.), *Spirituality in Australia Volume 2: Directions and applications* (pp. 90–110). Sydney: ACSS/CHILD.

Proctor, M-T., Miner, M., McLean, L., Devenish, S., & Ghobary, B. B. (2009). Exploring Christians' explicit attachment to God representations: The development of a template for assessing attachment to God experiences. *Journal of Psychology and Theology, 4*(37), 245–264.

Proctor, M-T., Stevens, M., Nagy, S., Lord, B., & O'Riordan, E. (2008, July). *Spirituality and bereavement: Coping with the death of a child with a life limiting condition within a spiritual framework.* Peer-reviewed paper presented at the Spirituality, Human Development and Well-Being UWS Psychology and Spirituality Society 2008 Conference, Sydney.

Schore, A. N. (2001). The effects of a secure attachment relationship on right brain development, affect regulation, & infant mental health. *Infant Mental Health Journal, 22*, 7–66.

Slade, A. (1999). Attachment theory and research: Implications for the theory and practice of individual psychotherapy with adults. In J. Cassidy & P. Shaver (Eds.), *Handbook of attachment: Theory, research and clinical applications* (1st ed.) (pp. 575–594). New York: Guildford.

Stern, D. N., Sandler, L. W., Nahum, J. P., Harrison, A. M., Lyons-Ruth, K., Morgan, A. C., et al. (1998). Non-interpretative mechanisms in psychoanalytic therapy: The 'something more' than interpretation. *International Journal of Psychoanalysis, 79*, 903–921.

Stevens, M., Lord, B., Proctor, M. T., Nagy, S., & O'Riordan, E. (2010). Research with vulnerable families caring for children with life-limiting conditions. *Qualitative Health Research, 20*(4), 496–505.

Stevens, M. M., Rytmeister, R. J., Proctor, M-T., & Bolster, P. (2010). Children with life-threatening or life-limiting illnesses: A dispatch from the frontlines. In C. A. Corr & D. E. Balk (Eds.), *Children's encounters with death, bereavement, and coping* (pp. 147–166). New York: Springer.

CHAPTER 13

CONCLUSION

THE PROBLEM AND AIM

Flourishing is a perennial human concern. People throughout the ages and across cultures have desired a life that goes beyond mere existence.

> Confucius dreamed of a society in which the king and his subjects embodied the principles of the Tao. Plato wrote of a republic that perfectly embodied the ideal principles of reason. Isaiah dreamed of a time of peace in which wolves and lambs would lie down together. (Baggett, 2008, p. 313)

In our own day, true to the consumerist and hedonistic principles which pervade Western society, a bewildering array of lifestyle choices are offered, which—it is claimed—lead to flourishing. In these cases, the underlying reference point for understanding the "good life" is not some universal principle, or the state, or some divine demand, but the freedom of the individual to determine his or her own destiny. Thus, hedonism and freedom rather than virtue and moral restraint are thought to contribute to the good life. Against this pervasive orientation, some social science approaches to "the good life" consider quality relationships with oneself and one's neighbor as important for flourishing. However, these approaches are often constrained by the limits of perceiving spirituality within a one-dimensional framework. Alternatively, some "spiritual" invitations to flourishing adopt an overly-transcendentalist "otherworldly" approach, which rejects the body, or requires an esoteric and highly partisan perspective on

Beyond Well-Being: Spirituality and Human Flourishing, pages 257–260
Copyright © 2012 by Information Age Publishing
All rights of reproduction in any form reserved.

what constitutes human flourishing. Moreover, each of these approaches is difficult to validate from a scholarly perspective because each draws on idiosyncrasy or anecdote rather than closely-reasoned argument or empirical evidence. How, then, are we to understand the contribution of spirituality to human flourishing?

Religions themselves, even the older religious traditions, sometimes base their claims concerning the best way to live on prescriptions that seem more designed to promote the power and privilege of the religious elite rather than societies or humanity generally. Alternatively, in other traditions, ongoing ascetical denial of the needs of the body and the limitation of desire are probably too harsh and restrictive to promote genuine flourishing. Flourishing may be promoted by encouraging a wise and virtuous restraint in season, but also by encouraging celebration, feasting and *jouissance* in its time.

A key difficulty in assessing the contribution of those traditions that appeal to transcendent sources as primary contributors to human flourishing through spiritual piety and devotion it is that this contribution lies beyond empirical validation. For example, the Christian faith considers that a proper relationship with God is a precondition for a proper relationship with oneself and one's neighbor and world. Such claims cannot be proven, but belong to the wisdom resources of the Christian spiritual tradition, which—along with the Jewish spiritual tradition from which it springs—claim that "wisdom is proved right by all her children" (Luke 7:35, NIV). The only way of demonstrating whether one group of people is happier, more fulfilled and more truly human than another group is by finding some criterion with which to compare the claims and the groups making them. The resources for undertaking such large-scale research are difficult to obtain, and—until now—a largely secular society has not thought it necessary to undertake such projects.

Nevertheless, we have proposed that it is both reasonable and helpful to consider spirituality in both its reflexive and its transcendental, God-originated forms as a key contributor to what makes human beings flourish and excel in the art of living. In making this claim we recognize that the definition of spirituality is very important: if the definition is too broad, it may blur distinctions between important dimensions and modalities of spirituality; if it is too narrow, the range of dimensions and modalities and their applications may be artificially restricted. In this book we have considered definitions and related models of spirituality that are applicable to the experience and practice of spirituality in a wide range of contexts and settings. A key contribution of this volume is the consideration of spirituality as a complex psychological construct that is oriented towards transcendence, even as transcendence reaches towards human existence by enriching and energizing it.

Notably lacking in past treatments of flourishing is an analysis that combines relevant inputs from psychology, philosophy and theology in ways that: a) represent the strengths of each of these disciplinary areas, b) allow each discipline to speak in its own ways to the problem of human flourishing, c) attempt an integration of these variegated perspectives, and d) hold promise for applications to life that resonate with human need and contemporary expressions of those needs in diverse settings.

Hence, this book has sought to make a contribution towards overcoming conceptual, theoretical, and practical divisions regarding human flourishing. In keeping with this integrative orientation, we have defined flourishing as self-actualization in the service of the common good. Actualization denotes internal states associated with flourishing, whereas altruism denotes external traits associated with flourishing. Our definition of flourishing is broadly consistent with psychological, philosophical and theological treatments.

OUR CONCLUDING ARGUMENT

As opposed to atheists, who argue that religious spirituality is an impediment to flourishing, we argue that:

1. It is sensible to talk about spirituality and flourishing.
    A reductionist approach that considers spirituality to be a misattribution of natural events to a transcendent cause ignores the "evidential force" of spiritual experiences as reported across time and culture (see Davis, 1999). Hence it is reasonable to propose that something real and transcendent causes such experiences. These spiritual/transcendent experiences contribute to an overall sense of connection, meaning, and personal transformation (see Chapter 1). Moreover, theories of psychological development point to personal transformations and meaning-seeking as related to overall human flourishing (see Chapter 3).
2. Spirituality has an effect on flourishing.
    Spirituality is not just a benign cognitive-affective state of the individual, but it actively motivates behavior that in turn contributes to the welfare of others (e.g., in acts of charity or benevolence). In this way, spirituality orients people to what is good and provides moral direction in living as flourishing beings (see Chapters 2 and 4).
3. Spiritually is not just correlated with flourishing, but has some causal (real world) effect on flourishing.
    The volume as a whole proposes that spirituality is an important cause of flourishing. Some chapters reflect on published research suggesting causal linkages between spirituality and aspects of flourishing (Chapters 6 through 8). Other chapters provide findings of

causality from original research or case analyses. This evidence includes a large, longitudinal survey of Australians (Chapter 5); a phenomenological study of church leaders (Chapter 8); and case studies of individuals and communities where spiritual inputs and changes led to subsequent reports of flourishing (Chapters 9 through 12). From such diverse evidence it is reasonable to conclude that spirituality has definite, discernable, and developmentally helpful effects on human flourishing. We recognize that not all forms of spirituality and spiritual practices are helpful, but we also recognize that in a season when spirituality itself is flourishing, the stimulus which has caused our "spiritual turn" is a response to positive yearnings that lie beyond material definition. This point noted, distinguishing between positive and more negative spiritual influences is a further contribution of this volume.

4. Despite the previous qualification, it is important not to ignore spirituality if we want to fully understand flourishing and understand how to help people to flourish.
   Many practical guidelines for those who desire to help others to flourish can be found in this volume. In particular, concrete ways of promoting flourishing through spirituality are presented for use by teachers, counselors, life coaches, psychotherapists, pastoral carers, and community developers.

It is a sad feature of our contemporary Western world that while (presumably) everyone wants to flourish, few experience the actualizing and altruistic satisfaction of a truly flourishing life. However, as a positive sign for the future of humanity, a broad search for resources for optimal living is now under way. The contributors to this volume hope readers will be prompted to seek a positive spiritual experience as a key resource for human flourishing in their own lives, and to use their attained measure of flourishing to support positive spirituality and flourishing in others.

REFERENCES

Baggett, J. F. (2008). *Seeing through the eyes of Jesus: His revolutionary view of reality & his transcendent significance for faith*. Grand Rapids, MI: William B. Eerdmans Publishing Company.

Davis, C. F. (1999). *The evidential force of religious experience*. Oxford: Clarendon Press.

ABOUT THE CONTRIBUTORS

Alan Black was Foundation Professor of Sociology at Edith Cowan University (Western Australia) before his retirement at the end of 2003. His fields of research include religion, spirituality, wellbeing, social capital, and community life. As an Emeritus Professor he retains an active link with the School of Psychology and Social Sciences, Edith Cowan University.

Rick Brouwer has over 25 years of pastoral and community experience as an ordained Assemblies of God minister. He is the founder and director of the Total Wellbeing Medical and Counseling Center, which utilizes a total approach to healthcare. Rick has produced numerous resources detailing how to enjoy "Total Wellbeing." He speaks and consults regularly as a Total Wellbeing Coach. In 2004 Rick designed and implemented a community based mental health program "40 days to a happier, healthier mind." He is currently designing a small group program that provides a practical theology of Wellbeing for use in churches. Together with his wife Deanna, he has raised five children and enjoys exercise, caravanning, home renovating and good food!

Stuart Devenish holds a Ph.D. in Religious Studies from Edith Cowan University (Perth, Western Australia, 2002) on the meaning of religious experience. He teaches mission and spirituality at Booth Salvation Army College in Sydney. Stuart is connected with PASS (Psychology and Spirituality Society, University of Western Sydney), and ACSS (Australian Centre for Studies in Spirituality, Sydney). He has publications in the areas of Christian theology, ministry, spirituality, mission, psychology of religion, and philosophy/

Beyond Well-Being: Spirituality and Human Flourishing, pages 261–265
Copyright © 2012 by Information Age Publishing
All rights of reproduction in any form reserved.

phenomenology. Stuart is the founding executive editor of the online journal *Indo-Pacific Journal of Phenomenology.* He has presented papers at the International Association for the History of Religions in Durban, South Africa in 2000; at the Association for Phenomenological Associations in Prague, the Czech Republic in 2002; at the International Metanexus Conference in Madrid, Spain in 2008; and at the Society for Biblical Literature Conference in Auckland, New Zealand in 2008. Stuart's present research activities include the contribution of spirituality to human flourishing, and the human person in the Divine presence. He lives in Sydney, Australia with his wife, who is a theological librarian.

Martin Dowson is currently Wesley Institute's Academic Director, having previously held senior leadership positions at the Sydney College of Divinity (as Professor of Pastoral Theology) and the Australian College of Ministries (as Director of Higher Education). His most recent research encompasses educational psychology, psychological measurement, and the psychology of religion. Martin is author of over 140 peer refereed publications, including articles appearing in *Review of Educational Research, Journal of Educational Psychology, Contemporary Educational Psychology, Educational and Psychological Measurement, Review of Religious Research,* and the *Journal of Occupational and Organizational Psychology.* He is also co-editor of Volume 6 of International Advances in Education: *Religion and Spirituality.*

Alison Feldman is Director of Feldman and Associates, Senior Lecturer in Public Relations at the University of Southern Queensland, and a Director of Australian College of Ministries. Alison's research experience includes investigation of adult learning in tertiary institutions. She won the University of Southern Queensland award for excellence in teaching in 2004. She has undertaken design of organizational research projects relating to leadership, organizational culture, strategic communication, community consultation, and reputation management. During her 25 years as a communication specialist she has assisted organizations to understand the impact of their "archetype" on their people, culture, belief system, and their clients.

Diann Feldman is Managing Director of Feldman and Associates, Chairman of The Greenleaf Centre for Servant-Leadership (Australia and New Zealand), and Director of Arrow Leadership Australia. In her 25 years as an experienced and accredited organizational development consultant, she has facilitated mentoring, personal development and coaching experiences internationally. Di has appeared on talkback radio, current affair television, and satellite links, and has presented at international engagements in the United States, United Kingdom, Europe, South America, Asia and Mauritius. Her books include *Mentoring Future Leaders, Leader as Coach,*

MaxPotential, The Significant Woman, Leading with Leaders, Winning Working Women, and *Navigating the Career Maze.*

Tony George is Principal of St Stephen's School in Perth, Western Australia, a Christian multi-campus coeducational school catering to students from Kindergarten through Year 12. Tony's research interests lie in educational psychology and theology, particularly in validating the critical contribution of Christianity to education. Tony's doctoral studies (in progress) are in educational psychology with a particular interest in attachment to God. Tony is a Visiting Lecturer in the Faculty of Education at St John's University, Tanzania. He is married to Jennifer, and they live with their four children in Perth, Western Australia.

Grant Gillett (MBChB (equivalent to MD); MSc(Psychology); D.Phil. (Oxon); FRACS (equivalent to Board Certification in Neurosurgery); FRS NZ) has lectured in physiological psychology, bioethics, philosophy, and cognitive neuroscience. He qualified as a neurosurgeon in Auckland, gained a D.Phil. in philosophy and a fellowship at Magdalen College, Oxford in 1985, and now teaches at the University of Otago in bioethics, philosophical psychology, cognitive neuroscience, and the philosophy of psychiatry. He is author of *Representation Meaning and Thought* (Oxford University Press), *Reasonable Care* (Bristol), *The Mind and its Discontents* (Oxford University Press), *Bioethics in the Clinic: Hippocratic Reflections* (Johns Hopkins University Press), *Subjectivity and being somebody: Human identity and neuroethics* (Imprint Academic), is co-author of *The Discursive Mind* (Sage), *Consciousness and Intentionality,* and *Medical Ethics* (Oxford University Press), and has written over 200 articles in philosophy, neuroscience, and biomedical ethics.

Philip Hughes has been a research fellow at Edith Cowan University since 1997. He has also been a researcher with the Christian Research Association since 1985. He is the author or co-author of many books and reports relating to spirituality and religion in Australia, as well as various publications on community life. He is currently the Senior Research Officer for the Christian Research Association, and an honorary research fellow of the School of Psychology and Social Sciences, Edith Cowan University.

Peter Kaldor was the founding Director of the Australian National Life Church Survey (NCLS) and has been involved for 25 years in research and writing in the areas of spirituality, religion, social policy, wellbeing and effective leadership. The author of many books and papers, he currently works in leadership capacity building with organizations and young adults. He is the Director of the Leadership Institute of the Uniting Church in New South Wales and of New River Leadership, a not for profit capacity building and consultancy group. He is an honorary research fellow of the School of Psychology and Social Sciences, Edith Cowan University.

Sue Kaldor has a degree in social work and a postgraduate diploma in psychotherapy. She currently works as a counselor in the Blue Mountains in NSW. She is a mother of three and has been involved in community health and community development. Sue has initiated projects that empower communities in the inner city of Sydney, in public housing areas, and locally where she lives. She is passionate about community and seeing people discover their full potential.

Loyola McLean is a Consultation-Liaison Psychiatrist and Psychotherapist in public and private practice with interests in psychosomatics, attachment theory and stress system disorders. Her recent Ph.D. thesis studied the mediating haemostatic and inflammatory links between depression and coronary heart disease. Her research is exploring the psychophysiological and clinical applications of attachment theory. This includes research into health aspects of psychospirituality and the clinical utility of the construct of attachment to God. She also teaches in the Sydney Medical School and in the Masters of Medicine (Psychotherapy) Program of the University of Sydney.

Maureen Miner (M.Clin. Psych., Ph.D.) is Chair of the University of Western Sydney Psychology and Spirituality Society. An Adjunct Research Fellow in Psychology at UWS, and Director of Research at Wesley Institute, Sydney, Maureen both teaches and researches in the field of the Psychology of Religion/Spirituality, and supervises student theses in this area. She consults as a clinical psychologist with clients having a religious worldview. Current collaborative research projects include the antecedents of burnout and job satisfaction in church leaders; impact of attachment to God on psychological health and well-being; and the development of measures of Islamic attachment to God and spirituality.

Marie-Therese Proctor is a registered psychologist, academic, and researcher with interests in spiritual attachment and its assessment, spirituality and health, and psychosocial adjustment to illness. Her Ph.D. work studied implicit and explicit attachment to God representations, and included the development of the Attachment to God Interview Schedule (GAIS). Her research is exploring psycho-spiritual and clinical application of spiritual attachment in the context of health and trauma. She is Senior Lecturer and Assistant Head in the School of Counseling, Wesley Institute, Sydney and an Adjunct Research Fellow with the Social Health Research Program, Griffith University.

Brian Rosner is Senior Lecturer in New Testament and Ethics at Moore Theological College and Honorary Senior Research Fellow in Ancient History at Macquarie University, both in Sydney, Australia. In the 1990s he taught at the University of Aberdeen in Scotland. Along with a Cambridge University Ph.D. in biblical studies, he has a BA (Hons) in Psychology from the University of Sydney. He is the author or editor of ten books, including the *New Dictionary of Biblical Theology* (co-editor; 2000), *The Consolations of Theology* (editor 2008), and *Greed as Idolatry: The Origin and Meaning of a Pauline Metaphor* (2007).

Stephen Smith is the CEO of the Australian College of Ministries. He previously served as the Director of Health for Churches of Christ in New South Wales (NSW) Australia, where his responsibilities focused on the holistic wellbeing and effectiveness of ministry leaders and their "communities of fresh hope" (churches, aged care facilities, refuges, and ministry centers). He holds qualifications in theology and counseling, an MBA, a doctorate in organizational development, and is completing a post-doctoral Ph.D. in leadership health with the Faculty of Health Science at the University of Sydney. He also serves as a Director of The Centre for Leadership Development, an international consortium of consultants and researchers. Stephen has worked extensively in Australia, USA and New Zealand consulting with a broad range of non-profit, government and corporate organizations.

Printed in Great Britain
by Amazon